KT-373-512

Debrett's

Family Historian

Debrett's

Family Historian

A GUIDE TO TRACING YOUR ANCESTRY

NOEL CURRER-BRIGGS
and
ROYSTON GAMBIER

INTRODUCTION BY
Sir Iain Moncreiffe of that Ilk, Bt

FOREWORD BY
Lord Teviot

COLLINS
TORONTO

A Webb & Bower Book
Edited, designed and produced by
Webb & Bower (Publishers) Limited

First published 1981 by
Webb & Bower (Publishers) Limited
in association with Debrett's Peerage Limited

This edition published 1981 by
Collins Publishers
100 Lesmill Road, Don Mills, Ontario

Designed by Vic Giolitto

Picture research by Anne-Marie Ehrlich

Canadian Cataloguing in Publication Data

Currer-Briggs, Noel.
The Debrett's family historian.—

ISBN 0-00-216858-8

1. Great Britain—Genealogy. 2. Genealogy
I. Title
CS415.C87 929'.1'0941 C81-094700-5

Typeset in Great Britain by MS Filmsetting Limited,
Frome, Somerset, England

Colour and duotone origination by
Culvergraphic Limited, High Wycombe

Printed and bound in Great Britain by Morrison & Gibb Limited,
London and Edinburgh

Frontispiece: A studio portrait of a Victorian family *c* 1880.

Contents

Foreword

LORD TEVIOT

My wife had always wanted to go to Somerset House to begin tracing her family tree, but it was only after a holiday in the Yorkshire Dales, during which we visited a Church where we saw her mother's maiden name, Ramsden, on a memorial, that we were finally triggered off.

I remember clearly my first visit to Somerset House and being in awe not only of the building but of the atmosphere as well. The old search rooms had galleries going all around the walls, and the shelves seemed to be full of musty-smelling books. Inside the books were millions of names. Seldom have I had such an exciting experience—there seemed to be an aura of magic over the whole proceedings. Obviously much of that aura has now worn off, but the thrill of discovery is still there and will never really abate.

From time to time I have had recourse to the floor of the chamber of the House of Lords to raise a number of matters concerning genealogy. In 1971 I initiated a small debate on the preservation of parish registers and records. It was the first time for many years that the subject of parish records had come up, and there appeared to be a considerable amount of interest. A few years later I introduced a bill which made provision for these records to be deposited in County Record Offices unless the parish church contained a safe which not only offered protection from fire but also from humidity. (This bill was not pursued as the Synod of the Church of England presented their own measure.) In theory by 1 January 1984 all parish registers and records that are over a hundred years old will be transferred to record offices unless the parish can meet the new storage requirement. At present it appears unlikely that this will be completely achieved by 1984 because of the cuts in local government expenditure, but it is to be hoped that the majority of records will have been transferred by then.

At one time it was suggested that the search room at St Catherine's House should close and that all the records held there would be moved to Southport in Merseyside. This would have caused great inconvenience to many people and a closely fought campaign ensued. After the debate in the House of Lords, I headed a small delegation which discussed the matter with a junior minister. The delegation included representatives of the College of Arms, the Society of Genealogists, the Holborn Law

Society, the Cambridge Group for the History of Population and Social Structure, and last, but by no means least, the Salvation Army. In fact it was largely due to the sincerity of the latter that the day was won.

It was also suggested that when the registers of births, marriages and deaths became a hundred years old they should be transferred to the Public Record Office where the general public could consult them on microfilm. It is this scheme that I am still concerned with after making two unsuccessful attempts to introduce a bill to achieve this aim.

The safety of parochial records certainly now seems to be more secure but there are many other records connected with Family History, the safety of which is less assured and which gives rise to concern among those interested in the subject. We may ask ourselves, 'What is a family record?' The simple answer is that it is anything that has names on it. Documents in private hands seem to be facing the greatest risk of destruction. It is the duty of every one of us to keep as many of our family records as possible, especially photographs and family albums, and to pass them on to someone reliable. If you have something of special interest you should deposit it in a record office for safe-keeping.

One day, for example, a man came up to me in St Catherine's House and showed me a brown leather-bound book saying, 'I bet you have never seen one like this before.' I thought that it was some old rate book and was just going to be rather condescending when luckily I stopped. It was an account book that had belonged to his grandmother, who had been a midwife in the East End of London during the 1850s and '60s, and gave the addresses that she had visited. A surviving record of that kind is rare and deserves to be kept for posterity.

We must be very grateful to people like Percival Boyd who produced the marriage index and countless other indexes and transcripts. More recently the work of the Church of Jesus Christ of Latter Day Saints (the Mormons), in building up their microfilm records, has proved to be of great value to researchers. Every encouragement must be given to all those who help to make these records more accessible.

Debrett's Family Historian will, I hope, make you feel that a most useful contribution has been made to the teaching of family history. After reading this book you should have the necessary knowledge to be able to embark on research of your own. Do not be afraid to use a new source and do not leave a stone unturned. There is bound to be a time when you reach a point at which you feel unable to proceed further. Do not despair, you may still crack your problem in the end. You must not be hidebound in your choice of records. Parish registers are a wonderful source of information but they are not the only records available. There are quite often other avenues of research to be explored such as those described in the chapter on Celtic Ancestors.

I wish you luck!

Introduction

SIR IAIN MONCREIFFE OF THAT ILK, BT, ALBANY HERALD

Genealogy is fun. Just as a piece of furniture or a picture takes on much more interest if you know its provenance, so does an individual the more the diverse ancestral elements that went to form him or her are known. The provenance of genealogy lies within the greatest gift of all: life. True family history in depth is a tapestry of *all* those who ever lived and to whom we owe our existence, and the threads woven across it are the connected lives of their interwoven generations. Tracing it, to change the metaphor, is like a detective trying to fit together a jigsaw puzzle whose pieces have been scattered throughout the world over the centuries. It is not only natural but instructive to want to know not just the broad generalized history of the country in which you live, but the actual life-histories of the people from whom you derive your individual existence.

When you have discovered who as many as possible of your ancestors were—not merely the line of your father's surname—you will find a new thrill in learning the strange vicissitudes of their lives in diverse walks of life. Visiting the houses or places where they lived, seeking out their likenesses or their graves, handling the coins they used centuries ago—everything takes on a special interest when you know that, as it were, something of you has been there before. For families are seldom static; the rich are not always rich, nor the poor nothing but the offspring of untold centuries of poverty.

Sir Anthony Wagner, former Garter Principal King of Arms, has pointed out in *Pedigree and Progress* that it is a myth to think of social classes as distinct, self-perpetuating, hereditary corporations. On the contrary, it is easy to demonstrate that this is no more than a figment of the imagination, fostered by politicians of both Left and Right to serve their own party dogmas. Even the middle classes, whose social movement up or down was often rapid enough to be visible to the naked eye, did their best to hide this movement in the anonymity of city life.

And never forget that you each owe your very existence not just to your parents, but to *every single one* of your personal ancestors since mankind began. It is impossible to knock out one brief link at any time in history and keep the whole chain together. Abraham Lincoln and the Aga Khan, and many more readers of these words than perhaps realize it, could never have been born had Alfred the Great's mother died in childhood.

LEFT
The statue of King Alfred at Winchester. Many people claim their descent from Alfred the Great, including Abraham Lincoln and the Aga Khan.

OPPOSITE
A reliquary of Charlemagne, Aachen 1350. Charlemagne united western and central Europe and was the first Holy Roman Emperor, reigning from AD 800–814. Many of the great families of Europe and America can trace their descent from him.

Ponder this. None of you could ever have been born if your mother's mother's mother's mother had died in infancy. But do you know offhand who she was? It would have been no good your direct maternal great-great-grandfather marrying somebody else instead, for the child of such a marriage would have been quite different genetically from your real great-grandmother, and no descendants could ever have been *you*.

The extraordinary variety of genealogy may perhaps be illustrated by a case well known to me. The child of a Kenya settler wanted to find out about his mother's side of the family. She vaguely believed herself to be of a titled family ultimately French in origin, and her mother, a British general's daughter, believed herself to descend maternally from Admiral Bradley who had taken part in the first coastal survey of Australia and after whom Bradley Head, a landmark at Sydney in New South Wales, was named. It seemed a fairly solid Victorian background.

Admiral Bradley turned out to be a *Sergeant* Jonas Bradley who had settled in Australia and whose son had been so successful as a sheep farmer that he has an entry in the Australian *Dictionary of Biography*. Young Bradley married the daughter of an Australian explorer called Hovell; her natural brother Albert Hovell, Master Mariner of the good ship *Young Australia*, was convicted in 1869, together with two of his crew of aborigines, of murdering three persons, names unknown, on the high seas: a story reminiscent of an adventure by Joseph Conrad. The farmer Bradley's daughter married General Pearse, of the 'Fighting Fifth'; and their daughter married the natural son of a dashing Austrian count of French origin called Rességuier de Miremont, whose father sprang in the female line from industrious Pierre-Paul Riquet (1604–1680), the Baron de Bon Repos who had built the Canal du Midi from the Mediterranean to the Atlantic. The Austrian count's mother, a Hungarian countess, Amelie Festetics, belonged to what had become a very grand family (descended in the female line from Erszebet Báthory, the 'Bloody Countess' who tops the list under 'murderer' in the *Guinness Book of Records*) whose founder had been Peter Ferstetych, born before 1504, a manumitted *serf* of the Bishop of Zagreb at Sassinovec in Croatia (now Yugoslavia). This then, was my mother's background, for I was that Kenya settler's son. The Midi of Languedoc, the Carpathians, the Balkans and the Australian outback alike took on a new interest for me.

It is a pity that some people seem interested only in grand descents, others only in respectable ones. Yet others seek only what is rare. I once told somebody that he descended from Charlemagne, which he hadn't known before. His only reaction was a shrug since an enormous number of other people must share in that descent. It seemed dull to me not to be excited, or at least interested, in identifying an actual flesh-and-blood forefather who lived in the eighth century, and to be able to know so much about him and even visit the chapel where he worshipped, whether he was a serf or an emperor. Indeed, quite literally, Charlemagne can be regarded as the Father of Europe; his was a most vigorous stock. If he and his third Queen, Hildegard, had never been born, no single one of his descendants would ever have been born; not George Washington, nor George III, not Herman Goering nor Winston Churchill, not Bonnie Prince Charlie nor President Nixon. Moreover, neither could any of these people have been born if the future William the Conqueror had never been born as William the Bastard, illegitimate son of the original Harlot (Harlotte of Falaise) the tanner's attractive daughter to whose prowess in bed one single night in 1027 so many of us thus owe our very being. All our ancestor's are interesting, for they were *all* necessary in handing down life to us even if they lived long, long ago.

In the quest, there are so many things that are fun too. As I have already observed, there is the discovery, if possible, of their photographs or their portraits: their iconography, as it is called. Then there are pictures of their houses or belongings. One of the oldest residences whose former occupants can still be traced is the drystone fortress of Ailech in Northern Ireland, where the ancestors of the present O'Neills of Clanaboy had their stronghold from the fifth until the eleventh century. To come to more recent times, I was shown on Lake Toba in the interior of Sumatra the ancestral stone table, stone benches and decapitation stone where cannibal feasts had been held until 1912 by the family of our hosts, the elder members of which recollected them well and described them shyly: 'But this was before we became Lutherans.'

There are so many side-lines of genealogy. I have noticed, for example, that a characteristic handwriting can sometimes be inherited as in the case of some of the Argyll family. Any study of genealogy among the early Celts requires an understanding of what social anthropologists call the 'classificatory' system, which extended among Indo-European peoples from India to Ireland, and was patrilinear. It seems probable that the Picts had a similar 'classificatory' system for purposes of succession law, but that it was matrilinear—such a system still exists among the Bemba of Zambia—which is of genealogical importance in working out the ramifications of the Pictish royal house because innumerable people now living in many countries can trace themselves back to Kenneth MacAlpin's Pictish grandmother, who was alive *c* AD 800. Again, heraldists seeking to disentangle relationships of heraldry should be aware that great houses often had two coats, probably one for their shield and one for their flag; the one having a device such as an eagle or a lion, the other a geometrical pattern, usually of the same colours in each case. Later branches of such families, sometimes taking different surnames in those early days bore one of the coats alone.

However, this book is concerned with the main stream of genealogical enquiry today. It describes the sources that can be consulted, and gives an outline of the way in which you can embark upon a search of your own. I will now content myself with some introductory general observations. First, I would like to stress the universal brotherhood of Man, that all human beings belong ultimately to the same family, if only we could trace everybody down from our common source. And second, I would like to indicate the sort of lines, usually sacred or royal, through which we can trace really quite a lot of people in all walks of life today back and back into the mists of early civilization.

Einstein said 'Science without religion is lame, religion without science is blind.' And early human genealogy and religion are inextricably entwined, as I will explain. This is not perhaps the place to discuss in detail my agreement with the scholastic axiom of my twenty-five times great-grand-uncle Saint Thomas Aquinas that (to quote Dr T. M. Lindsay) 'while reason and revelation are two distinct sources of truths, the truths are not contradictory: for in the last resort they rest on *one* absolute truth—they come from the one source of knowledge, God, the Absolute One'. But it has a profound bearing on the evolutionary theories of my fifth cousin four times removed—Charles Darwin—with whom I am equally in general agreement.

For nobody can fail to observe how extraordinarily the allegory of creation in the book of Genesis fits the sequence of evolution as revealed for us by the scientists. Epochs are poetically expressed as days, in much the same way as we say 'in Neanderthal Man's day'. We are told in Genesis that in the beginning 'there was light'. The scientists say that the Earth was a ball of fire. In the second epoch, as the Earth cooled, there was vapour: when the waters beneath were divided from 'the waters which were above'. Next, the waters gathered together to form seas, and the dry land appeared. Then vegetation sprang up, depending on the sunlight of the firmament for life. Next *out of the seas* came forth amphibious reptiles—'let the waters bring forth abundantly the moving creature that hath life'—and from these reptiles evolved, notice how the order in Genesis is still correct, 'fowl' before 'beast of the earth', i.e. birds before mammals. And the last in time to be evolved was Man.

How the correct sequence of evolution was revealed to the talented Hebrews centuries before Darwin's explorations, and how much of it was known to even earlier civilizations, is beyond our present knowledge; but their poetic use of the words 'day' for 'epoch' and 'created' for 'evolved' should not obscure the wonder of it.

A moment's reflection will show that, at some single stage and in some single place, within a little family group of primates, the single anthropoid common forefather of every man living today walked this Earth. Nobody really thinks different human beings, all with ten fingers and an appendix, were separately evolved from different amoebae in separate parts of the world. The myriad coincidences would be beyond ordinary mathematical comprehension. However much other warm-blooded mammals may have branched off as our yet more remote kin at some far earlier pre-anthropoid primordial stage, 'a man's a man for a' that'. To paraphrase Kipling: we are all brothers under the skin. And to quote him: 'We be of one blood, thou and I.'

So it cannot be stressed often enough that no family is older than any other family. Some lines can be traced back further than others, but none for much more than just over a couple of millennia. Some people adopted surnames earlier than others, so that one can trace the history of an old name, especially if it is mentioned in surviving records over a long period. But I repeat for emphasis, nobody suggests that two separate human families were evolved from two different amoebae, or even from two different quadrupeds, or even from two different monkeys. If every man alive today was able to trace back the source of his Y-chromosome—the

A meeting of the two great Chinese philosophers, Confucius and Lao-Tzu. Confucius himself was a descendant of the Shang dynasty (1766–1121 BC), through the dukes of Sung, and was the ancestor of the K'ung clan, who recorded their genealogy in the Chia Pu, or family name book over 2,500 years.

chromosome which can only be given him by his father and which alone can make him a man, and which his forefathers in turn could only have received from their forefathers—we would all find that we had each inherited our individual Y-chromosome from the very same source in the testicle of a single, joint, man-like ancestor, one individual at the anthropoid stage of evolution. That individual anthropoid's issue may have had to intermarry for generations before his distributed Y-chromosome produced men who were fully entitled to be called *Homo sapiens*, but we may nevertheless accord him the archaic name of Adam. For we all descend from him. All families spring from his. And to the age-old question, 'When Adam delved and Eve span, who was then the gentleman?' the answer is clear: Adam. How could it have been Eve? From that illustrious Y-chromosome sprang all the immemorial nobility in the world.

Throughout the world the early legends of every civilization attribute the discovery of agriculture and the arts to God-like royal ancestors. These early food producers perceived divine power in the life force which impregnated matter with energy. By concentrated prayer and ritual, part of this life-force, as it were the lucky spirit of the community, was embodied in the talisman king, successor to the wise horned-priest figure of Stone Age cave paintings. Respect for sacral royalty is the earliest religion of which there is any certain knowledge. It spread with civilization throughout the world. Sacral royalty 'was the early inspiration of drama, astronomy, architecture, sculpture, painting, music, dancing, games and costume'. It also inspired the earliest ancestral records, whether oral, passed by repetition from generation to generation by bardic herald-priests, or kept by them in newly invented writing.

It is not surprising, therefore, that the earliest genealogies that have come down to us are royal ones, or those of sacred families. And since kings have tended to marry princesses and often foreign ones, throughout the centuries, it is usually through royal intermarriages over the millennia that we can trace the most ancient descent of people actually living today. Most people have royal blood; the difficulty is to trace it.

Thus nearly all the longest traceable direct male-line descents, invaluable for the tracing of the human Y-chromosomes over long periods, are those of royal or sacred houses. In Japan, for instance, the oldest great historic families go back to the imperial house itself and to priestly court nobility, all traceable since the very first written records, and already then immemorial.

When I was a Guards Officer during the Second World War, one of my comrades was Lieutenant Louis Kung, Scots Guards, *alias* K'ung Lingchieh. His parentage linked modern Chinese history with the remote past. His mother was one of the three sisters of T. V. Soong, the former Foreign Minister of China; the other two Soong sisters had married respectively Sun Yat Sen, first President of China after the overthrow of the Manchu

Prince Constantin Alexandrovitch Bagration-Mukhransky, who was killed in the First World War, with Princess Tatiana Constantinova. The Bagration family can trace their descent in the direct male line to the fourth century AD.

dynasty in 1912, and Generalissimo Chiang Kai-shek. His father was Dr H. H. Kung, then Finance Minister, and I understand that they belonged to the K'ung clan who have evolved over more than seventy-five generations around the tomb of their illustrious forefather K'ung tsze, better known as the sage K'ung Fu-tze or Confucius (551–479 BC) and their genealogy had been treasured by Chinese scholars throughout two and a half millennia in their great Chia Pu or family name book. But I don't know whether any copy of this has survived the Communist 'burning of the books' throughout China. Moreover we are told that Confucius himself was a scion in the direct male line, through the dukes of Sung, of the proto-historic Shang dynasty (traditionally 1766–1121 BC). It was estimated in 1911 that some forty to fifty thousand male-line descendants of the K'ung family were living in the neighbouring city of K'iuh-fow; I would add, with possibly the oldest traceable human Y-chromosomes in the world.

In this connection, incidentally, I cannot sufficiently stress the grievous mental injustice, and the heartless blocking of all scholarly research, including medical and scientific research, caused by the operation of the

Adoption Acts, even as amended by the Children Act (1975). Briefly, an adopted child, after reaching the age of eighteen, can with great difficulty obtain access to some legal information about his true parentage. The reasons for and against this are well understood. But the *descendant* of an adopted child, long after the need for concealment is dead, has no means of gaining access to the important original birth certificate of the adoptee. The unnecessary cruelty of this thoughtless ban is obvious.

To return to descents traceable over a long period, ancient dynastic families of the Caucasus have survived into the twentieth century. Some of them, such as Bagration, are traceable in the direct male line since before the Conversion of Armenia in AD 314. For these, see Cyrille Toumanoff's indispensable *Manuel de Généalogie et de Chronologie pour l'histoire de la Caucasie Chrétienne* (Rome, Edizione Aquila, 1976) to be read in conjunction with his *Studies in Christian Caucasian History* (Georgetown University Press, 1963).

Excellent examples of groping backwards through the female line by way of ancient and medieval Caucasia are to be found in Sir Anthony Wagner's *Pedigree and Progress*, already referred to, which is based primarily on Professor Prince Toumanoff's works. It contains a fascinating series of tabular pedigrees indicating 'Bridges to antiquity' whereby very many people, including once again all the present royal families of Europe, almost certainly descend, by way of crusader intermarriages with the princely houses of Armenia, from the Arsacid dynasty of Parthian monarchs such as Mithridates, who were great kings of Persia from the third century BC. This is mobility of ancestry on the grandest scale. But above all, Sir Anthony Wagner's book stresses the mobility of this ancestry between classes as well as places.

Yearning backwards to the earliest sources of identifiable ancestors, I have so far discussed mainly royal or sacred lineages, only because it is usually through them that there is the best chance of getting furthest back, following all possible lines, male or female. To recapitulate: kings marry into even older dynasties across nations, their daughters marry local nobles whose daughters in turn marry lesser landowners in their districts, and so on downwards to the farmer's younger sons' daughters who marry labourers in the villages. Thus a given Mackay clansman living in Strathnaver in the remotest north-west of Scotland in 1370 was not likely to be the ancestor of a given Robertson clansman living in Atholl in the central highlands by 1870. But King Robert II, living in 1370, had a daughter who married the Macdonald Lord of the Isles, and their daughter married the Mackay chief. As a result of local intermarriage generation after generation among the Mackay cadets in Strathnaver, there is a strong likelihood of a given clansman there in 1870 descending from King Robert II. Similarly, another of Robert II's daughters married the thane of Glamis, and in the following century Lord Glamis's daughter married the Robertson chief: again, owing to local intermarriage generation after generation among the Robertson cadets in Atholl, there is a similarly strong likelihood of a given clansman there in 1870 descending from Robert II. And from Robert II, the genealogy can of course then be carried back without difficulty into the Dark Ages. It is the royal house that is the most probable unifying factor between the two widely separated clansmen's genealogies.

Two tabular pedigrees below illustrate the way in which royal ancestry links very diverse people together across great distances in both space and time. They are selected from the very many traceable ancestors of Mr Frederick Ray Howkins, living at 21616 Kramer Avenue, St Clair Shores, Michigan, USA, whose father matriculated Arms in Lyon Register in 1968. The one shows Mr Howkins' direct male line, father-to-son, back for thirty generations over more than nine centuries. We each have of course two parents, four grandparents, eight great-grandparents, and so on backwards in time: I understand that the number of theoretical ancestors we have thirty generations back is 1,073,741,904. Since there were not that number of people in the whole wide world thirty generations ago, it follows that we are all made up of innumerable cousin marriages. But it is of extraordinary interest that, with over a thousand million (over an American billion) theoretical choices in the thirtieth generation, we can pinpoint the exact individual living in 1045 from whom this particular American citizen living today has actually inherited his Y-chromosome. Since it can only come down father to son, Mr Howkins derives his Y-chromosome from the Breton noble Alan, Seneschal of Dol before the Norman Conquest of England; from whom such historic characters as King Robert II (cited above) founder of the Stewart dynasty, the Bonnie Earl of Moray and, for that matter, Bonnie Prince Charlie, also inherited their own Y-chromosome.

The second tabular pedigree shows how, in the female line, Mr Howkins' ancient roots can be traced back over twenty-two centuries to the Parthian imperial dynasty in the third century BC; and there is good reason to believe that they in their turn linked back through other princesses to even more ancient dynasties, stretching back immemorially into the human past. At four points in this second table, the generations have been linked by dots to indicate the probable affiliation. The general affiliation, however, is not in doubt, as Khachi'k Artsruni, Prince of T'ornavan in 1042, was undoubtedly a prince of the royal house of Vaspurakan, and thus a descendant of the Bagratid princess Rhipsime who married Hamazasp II Artsruni, Prince of Vaspurakan *c* 800; and Samuel, Prince of the Mamikonids and heir of the Gregorid domain (slain in battle 772) was undoubtably the descendant and indeed eventual heir of the marriage of Hamazusp I, Prince of the Mamikonids (307–432) to Sahakanoysh, the Gregorid heiress. Similarly, it is certain that Vologaeses IV, the Arsacid

Great King of Parthia AD 191–208, descended in the direct male line from Tiridates I, Great King 247–210 BC, son of Phriapites, son of Arsakes, but the exact relationship of each successive intermediate king of the dynasty is at present uncertain. Of the overall picture, however, there is no doubt. In both tables it has been an unexpected royal ancestor (King Charles II) who has functioned as the genealogical 'gateway to the past'. Similarly, more than three hundred thousand descendants of King Edward III of England (1312–1377) have spread his ancestral genes far and wide throughout the community and throughout the world.

Direct Male Line: Inheritance of 'Y' Chromosome

ALAN, hereditary Seneschal or Steward of Dol in Brittany, a Breton noble living *c* 1045

|

FLAALD, hereditary Steward of Dol (brother of Alan, one of the leaders of the First Crusade 1097)

|

ALAN fitz Flaald, feudal Baron of Oswestry, Sheriff of Shropshire on the Welsh border 1101

|

WALTER fitz Alan, 1st Great Steward of Scotland, granted great estates by King David I, and died 1177

|

ALAN fitz Walter, 2nd Great Steward of Scotland, a Crusader with Richard Coeur-de-Lion

|

WALTER, 3rd Great Steward of Scotland, first to take the surname of Stewart, died 1241

|

ALEXANDER, 4th Great Steward of Scotland, co-Regent of Scotland died 1283

|

Sir JOHN Stewart of Bonkyl, 'whose bravery Wallace praised above all men', killed at Falkirk 1298

|

Sir ALAN Stewart of Dreghorn, killed at the battle of Halidon Hill 1333

|

Sir ALEXANDER Stewart of Darnley, feudal Baron of Darnley 1371

|

Sir ALEXANDER Stewart of Darnley, feudal Baron of Darnley, d. *c* 1404

|

Sir JOHN Stuart of Darnley, Seigneur d'Aubigny and Count of Evreux, killed commanding the Scots in France 1421

|

Sir ALAN Stuart of Darnley, Seigneur d'Aubigny, murdered in a feud with the Boyds 1439

|

JOHN, 10th Earl of Lennox (by descent from its heiress) 1495

|

MATTHEW, 11th Earl of Lennox, killed at the battle of Flodden 1513

|

JOHN, 12th Earl of Lennox, captured and murdered by the Hamiltons at the battle of Manuel 1526

|

MATTHEW, 13th Earl of Lennox, Regent of Scotland, mortally wounded by the Hamiltons 1571

|

HENRY, King Consort of Scots (married Mary Queen of Scots), previously Lord Darnley, assassinated 1563

|

JAMES I, King of Great Britain, united the Crowns of England and Scotland, 1625

|

CHARLES I, King of Great Britain, beheaded 1649

|

CHARLES II, King of Great Britain 1685

|

CHARLES, 1st Duke of Richmond & Lennox, Duc d'Aubigny (natural son) 1723

|

CHARLES, 2nd Duke of Richmond & Lennox, Duc d'Aubigny 1750

|

WILLIAM Howkins, born 1747 (natural son) farmer and carpenter

|

JOHN Howkins, contractor, born 1782

|

JOHN Howkins, civil engineer, born 1807

|

JOSEPH Howkins, coppersmith, born 1827

|

JOHN BARTHOLOMEW Howkins, coppersmith, born 1847

|

JOHN BARTHOLOMEW Howkins, electrical contractor, born 1889

|

JOHN DELMARE Howkins, born in Ontario 1920, resident in Michigan USA

|

FREDERICK RAY Howkins, citizen of the USA, born 1948

|

Descent through the female line

Arsakes Vologaeses IV Dikaios Epiphanes Philhellen, Great King or Shah of Persia AD 191–208 (36th Great King of the Parthian imperial dynasty founded in 249 BC)

|

Chosroes I, King of Armenia AD 191–216, maintained the old pagan fire-altars

|

Tiridates II, King of Armenia 216–252, still a pagan Zoroastrian

|

Chosroes II, the Valiant, King of Western Armenia, slain by his brothers in 297

|

Tiren (Helios) Tiridates IV, first Christian King of Armenia 298–350

|

Chosroes III, King of Armenia 330–339

|

Bambishn of Armenia (married Athenoganes, son of Hesychius, Primate of Armenia 342–348)

|

Saint Narses the Great, hereditary Bishop and Primate of Armenia 355–373

|

Saint Isaac the Great, hereditary Bishop and Primate of Armenia 378–438

|

Sahakanoysh, the Gregorid heiress (m. Hamazasp I, Prince of the Mamikonids 387–432)

|

Hamazaspian, Mamikonid prince (brother of Saint Vardan and Saint Hmaycak)

|

Hmaycek, Mamikonid prince

|

Mushel, Mamikonid prince, 555

|

David, Mamikonid prince, *c* 600

|

Hamazasp II, Prince of the Mamikonids and heir of the Gregorid domain, Prince of Armenia 655–658

|

Hrahat, Mamikonid prince

|

David, Mamikonid prince, d. 744 (brother of Gregory I, Prince of the Mamikonids)

|

Samuel, Prince of the Mamikonids, heir of the Gregorid domain, killed 772

|

Mamikonid princess (m. Smbat VI, Prince of the Bagratids, Constable of Armenia for the Caliph, k. 772)

|

Ashot the Carnivorous, Prince of Armenia 806–926

|

Rhipsime, Bagratid princess (m. Hamazasp II Artsruni, Prince of Vaspurakan *c* 800)

|

Ashot I Abulabus Artsruni, Prince of Vaspurakan 836–874

|

Grigor Derenik Artsruni, Prince of Vaspurakan 857–868 and 874–886

|

Gagik III Artsruni, Prince (908) then King of Vaspurakan 943

|

Ahusahl Hamazasp III Artsruni, King of Vaspurakan 958–968

|

Derenik, Artsrunid prince (brother of Sennecherib John Artsruni, King of Vaspurakan 1003–1021

|

Khachi'k Artsruni, Prince of T'ornavan 1042

|

Hasan, Artsrunid prince, eleventh century

|

Abulgherib Artsruni, Byzantine Governor of Tarsus

|

Artsrunid princess (m. Oshim I, Prince of Lambron *c* 1071–1110, Sebastus)

|

Hetum II, Prince of Lambron and Tarsus 1110–1143, Sebastus

|

Oshin II, Prince of Lambron 1143–1170, Sebastus

|

Hetum III, Prince of Lambron 1170–1200 d. 1218

|

Constantine the Thagadir, Prince of Lambron 1220–1249

|

Hetum IV, lord of Lambron, died 1250

|

Alice of Lambron (m. the Crusader baron Balian d'Ibelin, Seneschal of Cyprus, died 1302)

|

Guy d'Ibelin, Seneschal of Cyprus, 1309

|

Alice d'Ibelin (m. Hugh IV de Lusignan, King of Cyprus 1324–1358 titular King of Jerusalem)

James de Lusignan, King of Cyprus 1382–1398, titular King of Armenia

Janus de Lusignan, King of Cyprus 1398–1432

Anne de Lusignan, pricess of Cyprus (m. Louis, Duke of Savoy 1468)

Margaret of Savoy (m. Pierre de Luxembourg, Count of Saint Pol, who died 1482)

Marie de Luxembourg, Countess of Saint Pol, died 1546 (m. François Count of Vendôme)

Charles de Bourbon, Duke of Vendôme, died 1537

Antoine de Bourbon, King Consort of Navarre, Duke of Vendôme, died 1562

Henri IV, King of France and Navarre, assassinated 1610

Princess Henrietta Maria of France (m. Charles I, King of Great Britain, beheaded 1649)

Charles II, King of Great Britain, died 1685

Charles, Duke of Richmond & Lennox, KG (natural son, by Louise de Kéroalle, Duchess of Portsmouth)

Charles, Duke of Richmond & Lennox, KG died 1750

William Howkins (natural son, by Sophie Howkins), farmer and carpenter, born 1747

John Howkins, contractor, born 1782

John Howkins, civil engineer, born 1807

Joseph Howkins, coppersmith, born 1827

John Bartholomew Howkins, coppersmith, born 1847

John Bartholomew Howkins, electrical contractor, born 1889

John Delmare Howkins, born in Ontario 1920, resident at St Clair Shores, Michigan

Frederick Ray Howkins, citizen of the United States of America, born 1948

Ancient Roots

Finally, there is the question as to which are the oldest traceable native American descendants. Many noteworthy people including modern Europe's great benefactor General Marshall of the Marshall Plan have sprung from the marriage of the colonist John Rolfe and the famous Virginian princess, Pocahontas (1595–1619), daughter of Powhatan, king of all the redskin tribes from the Alleghenies to the Atlantic seaboard. There are also the Spanish dukes of Moctezuma, descended from the maternal grandson of Halco Hucpantzin (Don Pedro of Moctezuma), son

A portrait of the Red Indian princess Pocahontas by an unidentified artist. Pocahontas, as a result of her marriage to the Englishman, John Rolfe, was the ancestress of many notable Americans, including General George C. Marshall, who was responsible for the Marshall Plan while Secretary of State after the Second World War.

of the celebrated Montezuma, actually Moteuczoma II, Emperor of Mexico, who perished in 1520; and whose ancestry, we are given to understand in Stokvis' *Manuel d'Histoire, de Généalogie et de Chronologie* (Leyden, 1888), was traceable through twelve further generations by way of the Aztec king Acamapechtli of Tenochtitlan (1350–1404) back to the Toltec king Totepeuh II (985–1026). By a happy combination of the proud native and the conquistador, the then Conde de Moctezuma was Spanish Viceroy of Mexico 1696–1701. It is to be hoped that as many other people as possible who have any redskin ancestry will record as much of it as is known while there is yet time.

We should all set to and emulate the effort behind Alex Haley's remarkable *Roots*, where he may have been misled about the exact village in Africa but nevertheless tracked down his American slave ancestry across the wide Atlantic to the aristocratic Mandinka kindred who bore the surname of Kinte in the former kingdom of Baddibu on the Gambia. And Mandinka history in general is known for the last thousand years,

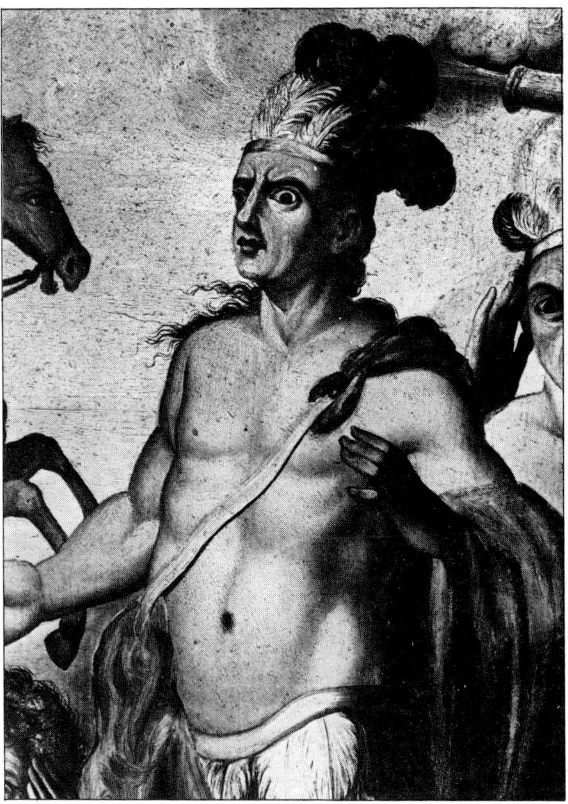

A print showing the South American Indian Chief, Moctezuma, who was the ancestor of the Spanish dukes of Moctezuma.

though it is rather an irony that although they abolished cannibalism throughout their conquests in West Africa they were themselves famous as slave-traders. Apart from the records kept in the Moslem and Christian north, such as those of the sultans of Morocco and the former imperial dynasty of Ethiopia, most black African genealogies are oral (as in Polynesia), but none the less valuable for all that, as their keeping was a sacred task. Thus the forefathers of the present Sabataka of the Baganda, son of my late friend 'King Freddie', the last Kabaka of Buganda, at whose ancestral court some of the ritual ceremonies went back to Ancient Egypt, are known through some thirty-five generations back to prince Kintu, the first Kabaka about 1300, an incoming royalty from a neighbouring kingdom whose dynasty is believed to have come by way of Abyssinia. In Africa, we may have come full circle, back to the cradle of Mankind.

In this Foreword, I have led you from the beginning of mankind up to some of the earliest traceable sources of present-day individual genealogy. This book takes over and leads you onwards from there.

CHAPTER ONE

Family History Yesterday and Today

Not for many centuries has the family as an institution been under such heavy and sustained attack as it is today, and nowhere is loneliness and the sense of rootlessness more complete than in modern cities. Twentieth-century urban civilization threatens family life in much the same way that traditional Roman values and family traditions were destroyed during the early years of the Empire. Since Western European civilization owes as much to Rome, and especially to Roman ideals of family life, as to the Jews, we should, perhaps begin by examining the role of the family in these two cultures.

The religion of ancient Rome was first and foremost the religion of the family. The very word religion means binding together. By extension, this religion of the family became the religion of the state. The central concept of Roman religion was the idea of genius, which begins from the paterfamilias who, in begetting children, becomes the head of a family. His essential character was isolated and given a separate spirit-existence; he carried on the family which owed to him its continuity and looked to him for protection. Thus, as a link in that mysterious chain of father-son-father-son, each individual gained new significance, setting him against a background which, instead of being a continuous surface, was broken up in such a way that one of its pieces became himself. His genius, therefore, was that which placed him in a special relationship to his long-dead forebears and to those of his progeny as yet unborn. Genius was thought of as a chain of mysterious power, linking the family from one generation to another; and it was because of this that the Roman father could see himself as a link in this unseen chain.

The traditional function of the family in Jewish culture was to propagate the race, and the family itself was a close-knit one in which the home was—and still to a large extent is—regarded as the basic religious institution, in which the individual found the completion not only of his personality, but also of his highest personal fulfilment in marriage and the continuation of the larger family. Whereas in Roman society the veneration of one's ancestors was due on account of the example they had set and so was of paramount importance, in Jewish society, especially of the Diaspora, children were the chief concern of their parents, because through them the hope of Jewish survival in a hostile world could be kept alive.

Greek attitudes to family life and to marriage differed markedly from Roman and Jewish attitudes. In Classical times neither married nor unmarried women

A frieze showing the family of Antonio II and Drusus—their son Germanicus, their daughter Antonia and Lucius Domitius Aenobarbus with his sons. Although the Roman religion was centred on the family such family group portraits are rare.

were regarded as legally entitled to act independently. They remained subject all their lives to the authority of a male citizen, usually their father or husband, but in the absence of either, to a male tutor or near relative. In Periclean Athens women who had been born free had no more political or legal rights than slaves. Their position contrasted strikingly with that of women under the Minoan and Achaean civilizations, who although not considered the equals of men did enjoy much more liberty than they would have been allowed at Athens. Such was the

threat of misogyny in ancient Greece that strict laws were passed against celibacy. At Athens, while not prohibited officially, celibacy was, nonetheless, uncongenial to the custom of the country. The desire to have at least one son led most young men to marry sooner or later, though marriage, more often than not, was for convenience or for the promotion of business interests. In fifth-century Athens, at least, wives hardly ever saw their husbands, except in bed. The couple rarely ate together, unless a family reunion took place; children were educated outside the home, the boys in the gymnasia and the girls in the gynecea. Christianity rejected most of what it found in Greek family life, but blended with the Roman reverence for ancestral custom and standards of public duty the Jewish concept of the family, wherein God was seen as the Father of all mankind, who to show His love for His earthly children had sent His Son to teach them that all men were brothers and members of one family, the Church. By the nineteenth century it would be hard to say which element was the more dominant.

There are few who lack all curiosity about their forefathers and nowhere is this truer than among those who have been adopted or brought up without any knowledge of their parentage. It is the natural human instinct to speculate upon one's ancestors—where they lived and what they did—and it is not surprising that ancestral records and genealogies can be found in the earliest records of civilized man. The application of genealogical techniques to the study of genetics and hereditary characteristics from diseases to handwriting will be considered elsewhere, and this application is increasing as the efficiency of method and of diagnosis improves. The actuarial evaluation of risks in the insurance industry, accident proneness, health potential, longevity and even criminal and anti-social tendencies all appear to be inherited either genetically, or because of family,

OPPOSITE
A studio portrait of a Jewish family in the early twentieth century. The family is the basic religious institution of Judaism.

BELOW
A Greek pyxis showing a marriage procession. In ancient Greece women had no more political or legal rights than slaves, although they were honoured with splendid weddings if they belonged to important families.

economic and environmental considerations; the study of all these can be enriched by family history, for while much of human behaviour is governed by environment, heredity plays an equal, if not more important part.

The study of family history is relevant to the laws governing inheritance and intestacy. Peculiarities of custom for succession at various times and in various countries require accurate knowledge of family if correct descent is to be legally established. Lawyers, therefore, have need of the skill of genealogists in such circumstances. Sociology, economics, the study of population movement, demography and the compatibility of groups of different ethnic origin, likewise depend upon it. For example, a study of the effect upon Kentish coalmining families of the immigration of miners from Durham and Wales early in the present century showed that there was considerable friction due to differences in local customs, speech, culture and behaviour. Although there was integration by marriage, such marriages were never secure, and the consequently disrupted families may well have been a direct cause of a very high rate of delinquency found among their children.

As has already been mentioned, there are strong forces striving to undermine the family and the hereditary system. George Orwell points out in *Nineteen Eighty-four* that 'class privilege' against which Marxists are trained to fight is based upon the false assumption that what is not hereditary cannot be permanent. That hereditary aristocracies have always been short lived is overlooked, whereas adoptive organizations such as the Roman Catholic Church have sometimes lasted for hundreds or thousands of years. The essence of oligarchical rule, he rightly points out, is not father-to-son inheritance but the persistence of a certain world-view imposed by the dead upon the living. A ruling group is a ruling group,

The Morse and Cator Families by Zoffany (*c* 1784). By the eighteenth century the union of such families was an important factor in the preservation of wealth.

so long as it can nominate its successors. Marxists are not concerned with perpetuating their blood but with perpetuating their political system. *Who* wields power is unimportant, provided the hierarchical structure remains the same.

In the same way, a deeper knowledge of history, and especially family history, makes it harder for the Party to fool the people. Past events, as Orwell rightly says, have no objective existence, but survive in written records and human memory. An oligarchy in full control of the records can falsify history at will. Thus the more an interest in family history is encouraged the more people will understand the truth of history, and the less they are likely to be taken in by ignorant political claptrap.

The present attack on the family may not always be motivated by sinister political ends, for it would be grossly unjust to accuse those who seek easier divorce and abortion of wishing to destroy the family as an institution. But the danger is real, and people should be made aware of it.

The fact remains that those who lived in closely-knit communities, whether they were isolated, rural peasant villages or Jewish, shtetl communities, knew more about true equality and worried less about class differences than their modern urban descendants.

The threat to Jewish family life in the United States and Western Europe is somewhat different from that which faces Christians. In his study of Jewish family life in the United States, Judson T. Landis found that the percentages of divorced and separated parents were 3·3 per cent for the Jews, 7·7 per cent for Roman Catholics and 10 per cent for Protestants, and for those of no religious faith it was 18·2 per cent. But while until recently Jewish families were more closely knit than those of other faiths or none, and probably still are, nevertheless, in recent years the rate of intermarriage between Jews and Gentiles has greatly increased. This tendency, while it must be welcomed on one level as a sign that the Jewish minority is becoming assimilated into the majority culture, at the same time poses a threat to the traditional Jewish family values and, should persecution return, to the ability of the Jewish way of life to survive. In 1963 Erich Rosenthal published a study of intermarriage in the Washington DC area in the *American Jewish Year Book*, which showed that while the overall ratio of Jewish intermarriage was reasonably small, the actual rate among the younger generation, namely those actually marrying at the time, was very much higher. Intermarriage has since become a burning topic for American Jewry, but there is unanimous agreement that intermarriage is growing, will continue to grow, and represents a great danger to the future of the Jewish community.

Writing in *Enemies of Society* (London, 1977), Paul Johnson makes much of the need to use words correctly, describing it as one of the most important elements in precision of thought. Skill in thinking logically and precisely is what we mean by science. This criterion is equally applicable to the science of genealogy: unless the truth is precisely sought and revealed, genealogies are no better than myths or fairy-tales. Genealogy has only recently emerged from a period of unscientific abuse during which it pandered to the conceit of those who indulged in it. This undoubtedly contributed to the erroneous yet trendy belief that the British are living in an ossified, class-ridden society. Indeed, the Marxist doctrine of the class struggle, so far as British society is concerned, is based on an almost complete ignorance of the historical and genealogical facts.

The science of genealogy must therefore be based on objectively established foundations using rational methods and mature criteria of proof. Great as his achievement was in tracing his ancestry to West Africa, this is where Alex Haley, the author of *Roots* finally fails. The work of historical demographers, especially of men like Laslett and Wrigley in England or Ganiage and Goubert in France, has shown scientifically how the classes in Western European society are constantly changing and that these changes are no new phenomenon of the twentieth-century reformers nor the result of a particular economic or social dogma. This is not to deny the existence of tensions between groups of people with different social and economic interests and backgrounds, which are both inevitable and desirable for progress. The concept of the class struggle and the perpetuation of the myth that people with a certain background or education behave in a certain exclusive and anti-social manner against the interests of the working class (whatever that term may mean) are good examples of pseudoscientific half-truths. Both notions are based on premises which are largely untrue and almost totally illusory. Historians and sociologists have, to be sure, written about the rise of the middle classes and the decline of the aristocracy and so on, but what in fact they have done is to draw general conclusions from a few examples of individuals and their families who had the ability to influence national and international events, and who experienced economic success or failure on an exceptional scale. The power and affluence of the Cecils, Rothschilds or Wedgwoods were only marginally shared by the whole social class to which they belonged. Their success (or failure) was due to the ability and intelligence of a few individuals. If by assortative mating these families were able to retain their power and affluence for several generations, this was because the social conditions in which they lived enabled them to do so. If, however, we go back to before the Reformation, we find just as many or just as few examples of men of humble origin attaining great power and wealth: Wolsey and Becket to name but two. Had it not been for the Church's rule of celibacy, no doubt they too would have founded influential families.

The Need for Family History

The need for genealogy arose from peoples' curiosity about their origins. For a long time legends were enough, but genealogy is the purest form of history as it concerns individuals, and, eventually, the desire to find the objective truth concerning the actual ancestors was to exert itself. The personification of history, which was the original purpose of genealogy, is still its greatest fascination, all the more so now that it is (or should be) dealing in scientifically proven facts. Tracing the history of one family is an admirable way of learning history. The reflection of wars and great national events on a set of individual families can sometimes tell one much more than the wide-ranging generalizations of a theorizing politico-economic historian; similarly how much deeper an understanding of social history can be derived by reading the plain facts about families without having them interpreted and analysed by a sociologist, incapable of thinking in anything but twentieth-century terms.

The twisting of facts to achieve a more pleasing result in a pedigree is as old as genealogy itself and still, regrettably, not unknown today. The biblical genealogies came to be dominated by the idea of purity of descent, illustrating the continuity of the race in exile. The first records in Greece were genealogical by nature, but open to abuse and of little historical value. Before the Roman Empire collapsed, the falsifying of patrician pedigrees back to Aeneas was a noted feature of that civilization. Busts of bogus ancestors would be placed in the shrines rather in the way that latter-day parvenus purchased their family portraits in antique shops.

The growth of genealogy took place as nations established themselves with modes of government and legal systems. Royal genealogies, as set out in the chronicle books, were obviously of the utmost importance in deciding the succession of kings and princes. The desire to assert the privileges of an aristocracy by birth was a powerful factor in Roman and Greek times (even in the days of the Republic) and in the development of genealogy throughout modern history. Inheritance is the heart of the hereditary principle and to settle disputes as to the inheritance of property, particularly real estate, genealogy came into its own.

The sixteenth century saw the start of collections of genealogies in manuscript and printed volumes; and the scholarship of the antiquaries of the seventeenth century uncovered material of immense value to the genealogist and demographer. Dugdale's prototype *County History of Warwickshire* and the work of the versatile Gregory King, the father of population studies, are outstanding examples of this period. Dugdale was also the first to produce, in his *Baronage*, a decent collection of the pedigrees of titled families. The eighteenth-century aristocratic view of genealogy is best summed up by Lord Chesterfield, commissioning, in a sarcastic gesture, portraits of Adam and Eve de Stanhope; and it was not until the nineteenth century that the pride of *Peerages* grew to such remarkable proportions. The 1700s had seen the appearance of *Collins's Peerage*, a largely legendary work which was corrected quite reasonably by Sir Egerton Brydges in its fifth edition (1778), apart from the insertion of his own forged ancestry. This is a characteristic syndrome of genealogists who, though reliable on other people's pedigrees, often get so hooked up on their own family trees that they alter records to suit their delusions of grandeur.

The nineteenth century was the golden age of bad genealogy; a whole shoddy industry, propped up by the pretensions of the parvenus to social status, supplied bogus evidence of gentility. There was also the craving for medieval romanticism, and to satisfy the families (the customers) some lamentable exercises in 'Gothick phantasie' were perpetrated. Mythological twaddle was put into the beginning of the pedigrees, which would often begin with the dread phrase 'The origins of this ancient family are lost in the mists of antiquity . . .'; whereas it was often more likely—social mobility being one of the key factors in tracing a genealogy—that the origins were lost in the dust thrown up by their carriage wheels. Genealogy became almost irredeemably tainted with the stigma of snobbery.

The twentieth century has been the age of the genealogy of the common man. Everyone has ancestors, and to a genealogist the fourteen generations behind Harold Wilson are of as much interest as those of the 14th Earl of Home. The Society of Genealogists was founded in 1911 to promote interest among amateur family historians; in 1968 the first professional body (the Association of Genealogists and Record Agents) was formed to establish codes of practice. During the 1970s the number of family history societies and One-Name family associations in Great Britain has risen from two or three to well over one hundred, and the same increase in interest and activity is to be found throughout the English-speaking world.

CHAPTER TWO

Genealogy and Genetics

From the earliest times heredity was regarded as the most important factor in deciding a child's future. The reason for this was the observation that children often resemble their parents, and that brothers and sisters often resemble each other. This is particularly obvious in the case of identical twins, who are not only identical with respect to heredity, but also very similar indeed in their respective personalities and talents. Thus the study of heredity is closely linked with that of family history.

The characteristic lower lip of the Hapsburgs is a persistent genetic feature which is apparent in portraits of members of the family from the sixteenth to the twentieth centuries. This demonstrates the inheritance of physical characteristics in the offspring of inbred families— it being the rule that royal families usually married their royal relations.

1.

2.

1. The Holy Roman Emperor Charles V (1519–1558) by Titian

2. The Holy Roman Emperor Ferdinand II (1578–1637) by Velasquez

3. King Philip IV of Spain (1605–1665) by Velasquez

4. Emperor Franz I of Austria (1708–1765) by Kreutzinger

5. Emperor Franz Josef I of Austria (1830–1916) by Winterhalter

6. King Alfonso XIII of Spain (1886–1941)

This way of looking at the origins of personality was supported by the fact that certain types of ability run in families. One has only to think of the Bach, Russell or Cecil families or the descendants of Josiah Wedgwood and Charles Darwin. But it is not at all clear why family resemblances should be interpreted in terms of heredity rather than environment. It is, indeed, possible that the outstanding qualities of the Bachs, Darwins, Cecils and Russells may have been transmitted through the exceptionally favourable environment the parents

3.

5.

4.

6.

provided for their children and grandchildren. Conversely, the fate of children with feeble-minded parents may just as easily be explained in terms of unfavourable environment. It is clearly impossible to argue from the resemblance of children to their parents to the importance of either heredity or environment, simply because both these hypothetical causes would work in the same direction.

Studies of inheritance have revealed a phenomenon known as 'regression to the mean'. The children of exceptionally tall parents will be tall, but not quite so tall as their parents. The same applies to children with very short parents who will tend to be somewhat taller than their parents, though still below average height. This phenomenon is quite universal and has been found to obtain, not only in relation to physical characteristics, but mental ones as well, and intelligence, in particular, has been studied exhaustively in this respect. The children of very bright and very dull parents respectively regress to the mean. This regression also obtains in the field of personality, so that the children of exceptionally unstable or of extroverted parents will be more stable and more introverted than their parents.

OPPOSITE

Josiah Wedgwood (1730–1795) by George Stubbs. As a result of marriages between his descendants and leading members of the intelligentsia, he can claim to be the ancestor of some of the most brilliant people ever born in Britain, including Charles Darwin and Ralph Vaughan Williams.

BELOW

The descendants of Josiah Wedgwood FRS.

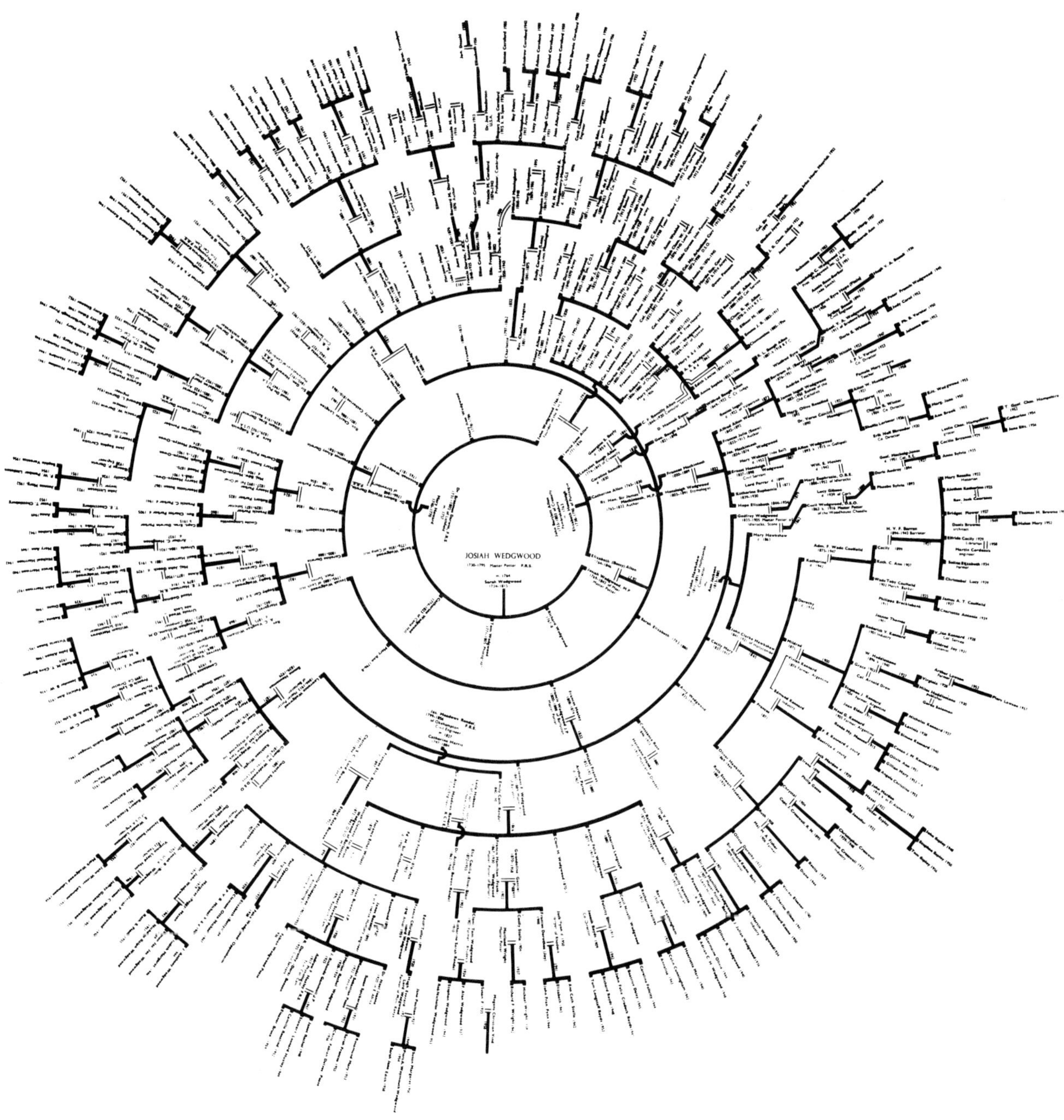

The truth is that genetic factors may produce dissimilarities just as readily as similarities. Each time a man and a woman beget a child, their genes are mingled in such a way as to produce a new and different combination which ensures that each individual is completely different from any other. Only identical twins have identical heredity. Brothers and sisters may be, and usually are, like each other, and may resemble their parents in some respects, but we can all point to people who are very unlike their parents and siblings. This is what would be predicted from our knowledge of the segregation of genes, and it is this dissimilarity that probably forms the strongest reason for asserting the importance of genetic factors. On the environmental hypothesis, brothers and sisters should be much more like each other than they usually are, especially if they have all enjoyed the same kind of home environment and upbringing. Environmental factors alone would not account for the very great dissimilarities often found between siblings who have been brought up together. Thus heredity produces both similarities as well as dissimilarities, and it is important to remember this when looking back on one's own family history.

It has often been asked how familial data can be used to substantiate the claim that heredity plays an important part in causing individual differences in intelligence. A knowledge of the degree of consanguinity between different types of kin makes it possible to deduce the precise amount of similarity that ought to be observable between them with respect to intelligence. Thus the highest degree of relationship should be found for identical twins; that between fathers or mothers on the one hand, and sons or daughters on the other, should be about half that seen for identical twins. The relationship between uncles and nephews, aunts and nieces should be smaller again, and so on. If genetic factors alone were the ones that were active, the degree of similarity should coincide with the degree of relationship. When this is done, observation comes close to theory, indicating that the effect of environment is not very strong. After all, the different members of a family enjoy broadly the same environment, yet the dissimilarities in IQ between them increase significantly the lower the degree of consanguinity.

Similar studies have been carried out with personality, in which identical and fraternal twins have been studied, and the outcome has usually been much the same. On the whole, genetic factors exert a powerful influence on the different aspects of personality and usually exceed that of environment, although the precise values depend upon the particular personality traits examined. The most convincing evidence for strong genetic determination is found in people's tendency to be sociable, impulsive and generally extrovert, as opposed to the contrary traits. Almost equally good evidence is available for emotional instability as opposed to sang-froid.

Another way of studying heredity and environment is by looking at the characters of adopted children. Those adopted in the first few months of life owe their biological inheritance to their true parents, but their environment is provided exclusively by their adoptive parents. The question arises whether

Identical twins not only look alike but also think alike and have very similar personalities. Fraternal twins, however, have no greater similarity to each other than ordinary siblings. By studying identical twins who have been brought up apart it is possible to assess the relative effects of heredity and environment.

Identical twins

Fraternal twins

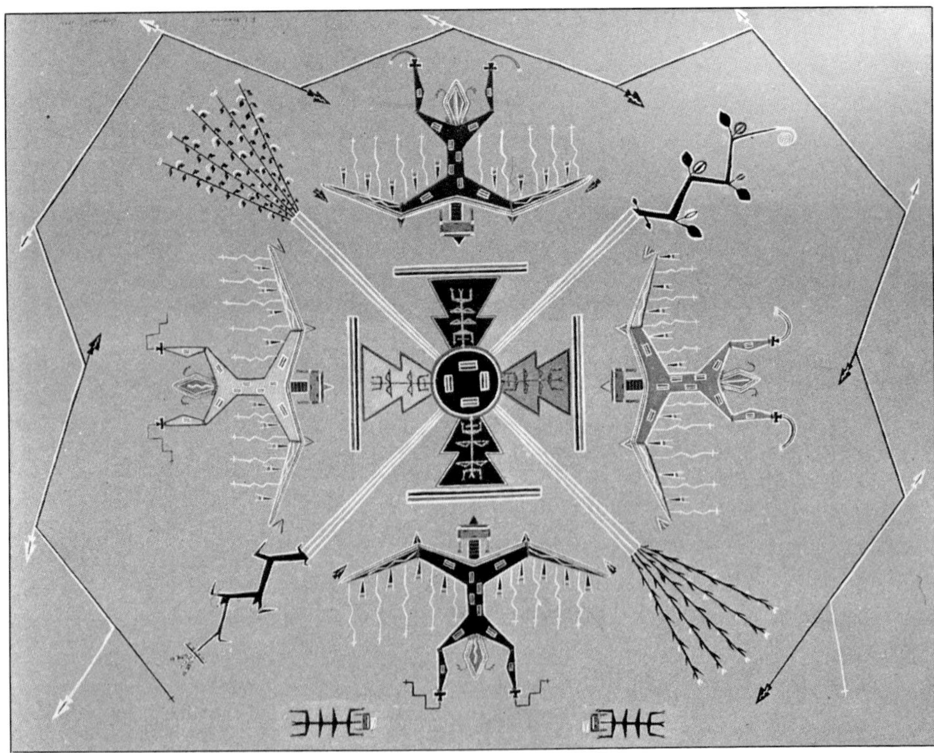

they resemble their true parents more than their adoptive ones. The answer is simple. Adopted children are more like their true parents in intelligence and do not resemble their adoptive parents to any notable extent. This often leads to adoptive parents being disappointed, for they hope that by providing a good environment, they will be able to bring up their adopted children to the level of their own. Of course, they may be lucky, and find they have adopted a genius, but the bright child may be held back if the adoptive parents are dull or intellectually much inferior.

The inheritance of intelligence can be studied in the offspring of inbred families. Some genes are dominant, others recessive. Intelligence, being obviously useful, is likely to show dominance in its mode of inheritance. If any kind of inbreeding takes place, the children of such marriages will show an increase of dominant characteristics, some of which may be desirable while others are undesirable.

An equally important consideration relates to the question of assortative mating. In other words, birds of a feather tend to flock together: intelligent men tend to marry intelligent women. This powerfully increases the heritability of this particular characteristic. However, no such assortative mating can be demonstrated in the field of personality. Extroverts do not tend to marry extroverts more often than introverts; emotionally unstable people do not tend to choose neurotic partners more often than stable ones.

OPPOSITE
Sand painting: North American Indian pictographs depicting a shooting chant.

RIGHT
Assyrian cylinder seals showing cuneiform writing, which was stiff and formal because the use of a stylus on clay made curved writing very difficult.

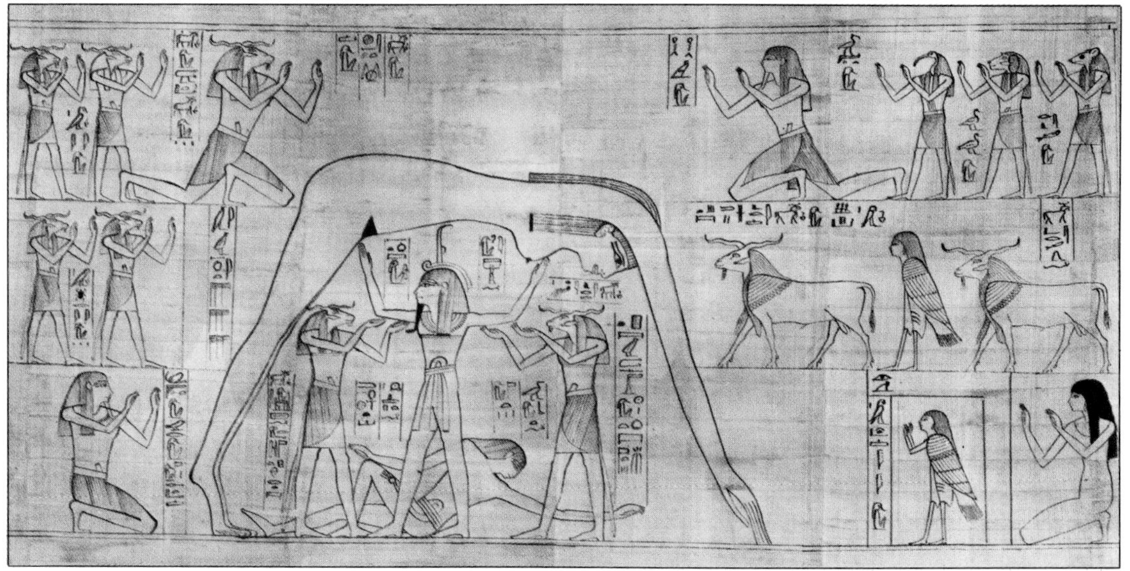

Egyptian hieroglyphic writing was based on stylized drawings of tangible objects. A combination was used to suggest abstract ideas. This detail from the Greenfield Papyrus depicts Nut, the sky god, holding up the sky.

OPPOSITE ABOVE
Egyptian heiroglyphs from *The Book of the Dead* (Papyrus of Hunefer). The illustrations show Hunefer before Ra.

A nineteenth-century screen painting showing the Chinese god of war, Kuan Ti. Chinese script is basically the same as Japanese script. The use of such writing allows people speaking different languages and dialects to communicate with each other as the signs bear no relationship to the words.

OPPOSITE BELOW
A bronze tablet (*c* 500 BC) recording the treaty between the Eleians and the Heraens of Arcadia. The Greek alphabet, like the Roman one, developed from earlier prototypes. It forms the basis of the Cyrillic scripts used by the Russians, Bulgarians and Serbs.

Given all these facts, genealogical investigations of single families, while having little or no scientific importance as such, can be all the more fascinating for the investigator who tries to discern in the pattern of family history the differing threads of heredity and environment. In individual cases these can never be conclusively demonstrated to be responsible for a particular characteristic, but we can reasonably argue from what is known about genetics to the individual case, and arrive at some plausible hypothesis about what, in our own make-up, we owe to our ancestors through the agency of genetics, and what through the agency of environment.

Graphology and Personality

More often than not the only 'artefacts' a person leaves for posterity which have emanated from him personally and are in essence uniquely 'of him' are his handwritten records. Handwriting is a record of the individual expression of his personality, and can be studied in detail if it appears in diaries and letters, and any changes over the years can be observed. A handwriting consultant with good historical background and knowledge, who understands the milieu and the copy-books of the time, can build up a picture of someone who died hundreds of years ago. For example, the disturbed writing of King James I and the writing of the ill-fated King Charles I of the United Kingdom brings their personalities to life in relation to the way they affected the course of history.

The study of human personality from handwriting is called graphology. An interest in the connection between handwriting and personality recurs throughout history. Aristotle and the Roman historian Suetonius Tranquillus are quoted as having shown interest in the subject, the latter in *The Lives of the Caesars.* John Keats said in a letter, 'I am convinced more and more day by day that fine writing is next to fine doing, the top thing in the world.' Disraeli, Goethe, Robert Browning and Baudelaire all flirted with the subject, which was intermittently a fashionable intellectual pursuit in Europe at the time. Sir Walter Scott obviously had serious thoughts on the matter as can be seen in this quotation from *Chronicles of Canongate:*

> Nay, my first impression was to thrust it into the fire . . . a little reflection made me ashamed of this feeling of impatience, and as I looked at the even, concise yet tremulous hand in which the manuscript was written, I could not help thinking, according to an opinion I have heard seriously maintained, that something of a man's character may be conjectured from his handwriting. That neat, but crowded and constrained, small hand argued a man of a good conscience, well-regulated passions, and, to use his own phrase, an upright walk in life, but it also indicated narrowness of spirit, inveterate prejudice, and hinted at some degree of intolerance, which though not natural to the disposition, had arisen out of a limited education. The passages from Scripture and the classics, rather profanely than happily introduced, and written in a

half-text character to mark their importance, illustrated that peculiar sort of pedantry which always considers the argument as gained if secured by a quotation.

Around 1840, a pioneer movement interested in the subject developed in France as a result of the studies of the Abbé Flandrin and the Abbé Jean-Hippolyte Michon; the latter spent many years of his life making a dossier of handwriting and the personality quirks of the writers. He coined the word 'graphology' and after the publication of his books *Les mystères de l'écriture* and *La methode pratique de graphologie* there was a great deal of interest in the subject in France.

With the end of the nineteenth century, the focal point of interest in graphology moved from France to Germany. Dr Ludwig Klages, who had already published several works on philosophy, wrote five books on graphology and became the leading force in Germany on the matter. Now in the second half of the twentieth century handwriting analysis is, and has been for many years, accepted in Germany as a valid subject for scientific study and as a commonplace tool for use in the business of personnel selection and vocational guidance.

Graphology is thus a science and an art. Handwriting is fixed and can be measured and it is possible to classify it in terms of size, proportions and angles with reference to age, sex and profession. But handwriting analysts have to draw up their reports in words, and it is often difficult to transpose scientific data into clear, concise language. Herein lies the art of interpreting handwriting, and it is because some analysts lack the gift of clearly expressing what the analysis of the writing tells them, that the subject has so often been led into disrepute.

The roots of our writing today can be found in early cave paintings and drawings. A picture that tells a story is called a pictograph, many examples of which survive among primitive peoples to this day. American Indian culture is particularly rich in the number of surviving pictographic documents. But it is important to understand that pictographs were visual images in no way connected to speech or language. Pictures and symbols, in time, came to stand for ideas and also became associated with sounds and syllables. Eventually individual alphabets developed with a sign representing each sound. Ironically the pictorial symbol has now reappeared for traffic signs, etc., and is universally understood bridging national languages and drawing people together.

Handwriting fashions change like those of costume and architecture. They are shaped by the social climate and changes in taste reflecting the spirit of the times and also by the technology of the day and materials available. When paper was scarce and expensive it was cheaper to write with a stick in damp clay; when feathers were made into pens and the art of turning skins into vellum was discovered the style changed again. The ball-point pen has similarly changed modern writing radically. The thick, rounded letter-forms of the Carolingian hand which developed in France in the early Middle Ages changed imperceptibly into a more angular Gothic style at about the same time that round arches gave way to pointed ones in ecclesiastical and military architecture. Gothic, in turn,

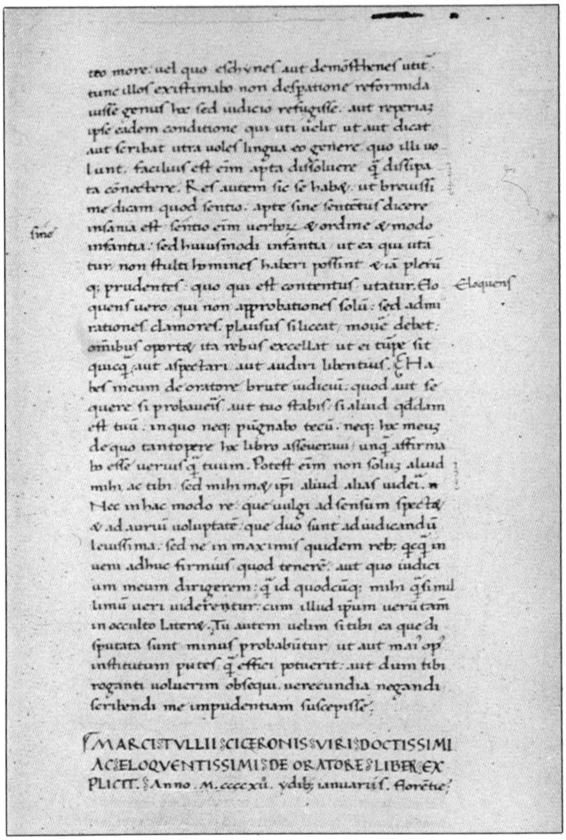

ABOVE

Gothic script: an extract from the beginning of The Book of Leviticus in the Bodleian Library. Gothic script was first used in France at about the time that the round arch gave way to the pointed one in architecture and spread from there to the rest of Europe. This writing survived in Germany with only small modifications until the end of the Second World War.

LEFT

Italic handwriting: an extract from a manuscript dated 1412.

An example of early nineteenth-century copperplate handwriting from a child's copy-book.

gave way during the Renaissance to a more flowing and graceful style influenced, no doubt, by the severe simplicity of the classical architectural forms which inspired the new movement. It is perhaps not insignificant that the Germans had a preference for the disciplined, iron-hard Gothic script right up to the time of Hitler.

In England a number of different 'hands' emerged around the middle of the sixteenth century. There was a native plain hand for correspondence, secretary hand and italic script for formal documents such as wills and parish registers, and court hand for legal documents, especially those written in Latin.

With the invention of the steel nib at the end of the seventeenth century, commerce and the law adopted copper-plate script which endured to the end of the nineteenth century and beyond. The early twentieth century saw the introduction of school copy-books written in a flowing, connected style with a rightward-moving slant and tall uppers with a confident look about them. This style admirably reflected the optimistic materialism, integrity and dedication of the great Empire-builders. Following the catastrophe of the First World War there was another significant change in writing style with the emergence of 'print script', an upright, disconnected and rounded style which did not lend itself to cursive elegance. Its introduction into the class-room was to herald the arrival of our uncertain modern age and of the utilitarian ball-point pen. In women's fashions it was the age of the short skirt and 'separates' which took over from matching suits. In the world of art it was the age of abstract cubism, surrealism, dada and ultimately nihilism; in architecture it was the age of By-pass Variegated, Stockbroker's Tudor and Gaumount-British Glossy.

Today people write smaller than they did a century ago. Personalities tend to be smaller because they tend to specialize. In fashion both men and women favour jeans, and captions on films are often written without capital letters. Victorian corsets have been consigned to the flames along with bras, and handwriting, like architecture has lost its beauty in the cult of punk, lack of delight and overwhelming cynicism.

In the West we write from left to right, so in the field of handwriting the future, where we are going to, is on the right, the past, where we have come from on the left. Lack of discipline and a sense of purpose for the future is reflected in a notable increase in 'left' tendencies, an increase in left-handedness and backward (or leftward) sloping writing. People are more concerned with the past and what has gone before; this is epitomized by the great popularity of historical spectaculars and what has loosely been called the nostalgia business. If we think of paternalism as being associated with the right (not necessarily in the political sense, of course), then maternalism can be associated with the left. It is significant, therefore, that we live in the age of the first British woman Prime Minister and of women's lib.

It can be seen that in families where correspondence and diaries have been kept, graphological examination of these documents can shed considerable light upon the characters of the people who wrote them.

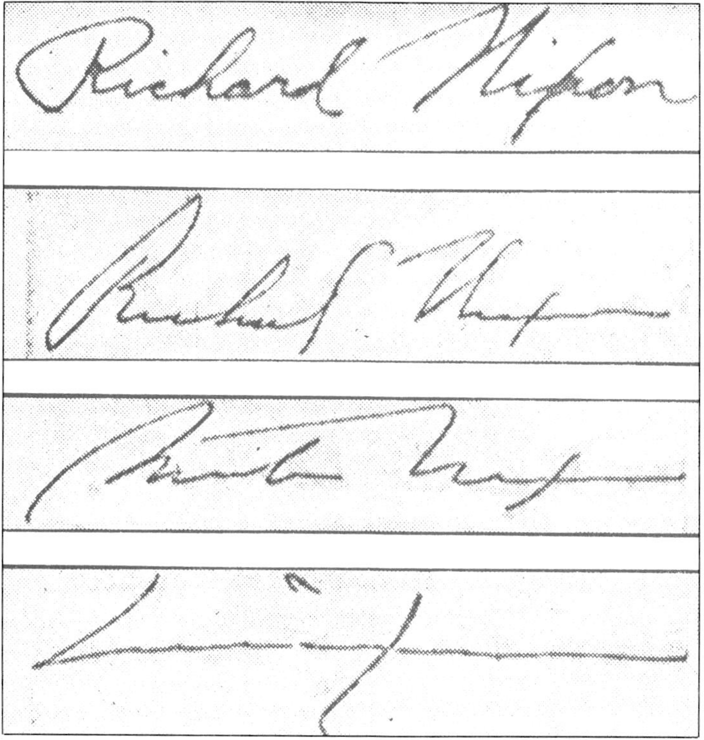

Four signatures of Richard Nixon covering the period 1959–1974: notice how the cross stroke of the 'x' becomes more exaggerated and the letter forms become simplified to the point of disappearing completely as the events in which he is involved become more desperate.

Adolf Hitler's signature before and after his rise to power. Like that of Richard Nixon it became less legible and shows a growing determination and obstinacy in the face of events.

Here is an example. Several dozen samples of writing covering five generations of a family were subjected to minute examination, in particular that of George, and his wife, Jane, and their son Simon. Simon was born when his two grandfathers were very old men, and he died before most of his grandchildren were born. Nevertheless it was possible to trace through these five generations certain characteristics. In the case of George, it was not possible to examine any examples of handwriting dating from the period before he met Jane, so any assessments had to be based on what survived from his maturity, and chiefly from the period 1873–1882. Each sample differed in style, but one was of particular interest, for George apologizes to his wife 'for the manner in which this letter is written'. It is the only one written naturally. The writing reveals a personality who had a mental picture of himself built up in youth, from which he never deviated. George saw himself as strong, reliable and friendly, and believed himself possessed of great charm. He wished to present this image to the world, and believed that others must see him in this light. His writing showed that he was a man driven by his desire for stature and professional prestige. In private he had to be the focus of attention and admiration. He was an incurable optimist, but beneath this façade his self-confidence fluctuated alarmingly. He possessed drive and ambition, but lacked a goal and purpose in life. He was clear-minded and objective, passionate, greedy and sometimes deceitful. The constant effort of playing a part tended to make him muddle-headed and compromised his judgment.

None of this was apparent from the content of the surviving documents themselves. Jane's writing, on the other hand, showed that as she matured she acquired an ease of manner and regularity of behaviour which she lacked in youth. Considerably more documents in her handwriting survive, and considerably more was known about her personality from these. Nevertheless, her handwriting suggested that she became dominated by a material and physical possessiveness, amounting in later years to an emotional sickness. This was something which the contents of her letters did not reveal, although the handwriting most certainly did. Comparing the handwriting of George and Jane, one finds some interesting similarities, which suggests that in many respects they were birds of a feather. In their personal standards, interests and depth of feeling, the evidence of their writing suggests that they were compatible. Both appear calculating and money-minded, but in their respective attitudes to personal distance the seeds of friction can be detected.

Their son Simon was a man of exceptional ability, both artistic and practical. He was an inventor and the founder of a successful business. In extreme youth (and letters from his fifth year to his death have survived as well as a mass of notebooks of a technical nature) Simon's writing is remarkable for the drive and vision it reveals. Research into the childhood environment of famous and successful men has shown that one parent frequently possesses a taste for research, experimentation or adventure, and a need for physical or intellectual activity. It has also shown that a possessive and ambitious mother can channel her thwarted wishes into ambition for her son. An unresolved Oedipus complex can, therefore, be the source of energy whereby the son tries to make the mother happy, feeling it to be his mission to succeed where the father has failed.

George had been a photographer, and his father before him a musician. He had absolutely no business sense, and had eventually gone bankrupt. The grandfather, however, had been a man of European stature, though likewise lacking in business acumen. In Simon's childhood writing an unconscious pull towards his mother is very apparent; so is his strong desire to excel. From a very early age he possessed a great capacity for thinking big and long-term planning. The writing suggests an exceptional ability for getting things done and seeing them through to their conclusion. He appears exceptionally thorough, and had a tendency throughout his life to make doubly sure, and to return constantly to correct what he had previously written.

Simon was a man prepared to observe the conventions of his age, where other men of equally great originality might disregard conventionalities. He was less original as a thinker, though better able to see the potential in other people's ideas and to exploit them with great imagination. This element of conventionality is one which permeates his writing throughout his life, suggesting a wish to proceed by orthodox routes rather than to strike out into fields beyond his own sphere. The writing reveals some strange alternations in his character. On the one hand there is aggression, and on the other humanitarianism, a hard streak balanced by something almost amounting to gullibility, but resulting in an impressionable, easily accessible personality.

About 1884, at the age of twenty, certain changes in his writing began to appear, indicating a versatility of the mind within a set framework. Later these variations increase, reflecting, by 1890, a nervous stress and strain. The most striking feature is the appearance of a halo-like loop above the letter 'k'. This detached movement is a characteristic of the writing of his son Bernard and daughter Sarah, and can even be detected in an embryonic form in his own childhood writing as early as 1872, when he was eight. This and other unconscious features detected in Simon's writing and that of his children, can be clearly observed in the writing of his father and grandfather, suggesting that the origin of certain character attributes can be traced genetically from particular sources by a study of handwriting.

CHAPTER THREE

Surnames: Their Origin and Meaning

Ever since antiquity, one of the chief requirements of society has been the ability to distinguish individuals by their own name. Originally people had only one name, but as society became more complex, this name became peculiar to the person concerned. At the dawn of Roman history, individuals were given one name only, but with the development of Roman society, a system was perfected to distinguish individuals from each other which resulted in their having up to four names. The first of these was the *praenomen*, followed by the *nomen*, then by the *cognomen* and frequently by an *agnomen*. The *praenomen* was a personal name chosen from a fairly limited number, possibly not more than thirty, and was often repeated within the same family. Typical examples are Caius, Publius, Marcus, Lucius, etc.

The *nomen* indicated the clan or *gens*, and was carried by every male and female member of the same *gens*, even by adopted children and by freed men and foreigners who had become Roman citizens as a result of service to a particular *gens*. The *nomen* is the most important part of a Roman individual's name. It links him directly with his clan, and also to both his ancestors and descendants. It is the symbol of the unity and continuity of the clan. For example, the full name of the Roman Emperor Claudius—Claudius Nero Drusus Germanicus—tells us a good deal about his ancestry.

The *cognomen* or surname indicates divisions of the clan into various families, and in general originated from a physical or moral attribute. The *agnomen* was added to indicate a particular situation, quality or relationship of a person who had been adopted.

Roman society, therefore, perfected rules for the distribution and succession of names comparable to our present system, and which were not found anywhere else amongst the peoples of antiquity.

The Greeks, in contrast to the Romans, tended to give people somewhat fantastic names, or names which had an idealistic ring to them. Many Greek names end in -cles (glory or fame) e.g. Pericles (very glorious); Sophocles (famous for wisdom); Callicles (famous for beauty). Other names began with Cle- such as Cleophanes (radiant with glory). Many Greek names incorporate the word 'aristos' (the best) e.g. Aristophanes (radiant with the best, or emanating goodness).

Whereas these names tend to be poetic, noble, fantastic or idealistic, the Romans in rugged contrast favoured much more prosaic names derived from

This tombstone of Aurelius Hermia and his wife gives an example of Roman names. Aurelius is his personal praenomen and Hermia his nomen or clan name.

mundane sources; for example Agricola (farmer); Cicero (a man who grows peas—maybe a peanut farmer!); Porcius (pig breeder); Rufus (red); Longus (tall); Crassus (fat); Balbus (stammerer); Claudius (lame); Plautus (flat-footed); Calcus (blind); Scaurius (club-footed); the list is endless and almost as if culled from the orthopaedic unit of a hospital. The ultimate in prosaic names must surely be those derived from numbers, such as Secundus (second); Tertius (third); Quartus (fourth); Quintus (fifth); Sextus (sixth) and so on. These names even became diversified into Quintilianus, Sextius, Octavianus and so on. It is almost as if fathers could not be troubled to find names for their offspring, so just called them two, three, five or whatever.

An element present in Greek names, but only in a minor way, reflects religion and an awareness of God. In the countries of the Middle East, and especially amongst Arabs and Jews, names referring in some way to God are extremely common. Many Jewish names incorporate the syllable Ja, Jo or Je, short for Jehovah or Jahwe, and begin or end with El, both of which mean God. For example Joshua (whose help is God); Jokanaan (John) (whom God has given); Jehosaphat (to whom God has done justice); Obadaiah (in Arabic Abdullah—God's Knight); Elimelech (to whom God is King); Eliezer (to whom God is help); Nathaniel (God-given); and Joel (a double reference to God, i.e. God is Jehovah). Even abbreviated names such as Nathan, which is short either for Nathaniel or Jonathan, contain this God element.

Ancient Teutonic names likewise reflect the characteristics of that warlike race. A strong preoccupation with heroes, war and fighting distinguish the Germans of antiquity. War and a thirst for adventure according to Tacitus (far from silent as his name implies), were what the Germans were best known for, and the 'Furor Teutonicus' is reflected in their names. The words for weapon, war, struggle and victory are at the root of most ancient Teutonic names. *Hild, gund, had, bad* and *wig* are ancient Teutonic words for struggle, battle and war, which have disappeared from the German language as it is spoken today, but which entered Britain with the Angles and Saxons, and which survive today, as for example in Wyman from Wigmund, and Hathaway from Hadawig.

Germans, more than other European peoples, have tended to keep their ancient names. Names such as Otto, Hermann, Heinrich, Adelbert, Dietrich and Bernhardt are all of Teutonic origin. These names spread outwards from Germany and by the time of the Crusades they were found belonging to Frenchmen, Italians and Normans. For example Godfrey (Gottfried) de Bouillon, Robert of Normandy, Raymond of Toulouse, Boemund of Taranto. In 991, many of the French bishops who gathered at the Synod of Reims had German names; e.g. Adalbert of Laon, Godermann of Amiens, Odo of Senlis, Ratbod of Noyon and several others.

After the fall of Rome, it was not until the eleventh century that it was again felt necessary to distinguish individuals by more than one name or to distinguish every clan or stock by a surname. The *cognomen* or family surname which has now been incorporated legally into society originated towards the end of the tenth century. It is true, however, that a few great families were distinguished by surnames as early as the ninth century, but only a very few documents have come down to us from this remote period to show which names were used as surnames transmitted from father to son and which were used as second names or nicknames.

The essential characteristic of a surname is its continuous transmission from father to son indicating the stock from which a family descends. In Italy, the Venetians were the first to use surnames. A document dated 982 signed by Baduarius Bragadino, Vitalis Greco, Johannes Bembo, Dominicus Maurocene and Dominicus Contareno among others, is the earliest surviving example.

There must be tens of thousands of differently spelt British surnames, but their modern form is comparatively recent, often preserving a phonetic spelling found two or three hundred years ago in some parish register or manorial roll. Some British surnames sound very foreign; indeed a great many are of German, French, Scandinavian and Jewish origin. But the name Pharaoh, for example, has nothing to do with Egypt but is a reconstructed spelling of Faro, originally Farrer, found also as Farrey, Farrah (made famous by the manufacturers of Harrogate toffee) and Farrow. The Sussex name of Van Ness has as little to do with Holland as its variant Venis has to do with Venice. Both are variants of a French place name Venoix in Normandy, where one of William the Conqueror's knights held land before the Conquest. Other variants of this name appear as Veness and Venus—nothing to do with the erotic activity of one of its bearers.

People nowadays are very particular about the correct spelling of their surnames, but a fixed spelling has generally only been adopted since Victorian times, and one cannot therefore assume that a distinctive spelling found in the past and continued to the present indicates continuity of line. The whims of scribes and the dictates of fashion had more influence on the spelling adopted from time to time than any other factor, particularly as most people were illiterate and signed with a mark.

We are fortunate in the English-speaking countries that the custom—though not the law—has long been that the children of a marriage assume the father's surname. Certainly in England this has been the case since medieval times, but in Wales there was a system of patronymics until recent centuries by which there was one name for each generation, linked to the previous one by the appellation 'son of'. The Scottish and the Irish clan/sept systems have resulted in the suppression of Celtic surnames, the acquisition or imposition of substitutes, and the limitation to a clan name.

Thus a surname, better than any pedigree, can take one back in the male line over twenty generations or more and then back again, more indefinitely, as a byname or forename, perhaps, to a person of Saxon or Norman or even Danish origin.

Surnames became fixed and hereditary over a long period and were in common use from about the beginning of the sixteenth century. No laws were made on the subject (and there are still none) and no conscious decision in any one generation to adopt a surname and make it hereditary; it was all very much a matter of

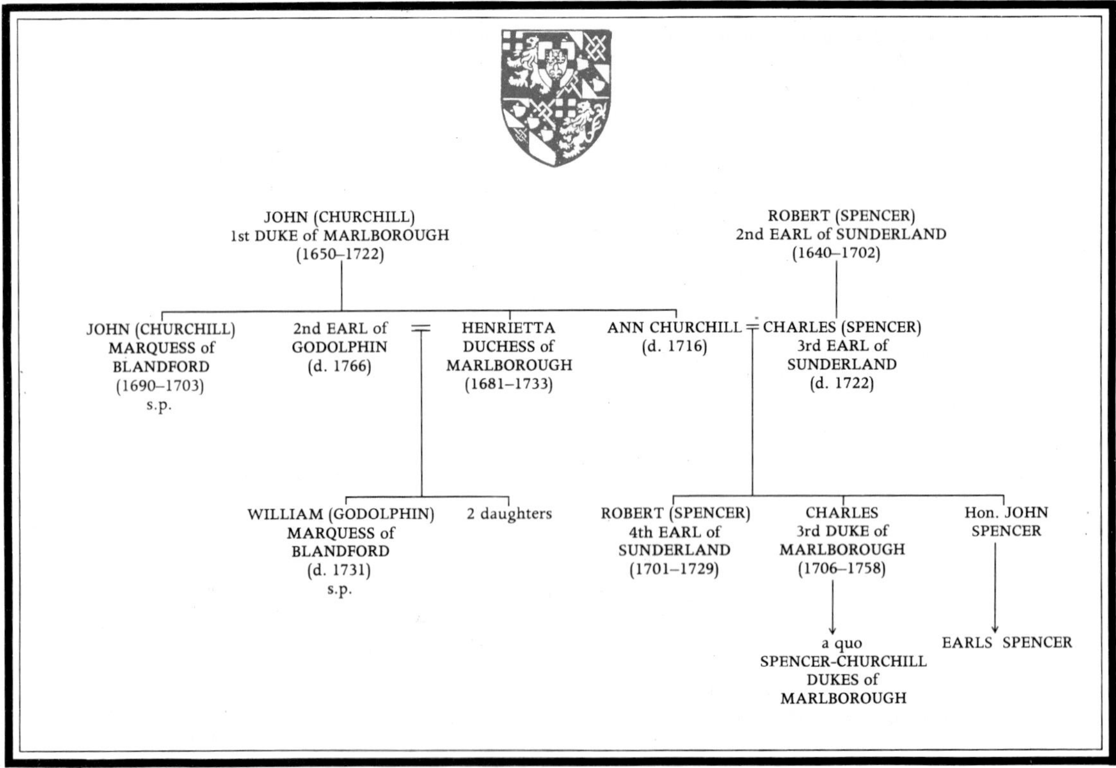

This extract from a family tree shows how the surname Spencer-Churchill arose. Charles Spencer, 3rd Earl of Sunderland married the younger daughter of John Churchill, 1st Duke of Marlborough. Following the death of her elder sister without surviving male heirs, the dukedom together with the names Spencer and Churchill came to the second son of the Earl of Sunderland. The earl's youngest son continued to use the name Spencer only and was the father of the 1st Earl Spencer.
The arms shown are those of Spencer and Churchill quartered together.

convenience, both personal and administrative. Before this time, as again is the custom now, 'Christian'-names sufficed for daily use.

Surnames may be divided into five main groups:

1. Surnames of relationship, that is to say deriving from the father's name (patronymic) or mother's name (metronymic)—Johnson, Alisson.
2. Surnames deriving from offices, titles, professions or trades—Judge, Lord, Parson, Tailor.
3. Surnames deriving from places or country of origin, from feudal fiefs and from topographical features—London, French, Ecclestone, Hill.
4. Surnames deriving from plants, fruits, flowers and animals—Quince, Bull, Tree. This is a particularly popular category among Italians, where an eccentric king of Naples once decided to award his courtiers titles of nobility, all of which were connected with vegetables, hence: Duca della Verdura (Duke of Greens), and Conte Carotti (Count Carrots).

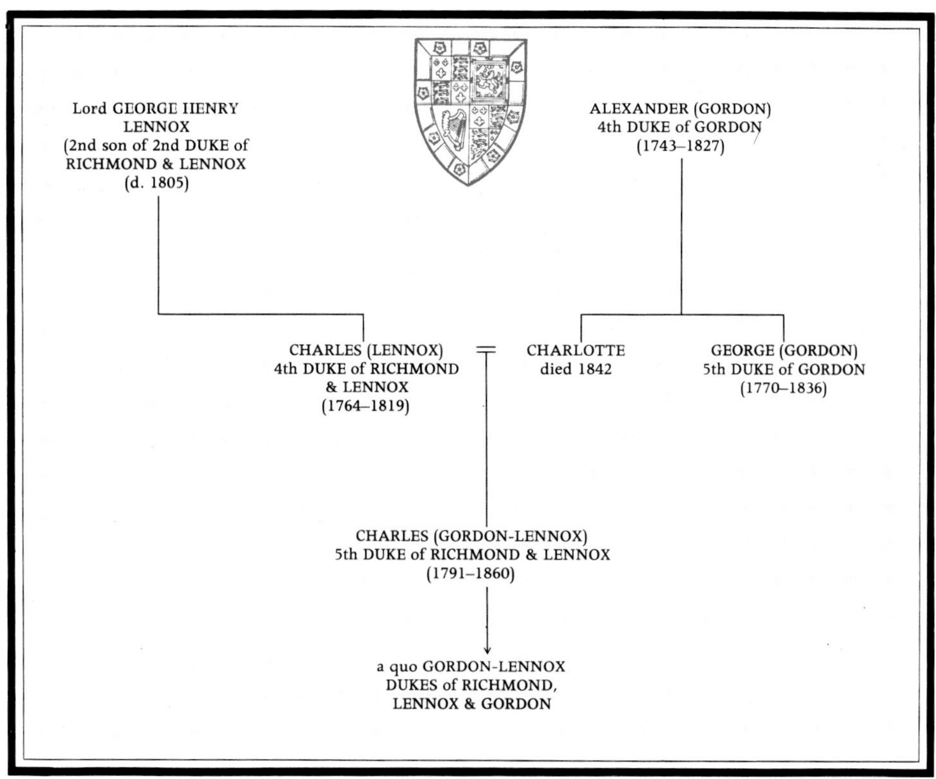

On the death of the 5th Duke of
Gordon without issue the title devolved
on his sister's grandson, the 6th Duke of Richmond and Lennox.
Thereafter the family took the two names Gordon and Lennox
and the triple title of Richmond, Lennox and Gordon.

5. Surnames deriving from nicknames—Cruickshanks, Goosey, Sharp, Wise. A sub-division of this category contains what may be termed phrase names, such as Purefoy—pure faith; Godsave or Godsalve. Such nicknames have the crudest of origins. There is the famous story told by John Aubrey in his *Brief Lives* of the courtier who, on making a profound obeisance before Queen Elizabeth I, had the misfortune to break wind. He was so overcome with embarrassment that he went into voluntary exile for many years. On his return home it happened that the Queen met him on one of her Progresses. With a tact not perhaps as great as that of her latter-day namesake Elizabeth II, the Queen said 'Sir, we greet you. We have forgot the fart.' It was no doubt an ancestor who committed the same faux pas at the French Court, who earned for Marshal Pétain the name of Roland Le Péteur.

In the nineteenth century the fashion for multiple surnames began to appear. One of the earliest examples is Ashley-Cooper, dating from the late seventeenth century, but with the union of aristocratic or politically influential houses, the habit increased. When John Churchill, Duke of Marlborough, died without a male heir, his daughter combined her surname with her husband's to produce Spencer-Churchill. They were followed by the Cavendish-Bentincks, Montagu-Douglas-Scotts, Twistleton-Wykeham-Fiennes, Ernle-Erle-Drax and even Cave-Brown-Cave. Generally speaking this custom grew out of the wish to perpetuate the name of a family which would otherwise have died out for want of male heirs. In earlier times the surname was given as a first name, so that one can find in the sixteenth or seventeenth century such names as Bassingbourne Gawdy, Moundeford Kirby, Seckford Gosnold, where the given name is usually that of the mother's family or more rarely the surname of a godparent from whom it was hoped the child would receive a substantial legacy. Nowadays the tendency is to drop one of the two surnames, as for example, the family of Lord Brabourne, the late Earl Mountbatten's son-in-law, who now call themselves Knatchbull, whereas they were formerly Knatchbull-Hugessen.

Some surnames that have disappeared in this country are still alive and well and flourishing in America and Australasia, while others have assumed different forms in those countries, particularly the United States, for a variety of reasons. Taken down by 'foreign' clerks, uttered by descendants unfamiliar with the place from which they originally hailed, if a locative name, they became distorted in the process and then formalized in this condition when spellings became fixed during the last century. Conversely, in many cases foreign names have accidentally or purposely become disguised as English names, so that now they cannot be told apart, with sometimes traditions or legends accruing to support their supposed origin, so that we are back again to the parallel of the modern Englishman who accepts unchecked family stories as to the origin of his own name and family. However, in general, the surnames of modern America reflect ethnic origins and though the United States and Canada are chiefly English-speaking, the names of their inhabitants reflect the polyglot nature of Europe.

CHAPTER FOUR

Where to Begin: Family Sources and Traditions

The first rule for the family historian is this: always work from the known to the unknown. This is the principle adopted by all police forces the world over, because it is the one which produces results which stand up to the most critical examination in courts of law. This may, perhaps, seem a somewhat stark approach to family history, but if you wish to create a pedigree that truly records your ancestry and which is worth handing down to posterity, then it is essential.

Probably most of us have family legends of lost fortunes and vast acres that should by right belong to us. Many have been told of an ancestress who was 'taken advantage of' by the Duke of Blankshire, or that we really belong to the landed gentry, or have blue blood in our veins. Grandmother, for example, may be convinced that her husband, long since dead, was a descendant of, shall we say, the Percys. On investigation, however, it may turn out that he was only the son of a man who lived in Alnwick. It is indeed possible that the descent is genuine, as in the case of Frederick Howkins mentioned by Sir Iain in the Foreword; on the other hand everything could be thoroughly above board and the only connection may turn out to be that of employer and employee.

A very large number of Americans are convinced that their ancestors came over the Channel with William the Conqueror, and over the Atlantic in the *Mayflower*. This is fascinating romantic stuff, but the genuine family historian should be seeking fact not fiction. Since a surprising number of people can genuinely trace their ancestry to King Edward III, as Sir Iain pointed out in the Foreword, the legend may not be so fanciful after all, but the point is it must be proved. Many traditions become exaggerated or diluted to become 'more acceptable', particularly the latter, for our Victorian ancestors were adept at locking skeletons in cupboards and sweeping dirt under carpets. It is therefore not advisable to accept everything at face value, yet traditions nevertheless carry a grain of truth, and should be borne in mind as they may help to point out a line of research which otherwise would be overlooked.

It is not always possible to establish a connection with a distinguished family of the same surname. This is a trap into which the descendants of many emigrants tend to fall. Howard, for example, is an extremely common surname, sometimes deriving from Hayward—an official found on every manor in the land—and sometimes from the old German for high or chief warden, and occasionally from the old French Huard which in turn derives from the old German, literally translated as brave heart. But because the premier English peer, the Duke of

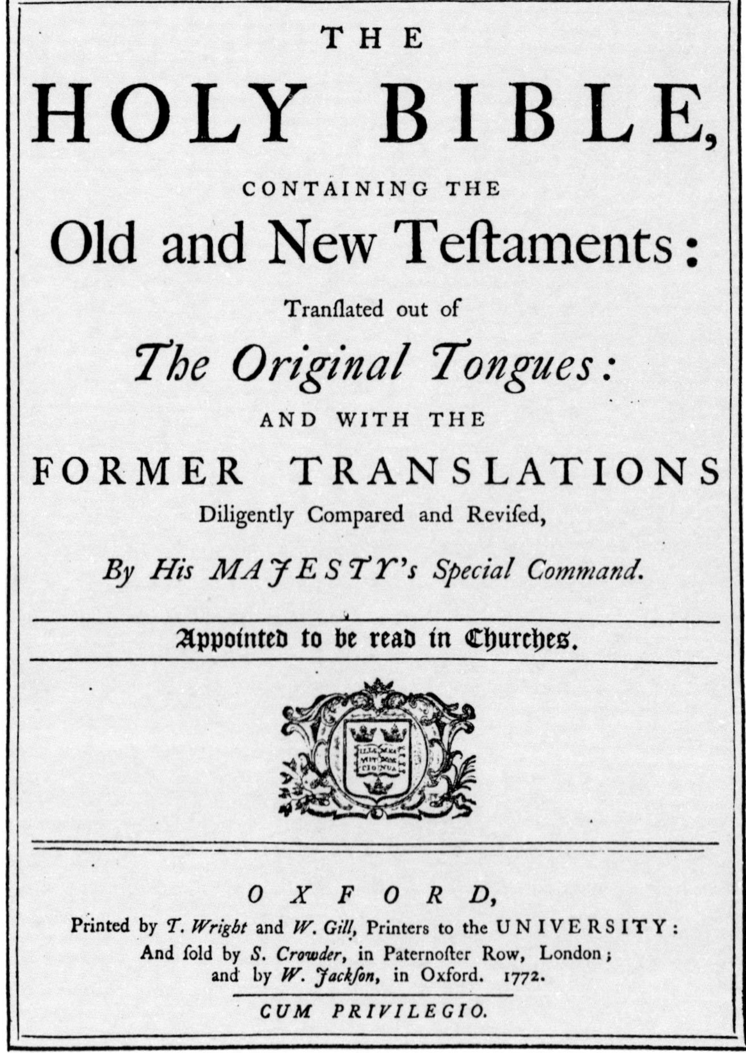

THE

HOLY BIBLE,

CONTAINING THE

Old and New Teſtaments:

Tranſlated out of

The Original Tongues:

AND WITH THE

FORMER TRANSLATIONS

Diligently Compared and Reviſed,

By His MAJESTY's Special Command.

Appointed to be read in Churches.

OXFORD,

Printed by *T. Wright* and *W. Gill*, Printers to the UNIVERSITY:
And ſold by *S. Crowder*, in Paternoſter Row, London;
and by *W. Jackſon*, in Oxford. 1772.

CUM PRIVILEGIO.

The title page and fly-leaf of an eighteenth-century family Bible, with the date of printing and entries recording births, christenings, and deaths of members of the family.

Norfolk, happens to have the surname Howard, people tend to jump to the conclusion that they are his kin. The chances of being related to such families is remote indeed. For names like Churchill, Townsend, Russell or Spencer derived in the first two instances from place names, Russell comes from red or 'russet', and Spencer from dispenser (of provisions), i.e. Steward or Butler. Indeed, what about Stuart and Boteler? If you are related to one of the prominent families bearing these names, the fact will automatically emerge in the course of research, and will be all the more rewarding for being accurate and substantiated by archival evidence.

William Currer married Elizabeth Swire March 18th 1777

Alice Currer born May 6th 1778 – babtized – died May 7th 1778.

Jennet Currer born March 2nd 1780 – at 20 min: past 12 in the Morning
babtized April 3rd – Sponsors Mr. Roger Swire
died May 13th 1791. aged 11.2.11 Mrs Currer
Mrs Swire – Proxy for whom Mrs [illegible]

Elizabeth Currer born March 27th 1782 – 10 Minutes before 7 in the Morning
babtized April 25th – Sponsors The Revd Wm Currer
died Novr 26th 1814 aged 32 8 — Jennet Swire
buried at Luddenden 1st Decr 1814 Mrs Higginson her Proxy [illegible]

Henry Currer born March 27th 1784 at five in the Morning. Died
babtized May 10th – Sponsors Revd Wm Currer Feby 12th 1817
N.B. The above Henry Currer laid the Roger Swire Ae. 32. 11. buried at
first stone of Boy Mill on Friday the Luddenden Feby 17th
18th of Feby 1803 Henry Currer Junr

Elizabeth the Wife of Wm Currer died Decembr 5th 1793 in the
50th year of her Age.

William Currer died Decr 13th 1807 in the 58 year of his
Age — buried at Luddenden on the 17th Decr

Fortunately it is unnecessary to start research from such abstract points, for by applying the principle of working from the known to the unknown, the search is taken backwards generation by generation to the most remote ancestor the records can reveal. Having decided which particular surname is to be researched, initial enquiries will be directed towards one particular family. However, if you are undecided which line you wish to trace, it will be necessary to obtain as much information as possible from all branches of your family group. In this way it is possible to chart your genetic descent from both parents, four grandparents, eight great-grandparents and sixteen great-great-grandparents—

A trade union membership certificate, like any other personal document, gives the researcher information about the individual to whom it belonged and can suggest new lines of inquiry.

always supposing you have that many. It is one of the ironies of genealogy that those with the bluest blood have the fewest ancestors, for the tendency among the aristocratic and dynastic families for cousins to marry each other reduces at a stroke the number of grandparents from four to two.

Those who attempt to trace their genetic ancestry frequently encounter the problem of a Jones, Smith or Brown ancestor, which effectively can block their path. At this point it is as well to pass on to a less common family surname, and undertake detailed research into that line instead. In practice, however, most family historians tend to keep to one surname only.

The most valuable and rewarding information will come from your eldest relatives, and it is logical to start by consulting them. If your surname is comparatively uncommon, it is often worth writing to people of the same name whose addresses you can find in the telephone directories. Some of these may well turn out to be remote cousins and they may have oral or documentary evidence to help in the building of a pedigree. As for family traditions, oral evidence is not always completely accurate, so allowance must be made for incorrect names, dates and places, which may have to be amended later when reliable documentary evidence is found.

An interesting example of this kind of problem relates to the American family of Langhorne. Family tradition, handed down over several generations, suggested that the family originated in the Welsh village of Laugharne and from a family of that name which owned large estates in Pembrokeshire in the seventeenth century. It is easy to see how this mistaken tradition arose, if one is unaware of the fact that the Welsh name is pronounced monosyllabically 'Larne'. The American family pronounces its name 'Langen' and the confusion arose from the mis-transcription of several documents in the printed Calendars of State Papers where a Colonel Richard Laugharne sometimes appears as Colonel Richard Langhorne. Anyone can be forgiven for confusing the written letters 'u' and 'n', and 'a' and 'o'. These were in fact two quite distinct families and it was not very difficult to disentangle the confusion once it was realized how the initial mistake had arisen.

Family Bibles are a most valuable source of evidence, for the records of births, christenings, marriages and deaths were usually made at or near the time of the event, and are therefore usually reliable. It is important, however, to check when the Bible was printed, for it is by no means unknown for the original Bible to disintegrate with wear and to be replaced by a new one, and for the entries either to be incorrectly transcribed or even entered from memory.

Copies of birth, marriage and death certificates may be found among family documents. Associated with these certificates may be baptismal certificates, wedding invitations and memorial cards, and because these are printed close to the time of the event, they are usually accurate records. The same applies to Confirmation and First Communion certificates, Barmitzvah cards, marriage contracts and settlements, and divorce settlements.

Records of academic and professional attainments are useful sources of

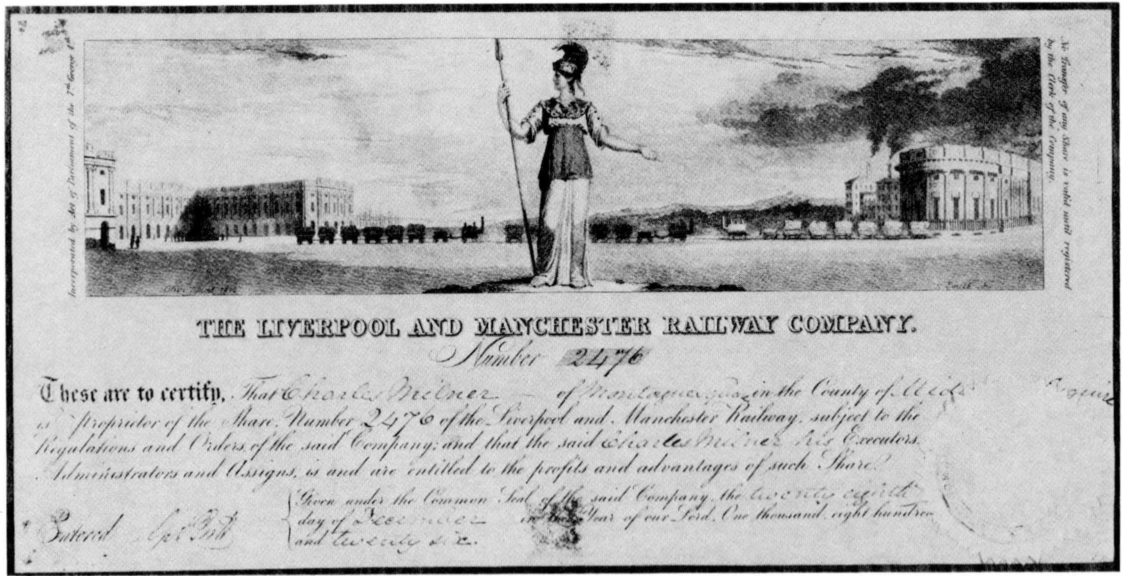

Incorporated by Act of Parliament of the 7th George 4th

No Transfer of any Share is valid until registered by the Clerk of the Company.

THE LIVERPOOL AND MANCHESTER RAILWAY COMPANY.

Number 2476

These are to certify, That Charles Milner of [illegible] in the County of [illegible] is Proprietor of the Share Number 2476 of the Liverpool and Manchester Railway, subject to the Regulations and Orders of the said Company; and that the said Charles Milner his Executors, Administrators and Assigns, is and are entitled to the profits and advantages of such Share.

Given under the Common Seal of the said Company, the twenty eighth day of December in the Year of our Lord, One thousand, eight hundred and twenty six.

Entered

information, particularly service records such as discharge papers. School prizes and certificates, university degrees, sporting prizes and cups, certificates of ordination, club and association records, trade union cards, apprenticeship indentures, trade and guild records, freedoms of cities, testimonials, civic awards, medals and decorations—all these add flesh to the bare bones of a pedigree and give clues to age and hence date of birth. In addition to these basic facts, they indicate abilities, interests and achievements in a way no other sources do. They can also point to the direction from whence some of your own interests and characteristics derive.

Records relating to property are valuable for the light they throw on the movements of a family from one place to another. Maps, passports, identity cards, denizations, naturalizations and letters, both personal and official, provide much information about a family, for they record major events in the lives of the individuals and families concerned.

Another type of record relates to wealth and health. These include bank books, stocks and share certificates, annuity (tontine) certificates, medical certificates, driving and other licences.

Finally, there are personal documents and mementos which may include pedigrees or notes on aspects of the family's history, which if not authenticated by a body such as the College of Arms, will need checking for accuracy. In this category fall diaries, personal letters and scrapbooks which, if subjected to handwriting analysis (see Chapter 2) can add greatly to one's knowledge of the character of the writers. Birthday books and cards, account books, book plates, samplers, which frequently include the age of the person who worked them and where and when they were made, armorial silver, china and glass, mourning and

OPPOSITE
This share certificate dated 1826 gives the name and address of the shareholder. This type of personal record is invaluable as it pinpoints the individual as being at a particular place at a particular date.

BELOW
A roll pedigree of the Hawley family in 1640 which was written in 1870. It shows the arms of related families; the Hawley arms are those with four lions on a bend.

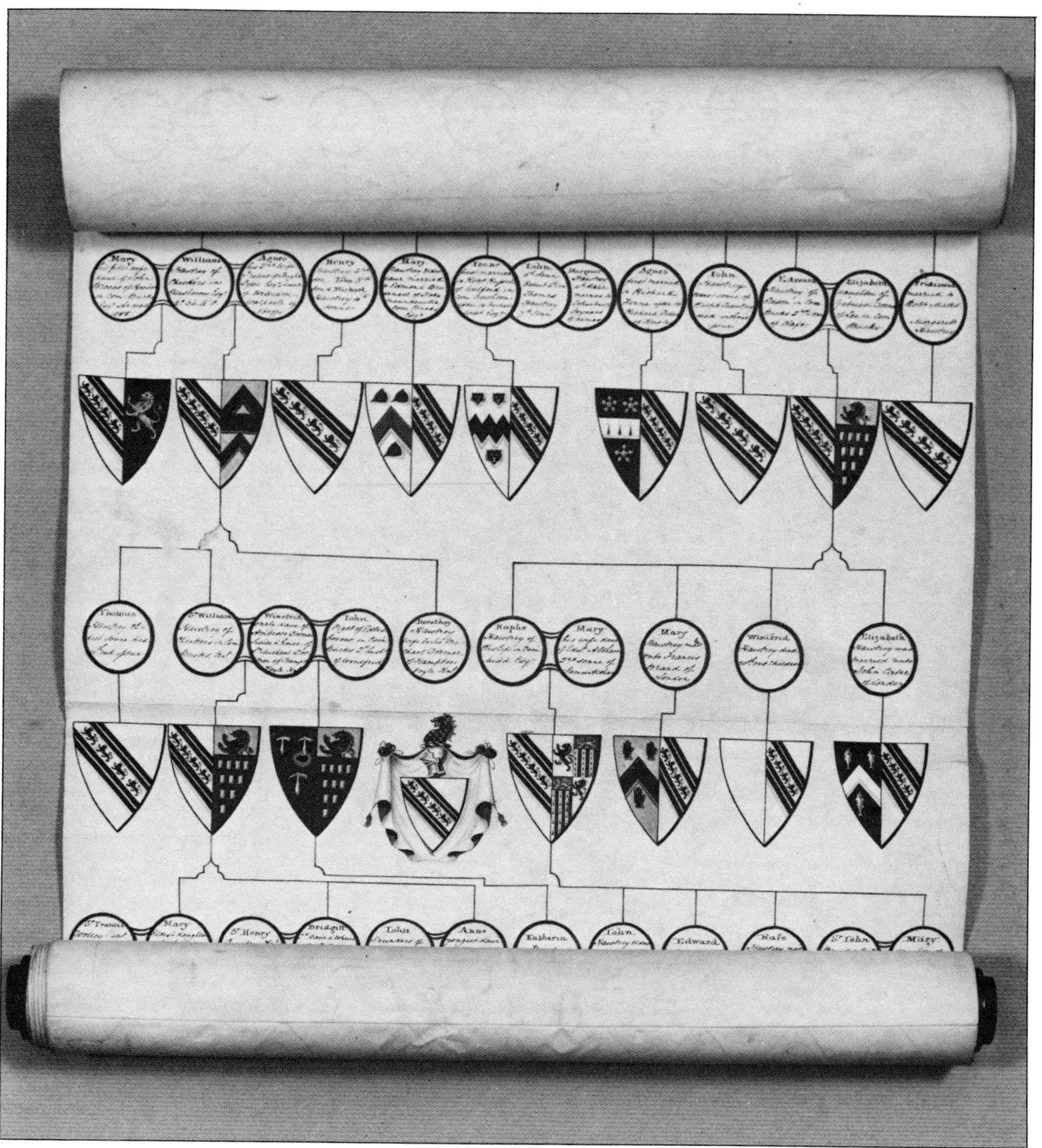

Pieces of armorial china, glass and silver that are handed down within a family help the family historian to establish links with those whose arms are on the items.

signet rings, seals and fobs, and of course portraits and photographs of people and houses are all very valuable. As an example of the way in which a picture of a house can help, a Canadian had a picture of a Georgian house in Somerset in his family album. It was taken about one hundred years ago, and the caption underneath it included the name of the house and the words 'God Bless our Home'. There was no-one in the family who knew why it was in the album, nor the name or the relationship of the person who put it there. A letter to the present owner elicited a number of interesting facts, including copies of the deeds from which it was possible to discover that the house had been let for twenty years between 1860 and 1880 to a family which, on investigation, proved to have been that of one of his great-grandparents, whose name he did not even know. From this it was ultimately possible to discover when this particular individual had been born, married and emigrated, and why.

Naturally, a number of these items could be in the possession of distant members of the family, possibly those who descend from female lines and whose surnames are different from your own. Care should be taken when approaching such people not to give the impression that as the family historian of your particular branch, you are the person to whom they should belong. Whenever possible, offer to have the material copied at your own expense, or make arrangements to photograph it yourself. Since much research of this kind must be carried on by correspondence, often with elderly people who may be easily bothered by

This earthenware dish bears the arms of James Brydges, Marquess of Caernarvon, and was made between 1759 and 1771.

receiving letters asking numerous questions, and who may not be in the habit themselves of writing long letters, the response may be negative. Wherever possible it is a good idea to seek a meeting, and to record your conversation on tape. An excellent example of this technique is to be found in Ronald Blythe's marvellous book on Suffolk village life *Akenfield*, which is almost entirely based on tape-recorded interviews. When approaching people for family information, it is advisable to take or send a separate pedigree of the family group, and ask for comments, corrections and additions where appropriate. Ask if there are any documents available for copying, and if your correspondent knows of any other members of the family who might have information to offer. Always enclose a stamped addressed envelope or two International Reply Coupons.

If you do not know of any direct contacts, but know the town or county from which your ancestor came, then an enquiry through the personal column in the appropriate local newspaper or county 'countryside' magazine could bring results. Head the advertisement with the surname you are researching in bold type. Most people stop to read anything about their own name, or one that is well known to them. Follow this with a brief explanation of the research project, asking anyone with information or similar interest to contact you at the address shown. If the surname is a common one locally, much of the information may be irrelevant, on the other hand it may put you in touch with distant kinsfolk who are unknown to members of your family.

CHAPTER FIVE

Printed Sources

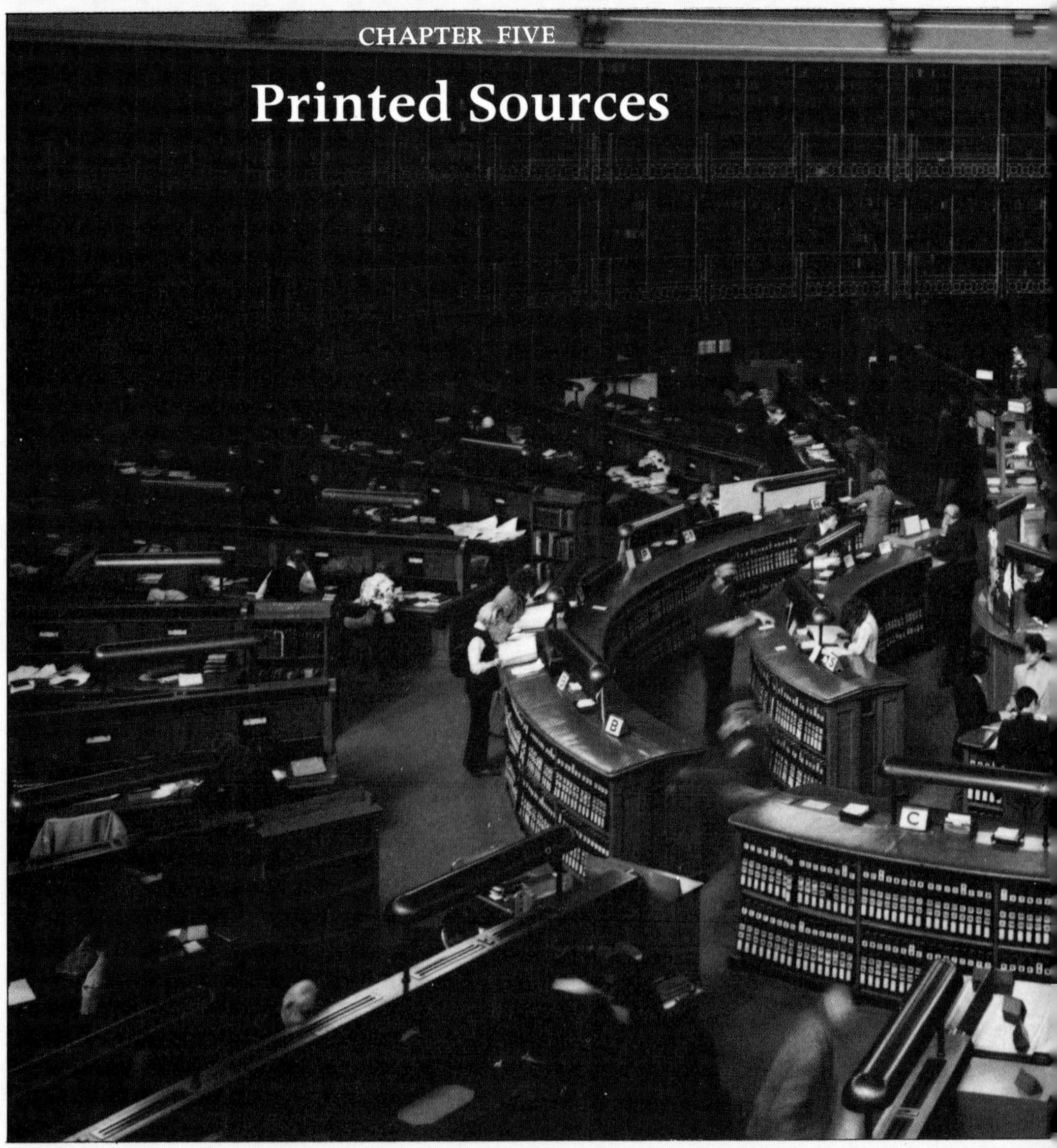

After getting all the information you can from family sources, and before embarking on extensive research in manuscript archives, it is wise to find out whether any work has been done before on the families in which you are interested, or whether anyone else is currently engaged in research with whom you might exchange information.

Two valuable books available at most principal libraries are G. W. Marshall's *The Genealogist's Guide*, and J. B. Whitmore's *A Genealogical Guide* which is a continuation of Marshall's work. These books form a valuable index to pedigrees of three generations in the male line that have appeared in print before 1953.

The Reading Room at the British Museum contains the main index of books in the British Library. The catalogue is held in the two concentric stacks of shelves which can be seen in the middle of the room.

T. R. Thomson's *A Catalogue of British Family Histories* and G. B. Barrow's *Genealogist's Guide* are more recent works containing additional information which complement Marshall and Whitmore. Margaret Stuart's *Scottish Family History*, Joan P. S. Ferguson's *Scottish Family Histories held in Scottish Libraries* and Edward MacLysaght's *Irish Families, Supplement to Irish Families* and *The Surnames of Ireland* are the appropriate works for those countries.

When you first set out to discover what printed books about your family there may be, time can be saved by a visit to the British Library at the British Museum, but admission to the Library is by pass which is available only if you are over twenty-one years of age. Provided you take proof of identity, such as a passport, banker's card or similar document bearing your signature, a pass can be obtained without much difficulty, once you have been photographed in the Research Admission Office. However, if you wish to have access to the Department of Manuscripts, you will need a written reference from someone of recognized position, such as a clergyman, lawyer, or schoolmaster, certifying that you are fit to use the Students' Room of this department. Because the demands on staff and accomodation in the Reading Room of the British Museum have increased so dramatically in recent years long delays in the production of books and documents must be expected.

In order to find out what printed sources on the particular family you are interested in there are, you must consult the main catalogue where printed family histories are listed under the relevant surname. These may include privately printed volumes of memoirs and diaries as well as family histories themselves.

Under the Copyright Act, the British Library is one of six libraries to which a copy of every book published in Great Britain since 1814 must be sent. The other Copyright Libraries are the Bodleian, Oxford, the Cambridge University Library, The National Libraries of Wales and of Scotland, and Trinity College Library, Dublin. You will thus find a number of extremely useful standard works, including *Walford's County Families*, *Victoria County Histories*, sundry county and parish histories, genealogical periodicals, the *Gentleman's Magazine*—a goldmine of information in the form of obituaries and articles of family interest, *The Dictionary of National Biography*, *Who Was Who*, and many more. The Manuscript Department is particularly valuable for collections of family papers, diaries, genealogies and the huge collection known as the Harleian Manuscripts which contain copies of many of the pedigrees taken at heraldic visitations extended by subsequent historians.

It is worth mentioning that once you have listed the books which interest you in the main catalogue, most can be obtained through the inter-library loan scheme from your local public library.

Many County Libraries and County Record Offices have collections of local family genealogies which are easy to locate as they are almost invariably indexed.

Many pedigrees, not all of them armigerous, are registered at the College of Arms in London, or at the Lord Lyon Court in Edinburgh, the two official bodies with jurisdiction over the granting of arms in England and Scotland. The corresponding body in Ireland is the Office of the Chief Herald of Ireland at Dublin Castle. The College of Arms does not allow public access for research, but searches can be undertaken by officers of the College on the payment of a fee. In Edinburgh and Dublin the registers are open to the public. Nevertheless, there are several standard reference books on heraldry such as, for example, Fox-Davies' *Armorial Families*, Debrett's and Burke's *Peerages*. Burke's *Family Index* is a general guide to family entries featured in their range of genealogical and heraldic publications since 1826 and is of great value to family historians.

The College of Arms in London is the headquarters of English heraldry. Although visitors may enter the building, the College's records are not open to public examination.

In addition to these generally available sources, there is a large collection of family histories and pedigrees at the Society of Genealogists in London, which houses the largest specialized library on the subject in Britain. Non-members can make searches in the Society's Library for a daily fee.

The recently established National Genealogical Directory, which is available through most local libraries, lists the names and addresses of about seventeen hundred family historians, and over twenty thousand surnames of families currently being researched. Similar directories of 'members interests' are published by many local family history societies, which are now established in every English county and parts of Wales, Scotland and Ireland. Now nearly every county has such a society, and the address of your local society, or the one in the county from which your family may have originated, can be obtained from The Federation of Family History Societies in Cambridge, Gloucestershire. For those who decide to embark on a definitive study of a particular surname, it is advisable to contact The Guild of One-Name Studies in Essex, which is the co-ordinating body for the growing number of family historians who concentrate their research on references to a single surname only.

CHAPTER SIX

Manuscript Sources

Civil Registration

No matter how much information has been obtained from family and printed sources, the exciting time will come when you have to embark on original research of your own. For the family historian the progression of research is in the main logical so long as the axiom of working from the known to the unknown is adhered to. Inevitably the first public records required to extend a family history are those of civil registration of births, marriages and deaths.

The starting date for civil registration was not uniform throughout the United Kingdom. In England and Wales it started on 1 July 1837, and the country was divided into Registration Districts under the control of a Superintendent Registrar whose records contain all the original certificates for the events that were registered within that district. At the end of each quarter—March, June, September and December—a copy of all registered events is sent to the Registrar General at St Catherine's House in London. These are collated into master indexes for births, marriages and deaths for the respective quarters, but it must be emphasized that the entries in them relate to when the event was registered, and not to the date it actually took place. If therefore you are looking for an event that happened near the end of a quarter, it may not be registered until the beginning of the next one.

Anyone can go to St Catherine's House to examine the indexes of births and marriages or to nearby Alexandra House to examine the indexes of deaths. Such searches can be carried out free of charge. It should be borne in mind, however, that these places become very overcrowded, particularly during school half-terms and holidays as well as between 12 and 2 pm. Therefore these times should be avoided as much as possible.

The distinctive bindings of the indexes—red for births, green for marriages and black for deaths—make it easy to locate the section required. Within each volume, all entries are arranged in strict alphabetical order. Because surnames are liable to variant spellings, however, it is advisable to make a list of all these so that each can be checked if the entry required cannot be located where you expect to find it. For example, a family named Langman might be indexed under Longman. The name Kirby can be spelt more than thirty ways phonetically. Because the letter 'b' in seventeenth-century script can be mistaken for 's' and 's' can be mistaken for 'f' the name could appear (and, indeed, has) as Kersie and Kerfitt, for 'tt' can be mistaken for a final 'e'.

CERTIFIED COPY OF AN ENTRY OF BIRTH — GIVEN AT THE GENERAL REGISTER OFFICE, LONDON

Application Number 4605 B.

REGISTRATION DISTRICT Woodstock

1874 BIRTH in the Sub-district of Woodstock in the County of Oxford

Columns:— No.	1 When and where born	2 Name, if any	3 Sex	4 Name and surname of father	5 Name, surname and maiden surname of mother	6 Occupation of father	7 Signature, description and residence of informant	8 When registered	9 Signature of registrar	10* Name entered after registration
388	Thirtieth November 1874 Blenheim	Winston Leonard	Boy	Randolph Henry Spencer Churchill	Jennie Churchill formerly Jerome	M. P. for Woodstock	Randolph S. Churchill Father Blenheim	Twenty third December 1874	George Foster Registrar	

CERTIFIED to be a true copy of an entry in the certified copy of a Register of Births in the District above mentioned.
Given at the GENERAL REGISTER OFFICE, LONDON, under the Seal of the said Office, the 23rd day of November 1976

*See note overleaf

This certificate is issued in pursuance of the Births and Deaths Registration Act 1953. Section 34 provides that any certified copy of an entry purporting to be sealed or stamped with the seal of the General Register Office shall be received as evidence of the birth or death to which it relates without any further or other proof of the entry, and no certified copy purporting to have been given in the said Office shall be of any force or effect unless it is sealed or stamped as aforesaid.

BXA 253978

CAUTION:—Any person who (1) falsifies any of the particulars on this certificate, or (2) uses a falsified certificate as true, knowing it to be false, is liable to prosecution.

Form A502M (S.355267) Dd.323476 110M 12/75 H/w.

CERTIFIED COPY OF AN ENTRY OF MARRIAGE — Given at the GENERAL REGISTER OFFICE, LONDON

Application Number 086 D

Registration District of St. George Hanover Square

1908. Marriage solemnized at The Parish Church in the Parish of St. Margaret Westminster in the County of London

No.	1 When married	2 Name and Surname	3 Age	4 Condition	5 Rank or profession	6 Residence at the time of marriage	7 Father's name and surname	8 Rank or profession of father
483	September 12th 1908	Winston Leonard Spencer Churchill	33	Bachelor	President of the Board of Trade	Board of Trade 7 Whitehall Gardens S.W.	Lord Randolph Churchill (deceased)	M.P. Sometime Secretary of State for India & Chancellor of the Exchequer.
		Clementine Ogilvy Hozier	23	Spinster	—	51 Abingdon Villas Kensington	Sir Henry Hozier (deceased)	Colonel

Married in the Parish Church according to the Rites and Ceremonies of the Established Church by Licence by me A. G. Asaph

This marriage was solemnized between us, Winston Leonard Spencer Churchill, Clementine Ogilvy Hozier

in the presence of us, Jennie Cornwallis-West, Ridesdale, D. Lloyd George, William Hozier, Blanche H. Hozier, Hugh Cecil Churchill

CERTIFIED to be a true copy of an entry in the certified copy of a Register of Marriages in the District above mentioned.
Given at the GENERAL REGISTER OFFICE, LONDON, under the Seal of the said Office, the 9th day of August 1977.

This certificate is issued in pursuance of section 65 of the Marriage Act 1949. Sub-section (3) of that section provides that any certified copy of an entry purporting to be sealed or stamped with the seal of the General Register Office shall be received as evidence of the marriage to which it relates without any further or other proof of the entry, and no certified copy purporting to have been given in the said Office shall be of any force or effect unless it is sealed or stamped as aforesaid.

MB 167994

CAUTION:—Any person who (1) falsifies any of the particulars on this certificate, or (2) uses a falsified certificate as true knowing it to be false, is liable to prosecution.

Form A513 (S.356449) Dd.437139 40m 11/76 Hw.

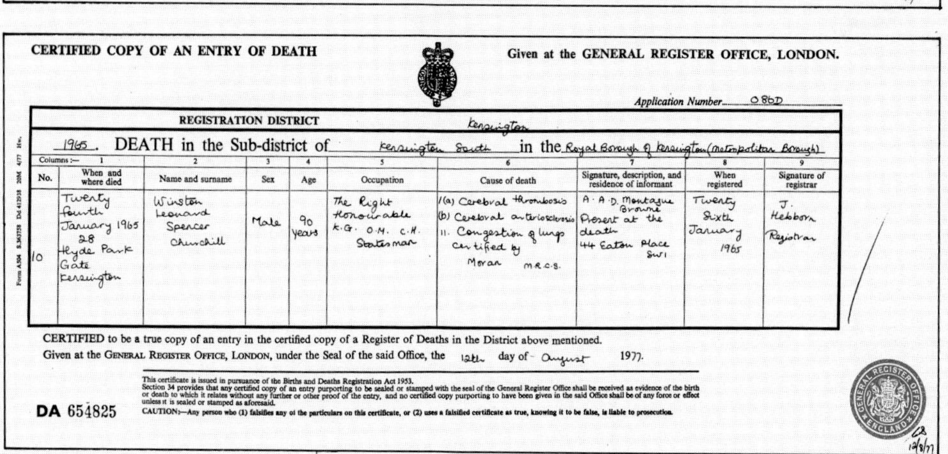

CERTIFIED COPY OF AN ENTRY OF DEATH — Given at the GENERAL REGISTER OFFICE, LONDON.

Application Number 086D

REGISTRATION DISTRICT Kensington

1965. DEATH in the Sub-district of Kensington South in the Royal Borough of Kensington (Metropolitan Borough)

Columns:— No.	1 When and where died	2 Name and surname	3 Sex	4 Age	5 Occupation	6 Cause of death	7 Signature, description, and residence of informant	8 When registered	9 Signature of registrar
10	Twenty fourth January 1965 28 Hyde Park Gate Kensington	Winston Leonard Spencer Churchill	Male	90 years	The Right Honourable K.G. O.M. C.H. Statesman	I(a) Cerebral thrombosis (b) Cerebral arteriosclerosis II. Congestion of lungs certified by Moran M.R.C.S.	A. A. D. Montague Browne Present at the death 44 Eaton Place SW1	Twenty Sixth January 1965	J. Hebborn Registrar

CERTIFIED to be a true copy of an entry in the certified copy of a Register of Deaths in the District above mentioned.
Given at the GENERAL REGISTER OFFICE, LONDON, under the Seal of the said Office, the 12th day of August 1977.

This certificate is issued in pursuance of the Births and Deaths Registration Act 1953.
Section 34 provides that any certified copy of an entry purporting to be sealed or stamped with the seal of the General Register Office shall be received as evidence of the birth or death to which it relates without any further or other proof of the entry, and no certified copy purporting to have been given in the said Office shall be of any force or effect unless it is sealed or stamped as aforesaid.

DA 654825

CAUTION:—Any person who (1) falsifies any of the particulars on this certificate, or (2) uses a falsified certificate as true, knowing it to be false, is liable to prosecution.

Form A504 S.363738 Dd 412938 20M 4/77 Hw.

The birth, marriage and death certificates of Sir Winston Churchill KG show that no differentiation is made for rank in these records, which are common to all citizens of England and Wales, including members of the Royal Family.

You should start by looking at the volume where you think you will find the entry of your known family member. When you have found the volume you require for the appropriate quarter and year, and the particular name of the person you are looking for, it will then be necessary to note the various references shown against that name. The full entry indicates the surname, forename(s), registration district and the volume and page number on which the actual entry is recorded. This information, together with the year and quarter, are required for completing the application form to obtain a copy of the full certificate. You will need the full certificate as the short one is of little value for genealogical purposes, since it omits details of parentage and gives the date and place of birth only.

There are certain 'peculiarities' for each main section of the indexes which are worth noting. The indexes from the September 1837 quarter to the December 1865 quarter are handwritten on vellum and are split into a number of alphabetical volumes (a note of caution: these can be very heavy to handle). The details given are as previously described. Unless there are more than three, each forename is written out in full. In the year 1866 the indexes are printed, and for this year only the second and any other forenames are only shown by initials. From 1867 to 1911 these indexes are printed with most of the forenames.

In 1911 we witness the beginning of typescript indexes with again only the first forename being shown. From 1912 onwards, the surname of the mother is recorded in the birth indexes, immediately following the surname and forename(s) of the child. This can be a valuable check that the entry is the correct one, provided, of course, that the mother's surname is known. This is also helpful in compiling a family group from the index entries without the expense of obtaining certificates for all the children born to a particular family. Some mothers' surnames are the same as the surname of the child. Although this can be a case of marriage between cousins, it quite frequently signifies a birth out of wedlock. In the Marriage Indexes the surname of the other party is also shown after 1912. This again is a check that the entries are correct, if both surnames are already known. With marriages, both parties are indexed under their respective surnames; therefore it is always essential to check both the entries (assuming both surnames are known), in order to obtain the certificate, the district, volume and page number for both parties must be identical. Here sometimes one has to search a number of years if your particular ancestor was the youngest of a large family. Do not despair if you do not find a marriage quickly. The Death Indexes show the age at death, after the forename(s) from 1866 to 1968. After 1969, the date of birth of the deceased is shown instead of the age at death, which may or may not be accurate.

The information shown on each full birth certificate is as follows:

1. When and where born;
2. Name, if any;
3. Sex;

4. Name and surname of father;
5. Name, surname and maiden surname of mother;
6. Occupation of father;
7. Signature, description and residence of informant;
8. When registered;
9. Signature of registrar;
10. Name entered after registration.

If at the time of registration the forename(s) of the child have not been decided, the 'Name, if any' column will be left blank, and the entry in the index will show the surname, followed by either 'male' or 'female'. However, if the forename(s) were ultimately notified to the registrar, then they would be recorded in the last column, headed 'Name entered after registration'.

If the child was born out of wedlock, in most cases the name of the father is not shown, and the child is registered under the surname of the mother. However, since 1875 the father's name may be inserted, in which case the birth is registered under both surnames.

If the mother had previously been married, then the column 'Name, surname and maiden surname of mother' would show, for example, Jane Brown, late Smith, formerly Jones. But if the informant did not reveal this information, it will not be shown, and could therefore read Jane Brown, formerly Jones.

If you cannot find the entry of the person required in the main index, but other members of the family group are known, it is worth looking for one of these entries, and if you find it, obtaining the certificate as this will provide you with the information regarding the parents. This procedure is recommended because of the surname variants previously mentioned, which, apart from phonetic misinterpretation, can be caused by incorrect copying from the original registration.

Full marriage certificates contain the following information:

1. When married;
2. Name and surname of both parties;
3. Ages;
4. Condition (bachelor, spinster, widow, etc.);
5. Rank or profession;
6. The residence of both parties at the time of marriage;
7. Fathers' name and surname;
8. Occupation of fathers.

If the names of both parties are known, then it will be easier to locate the relevant index entry for the less common surname first, and then cross-check this with the other party's index entry for the matching references previously mentioned. If the bride is a widow her surname will be that of her late husband; but if a divorcee then it may be her previous married surname or her maiden name. Sometimes a woman has been living with her husband before the marriage, and may have changed her name to his by Deed Poll. Consequently she will be listed in the index under her changed, but lawful surname, and if declared at the time of registration, also under her original surname.

If the name of one or the other or both fathers is missing on the full certificate, this may be due to several reasons: the party was born out of wedlock, the father was deceased, or at the time of registration the information was not recorded. The last two instances are cases of negligence, but such cases are known to have happened. Some marriage certificates will show the name of the father together with the word 'deceased'. There is, therefore, no point in looking for his death registration after the day on which the marriage took place. On the other hand, the fact that 'deceased' is not recorded on the certificate is not proof that the father was in fact alive, as at the time of registration this particular question may not have been asked.

The ages shown on marriage certificates can be misleading. They may have been increased or decreased at the whim of the parties involved. Unfortunately, many are recorded as 'of full age', meaning that the people were twenty-one years old or upwards. Often '21 years' can indicate the same thing, merely that the person was of full age. The 'Residence at the time of marriage' may not always be the usual place of abode of the bride and bridegroom, but may be a temporary address of convenience. It is well worth noting the religion and occupation shown on marriage certificates, since these may be important clues to other records, and to the identification of people elsewhere.

Death certificates contain the following information:

1. When and where died;
2. Name and surname;
3. Sex;
4. Age;
5. Occupation;
6. Cause of death;
7. Signature, description, and residence of the informant;
8. When registered;
9. Signature of registrar.

It should be remembered that the place of death may not be the usual residence of the person who has died. In fact you may find that the deceased died many miles away from home. This can be helpful if he was visiting relations at the time, since it could guide you to an area from which the family originally migrated.

The age given can be incorrect and allowance must be made for this when calculating the probable year of birth. It is of course very helpful if the informant is a relative as the relationship may be stated which can confirm a tentative link in your research.

All certificates show places of residence, and if the events occurred near the date of a census, they offer a useful clue for searches in the Returns immediately following or preceding them. Although the records of births, marriages and deaths registered in England and Wales since 1 July 1837 are the main class of records held by the Registrar General, there are others which are worth noting. Records of still-births registered in England and Wales since 1 July 1927 can be obtained only with the special permission of the Registrar General. Records of births and deaths at sea (known as the Marine Register Books) since 1 July 1837 relate to persons born on British ships whose parents were born in England and Wales. Records of births and deaths in aircraft began in 1949 (known as Air Register Books) and relate to these events occurring in any part of the world in any aircraft registered in Great Britain and Northern Ireland. Service records contain births, marriages and deaths among members of the armed forces and certain other persons, or occurring on board certain ships and aircraft. Royal Air Force Returns began in 1920. The registers of the army are in two series. Firstly, there are the straightforward registers of army records and chaplains' returns, and secondly there are the indexes of Regimental birth registers. Equally there are the equivalent registers of marriages and deaths which are not indexed but can be sought on personal application in the foreign department of St Catherine's House. There are also separate death registers of officers and men who died in the Boer War and Second World War for each of the services.

Entries of births, marriages and deaths for civilians which took place in foreign countries can be found in either the Consular Records which are kept at St Catherine's House or the Miscellaneous Records which are held at the Public Record Office. These comprise what is known as the Overseas Section which is probably the most apt term for describing a group of registers made up from various sources.

The Consular registers were started in 1849 by an Act of Parliament and continue until the present day. Miscellaneous registers are non-statutory ones which were sent into the Registrar General. They have now been sent to the Public Record Office and both the indexes and the registers can be seen at Chancery Lane unless they are less than thirty years old. The earliest of these are registers of births, marriages and deaths that took place at The Hague from 1627. There are also some eighteenth- and nineteenth-century records which begin before 1849. If you fail to trace your particular family in the Consular registers, then you should consult the Miscellaneous register.

Records for anyone born in one of the former or existing British Colonies are held by the Registrar General of that country except for those records held by the India Record Office for British citizens born in India before 1947.

The last registers to be mentioned here are of British persons, civil or military, in the Ionian Islands from 1818–1864 who were in either Cephallonia or Corfu.

Records of adoption consist of entries made in the Adopted Children Register, in accordance with the Adoption Acts, since 1 January 1927, and relate only to adoptions effected under these Acts.

In recent years the fee for full certificates has changed so frequently that it is advisable to ascertain the current charges from the Registrar General at the time of undertaking your research. Applications by post will be undertaken but the cost is currently more than double that of going to the General Register Office in person. Fees for searches are given in the free leaflet available from the Registrar General.

Divorce records in England and Wales date back to 1852. However, it is necessary to know full particulars of names and the approximate dates of the Decrees Nisi and Absolute. Applications for the Decree Absolute should be made in person or by post to the Divorce Registry in London.

Apart from the obvious information obtainable from certificates, there are a few points worth noting which could also be of use. A note should be kept of all witnesses and informants that are shown on certificates as they could be relatives or provide links with other evidence for future research. It is possible that a few events were not registered, especially births, and the possibility is greater before 1875 because from that date the penalties for non-registration were increased. If, even after trying all possible surname variants, the search in the general indexes fails to produce results, then the period of search should be extended progressively either side of the expected date of the event. If the district where the event took place is known, it is advisable to try the district Superintendant Registrar's Office, in case of errors or omissions in the general indexes. Lastly, it may be that the event took place abroad, in which case either occupation or family connections may provide a clue for further research.

The Channel Islands and The Isle of Man

In the Channel Islands civil registration is divided between Jersey and Guernsey, each having their respective Registrars General. In Jersey births, marriages and deaths have been recorded since August 1842, and information about them can be obtained from the Superintendant Registrar, in Jersey, but research enquiries should be addressed to the Société Jersiaise, St Helier.

The States of Guernsey has jurisdiction over the islands of Guernsey, Alderney, Brecqhou, Herm, Jethou and Sark. Registration of births and deaths is now governed by an Order-in-Council of March 1935 and registration of marriages by an Order-in-Council of May 1919. For the period before this, but after 1840, completed registers are held by the Registrar General in St Peter Port, Guernsey. It should be noted that some of the registers of Alderney were lost during the German occupation in 1940–45.

In the Isle of Man the statutory records of births and deaths relate to those registered since 1878 and marriages since 1884. In addition there is the Adopted

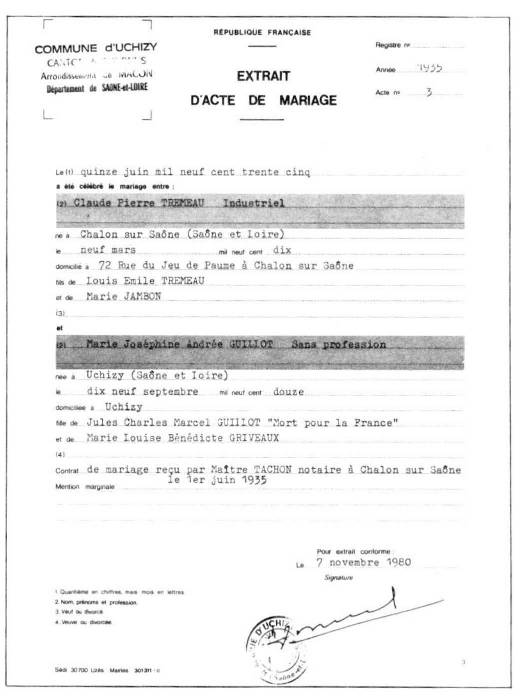

COMMUNE d'UCHIZY
CANTON de TOURNUS
Arrondissement de MACON
Département de SAONE-et-LOIRE

RÉPUBLIQUE FRANÇAISE

EXTRAIT
D'ACTE DE MARIAGE

Registre n°
Année 1935
Acte n° 3

Le (1) quinze juin mil neuf cent trente cinq
a été célébré le mariage entre :
(2) Claude Pierre TREMEAU Industriel
né à Chalon sur Saône (Saône et Loire)
le neuf mars mil neuf cent dix
domicilié à 72 Rue du Jeu de Paume à Chalon sur Saône
fils de Louis Emile TREMEAU
et de Marie JAMBON
(3)
et
(2) Marie Joséphine Andrée GUILLOT Sans profession
née à Uchizy (Saône et Loire)
le dix neuf septembre mil neuf cent douze
domiciliée à Uchizy
fille de Jules Charles Marcel GUILLOT "Mort pour la France"
et de Marie Louise Bénédicte GRIVEAUX
(4)
Contrat de mariage reçu par Maître TACHON notaire à Chalon sur Saône le 1er juin 1935
Mention marginale

Pour extrait conforme :
Le 7 novembre 1980
Signature

1. Quantième en chiffres, mais mois en lettres.
2. Nom, prénoms et profession.
3. Veuf ou divorcé.
4. Veuve ou divorcée.

Sedi 30700 Uzès Mariage 301311-0

French marriage, birth and death certificates. Such certificates can be extremely useful to the family historian because of the amount of information they give. Birth certificates give the hour as well as the date of birth and the dates and places of birth of the parents. Death certificates give the place and date of death, the name of the parents and of the widow or widower.

COMMUNE d'UCHIZY
CANTON de TOURNUS
Arrondissement de MACON
Département de SAONE-et-LOIRE

EXTRAIT
D'ACTE DE NAISSANCE

Registre N°
Année 1943
Folio

Le six mai mil neuf cent quarante trois
à 20 heures 40 en notre commune
est née Monique Jeanne Marie Pierre TREMEAU
du sexe féminin
de Claude Pierre TREMEAU
né le 9 mars 1910
à Chalon sur Saône (Saône et Loire)
(1) et de Marie Joséphine GUILLOT
née le 19 septembre 1912
à Uchizy (Saône et Loire)

Mention marginale : néant ~~marié séparé de corps divorcé décédé~~

Mentionner les références de la décision

Inscription au répertoire civil N° 3
Certifié le présent extrait conforme aux indications portées sur le registre par nous
Hippolyte JOSSERAND officier de l'état civil
de UCHIZY (Saône et Loire)
Le 7 novembre 19 80

(1) Cette rubrique ne doit être remplie que si l'extrait est délivré à une administration publique, à un héritier ou à une personne susceptible d'obtenir copie intégrale de l'acte de naissance.

24-07-20 (Simple)
24-07-22 (Bloc autocopiant) (7902)
IMPRIMERIES ADMINISTRATIVES CENTRALES
8, rue de Furstenberg - 75006 PARIS

COMMUNE d'UCHIZY
CANTON de TOURNUS
Arrondissement de MACON
Département de SAONE-et-LOIRE

EXTRAIT
D'ACTE DE DÉCÈS

Registre N° R
Année 1965
Folio

Le quatorze octobre mil neuf cent soixante cinq
à 11 heures en la commune de
Chalon sur Saône (Saône et Loire)
est décédée Marie Louise Bénédicte GRIVEAUX
né à LYON 7e (Rhône)
le 2 août 1887
profession sans profession
fille de François Claude GRIVEAUX
et de Marie Floride VILBERT
(1) ~~célibataire époux de ou~~ veuve de Jules Charles Marcel GUILLOT

Certifié le présent extrait conforme aux indications fixées sur le registre par nous
Hippolyte JOSSERAND officier de l'état civil
de UCHIZY (Saône et Loire)
Le 7 novembre 19 80

(1) Rayer la mention inutile et préciser s'il y a lieu : divorcé de

24-12-28 (Simple)
24-12-38 (Bloc autocopiant) (7903)
IMPRIMERIES ADMINISTRATIVES CENTRALES
8, rue de Furstenberg - 75006 PARIS

8

~~City or Borough~~ of

Parish ~~or Township~~ of East Peckham

Enumeration Schedule.

PLACE	HOUSES: Uninhabited or Building	HOUSES: Inhabited	NAMES of each Person who abode therein the preceding Night.	AGE and SEX: Males	AGE and SEX: Females	PROFESSION, TRADE, EMPLOYMENT, or of INDEPENDENT MEANS.	Where Born: Whether Born in same County	Where Born: Whether Born in Scotland, Ireland, or Foreign Parts.
			// Ann Graylund		15	F S	Yes	
Hextle House		1	Thomas Martin	35		Farmer	Yes	
			Maria do		30		do	
			Edwin do	5			do	
			Emily do		2		do	
			/ Frederick do	1 month			do	
			Ann Batchlar		20	F S	do	
			Caroline Colegate		20	F S	do	
			Louisa Excall		20	F S	do	
			William Greenaway	25		M S	do	
			// Henry Jupp	19		M S	do	
Mount Pleasant		1	/ Martha Andrews		60	Independent	Yes	
			William Dunk	62		M S	do	
			Caroline Wilson		25	F S	do	
			// Bathaney Cheesman		19	F S	do	
near the Court Lodge		1	George Scott	29		Ag Lab	Yes	
			Mary do		21		do	
			Mary do		3		do	
			Elizabeth do		2		do	
			/ Harriott do		2 Month		do	
			// Sarah Underdown		11		do	
do		1	George Bishop	28		Ag Lab	Yes	
			Harriott do		30		do	
			Robert do	8			do	
			John do	5			do	
TOTAL in Page 8		4		10	15			

Bc

37 10 R

1841 Census

Comparison of these extracts from the census returns of 1841 and 1851 for Hextle House, East Peckham, shows that Thomas Martin died between the two dates and that his wife Maria only gave her approximate age in the earlier census, as required by the rules. In the 1851 return the precise place of birth is given and the children Edwin and Emily appear to have died. Leslie's birth, which took place during 1848 or 1849, gives an indication of the approximate date of Thomas's death.

Parish or Township of East Peckham	Ecclesiastical District of	City or Borough of	Town of	Village of

No. of Householder's Schedule	Name of Street, Place, or Road, and Name or No. of House	Name and Surname of each Person who abode in the house, on the Night of the 30th March, 1851	Relation to Head of Family	Condition	Age of Males	Age of Females	Rank, Profession, or Occupation	Where Born	Whether Blind, or Deaf-and-Dumb
		Richard West	Servant	Un	21		Farmer Servant	Kent East Peckham	
68	Hextle Cottage	William Jupp	Head	Mar	33		Gardener	Kent East Peckham	
		Mary Jupp	Wife	Mar		42		Kent Penshurst	
		Matilda Jupp	Daur	Un		9	Scholar	Kent East Peckham	
69	Pond Farm	Robert Lipscomb	Head	Mar	54		Farmer of 130 acres employing 8 Labourers	Kent Tonbridge	
		Elizabeth Lipscomb	Wife	Mar		54	Farmer Wife	Kent Speldhurst	
		Martha Lipscomb	Daur	Un		19	Farmer Daughter	Kent Penshurst	
		Anne Saxby	Visitor	Un		20		Kent Penshurst	
70	Hextle House	Maria Martin	Head	Mar		42	Landed Proprietor	Sussex Hove	
		Anna Martin	Daur	Un		2		Kent East Peckham	
		Leslie Martin	Son		3			Kent East Peckham	
		Caroline Sandeday	Sister	Mar		43		Sussex Hove	
		Helen Murdoch	Servant	Un		19	Governess	Middlesex St Pancras	
		Ann Saunders	Servant	U		20	House Servant	Kent East Peckham	
		Ann Dean	Do	U		27	House Servant	Sussex Lamberhurst	
		Mary Rogers	Do	U		25	House Servant	Kent East Peckham	
		George Bevans	Do	U	21		Ag Lab	Kent Wrotham	

The End of that part of the Parish of East Peckham not included in the Trinity District Hadlow. Thomas Webb

Total of Houses 13 U — B — Total of Persons 5 12

1851 Census

Children Register which covers legal adoptions registered since 1928. Search fees are very reasonable and enquiries should be made to the General Registry, Douglas, Isle of Man.

Census Returns

The Census Returns have been described by some researchers as the most helpful and revealing records that the family historian is likely to encounter. As early as 1750 it was proposed that regular censuses of the population should be held, but it was not until 1801 that they were introduced. Since that date they have been held every ten years with the exception of 1941. Unfortunately the returns up to and including 1831 are generally of little use from the family historian's point of view as the names of residents were not recorded. It is therefore those from 1841 onwards that are of interest. In England and Wales the census returns are not available for public inspection until they are over one hundred years old.

The original returns are held at the Public Record Office in London, on microfilm, but before access to them is allowed it will be necessary to obtain a Reader's Ticket from the Enquiry Office or a day pass at the door.

It is at this stage in your research that the addresses revealed by previous work can be of such value. The nearer the date on the records which reveal such addresses is to the date of each census, the greater the possibility that the person being sought will be found at that address when the census was taken.

The census of 7 June 1841 records the parish or township, and the name of the city, borough, town or village at the head of each enumeration sheet. The columns beneath show:

1. The name of the street, place or road and the name or number of the house;
2. The name and surname of each person in the house;
3. Age and sex;
4. Rank, profession or occupation;
5. Whether born in the same county;
6. Whether born in Scotland, Ireland or foreign parts.

The ages of persons under fifteen years are stated exactly, but those above fifteen years are rounded down five years, i.e. someone aged sixty-four appears as sixty, twenty-three as twenty, and so forth. Places of birth are indicated by 'Y' (Yes) or 'N' (No) and 'S' (Scotland), 'I' (Ireland), 'F' (Foreign parts) in the appropriate columns.

The Returns of 1851, 1861 and 1871 are far more informative. They show the following additional information:

1. The schedule number;
2. Relationship to the head of the family;
3. Condition or matrimonial status;
4. The exact age of each person;
5. The exact parish and county of birth;
6. Whether deaf, dumb or blind.

In the 1871 census, provision was made to show if any person was an imbecile, idiot or lunatic.

All of the above applies to the 1881, 1891 and 1901 census returns as and when they become available.

It must be noted that those listed in the Census Returns are every person living in the house on the day in question, together with those engaged at their labour during the night, and returning regularly next morning. No member of a household who normally slept away from the house was included, such as domestic staff, residents at an institution, and so on. Such persons would be recorded on the appropriate enumerator's return, at such places as hotels, lodging houses, hospitals, institutions, aboard ships, and even in tents. Visitors and servants are often listed in the household and their places of birth are worth noting as there may be some form of family connection in that area. Occupations are frequently abbreviated, e.g. Ag. Lab for agricultural labourer; F.S. for female servant; Ind. for independent means; and so on.

The marks made by the enumerators after a list of names for a given address are to indicate, / the end of a household, and // the end of all households within the building. On some returns, particularly those for small villages, the name of the street or road is not shown, and the only identification given is that of the schedule number. To ascertain the likely location of the house or building concerned it will be necessary to check the 'description of enumeration district', which is to be found at the beginning of each such section of the census return. In any case, you can save many hours of searching by checking the description of each district first, to see if the street or road is listed as part of that particular enumeration. If it is not found, then each subsequent district should be checked until the place required is located. Roads of great length are invariably part of more than one district, in which case all districts may have to be checked before the required address is found. Sometimes an address cannot be found, owing to a change of house name or number, or even the name of the road itself, between the date on the source of information and the date of the census. In such cases, the Record Office should be consulted in order to find out whether a list of such changes exists for that particular locality. For large towns and cities, street indexes are available, and these are of considerable help in locating the section of the census return required to find a particular address.

It is also worth searching the area in the vicinity of the family residence. In the past, members of the same professions and family groups often lived near to each other, and the returns, by noting the trades or professions of those living in a locality, shed a great deal of light upon its social make-up. It must be stressed that the information recorded in the Census Returns is subject to varying degrees of error. False statements were made by those who had something to hide, or were just being awkward. Ages can be found to be only approximate; there is also the perpetual problem of surname variants due to spelling or phonetic misinterpretation.

Nicknames, stage names and noms-de-plume are sometimes found in Census Returns. In one case the individual's given name was Ernest but he was always known in the family as George because he liked this name better. Unless one has information of a private character it is usually impossible to identify such people with certainty, and much confusion is caused thereby. Bella for Isabella, Nelly for Helen and similar variants are very common and frequently found in returns.

In addition to the Public Record Office, most County Record Offices and many reference libraries have copies of the Census Returns for their areas. Although the Census Returns are only available for public inspection if over one hundred years old, it is possible to obtain information for more recent returns from the General Register Office, London. However, in these cases it is necessary to provide the surname and christian name of the person, and the precise address, together with written permission of that person or a direct descendant, and to sign a declaration that the information will not be used in litigation. The fee required for this is quite high, and consequently this is a source only to be used as a last resort.

Census Returns in the Channel Islands and Isle of Man are held in the Public Record Office in London.

These examples of the various spellings of the surname Yardley found in the register of of St Saviour's, Southwark for 1585–1603 show it spelt phonetically as Yearleye, Orley, Erley, Yardley, Yarly, and Earlye. The George baptised on 28 July 1588 became Governor of Virginia as Sir George Yardley.

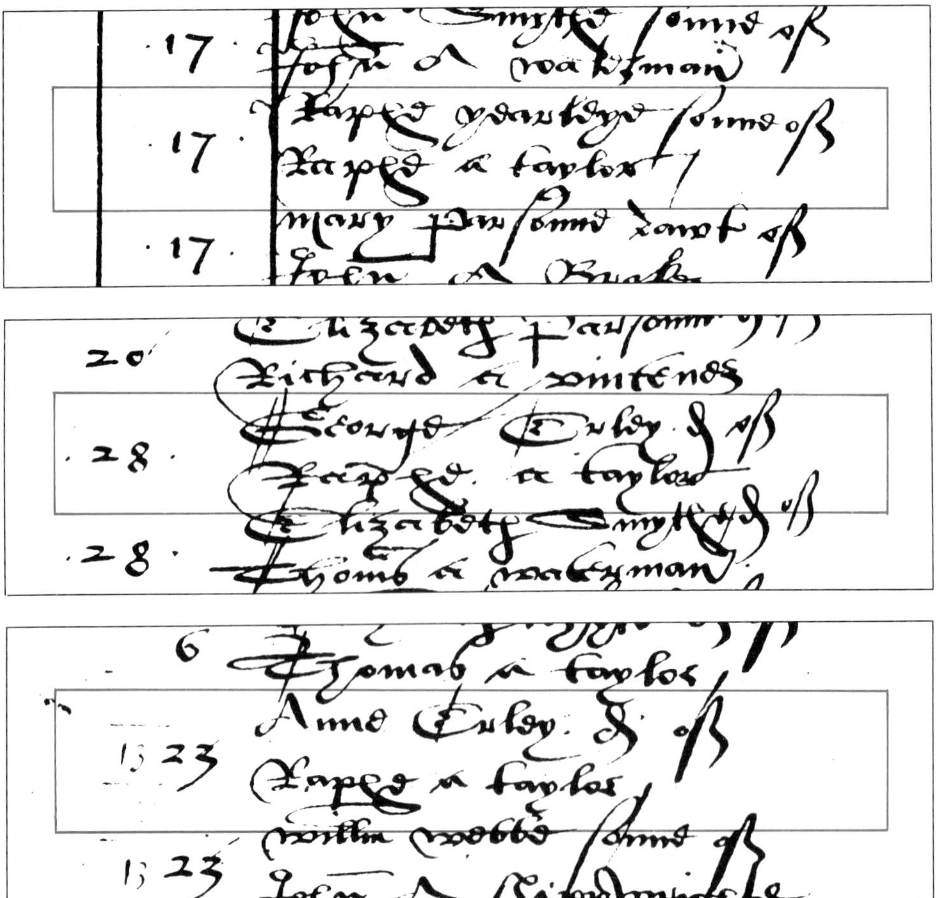

Parish Registers

At this stage of research, the accumulated evidence from certificates and Census Returns will provide the names of your ancestors and the approximate dates of events and places where they were living in the early nineteenth century or late eighteenth century. It is at this stage that the records of the Parish and its administration will provide the main sources for these and earlier generations.

Of the many parish records available for research, undoubtedly the Parish Registers are the most important. The earliest registers in England and Wales began in 1538 when Thomas Cromwell, Vicar General to Henry VIII, issued an injunction that records of baptisms, marriages and burials should be kept by the clergy of the Church of England. These early registers are generally paper books,

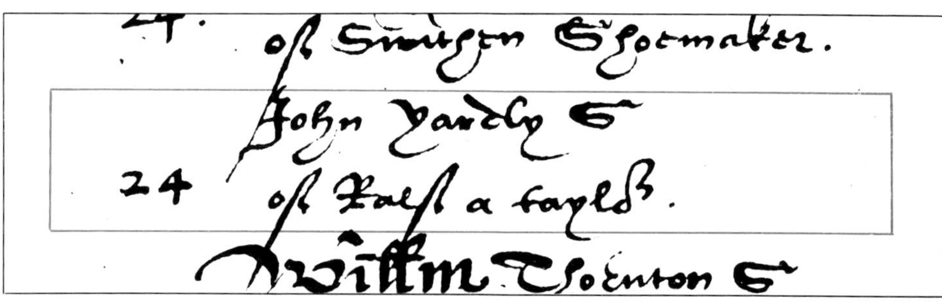

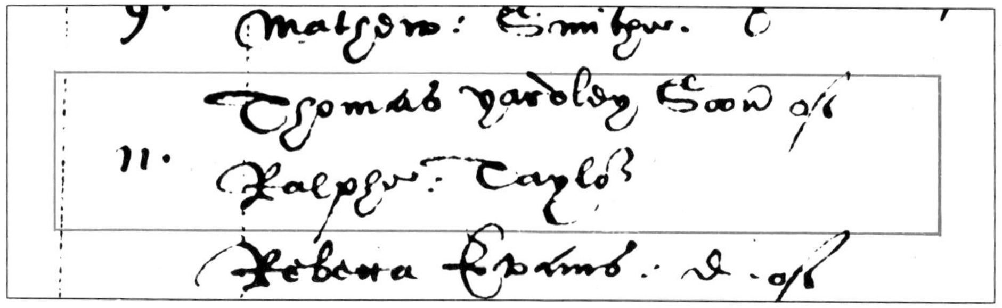

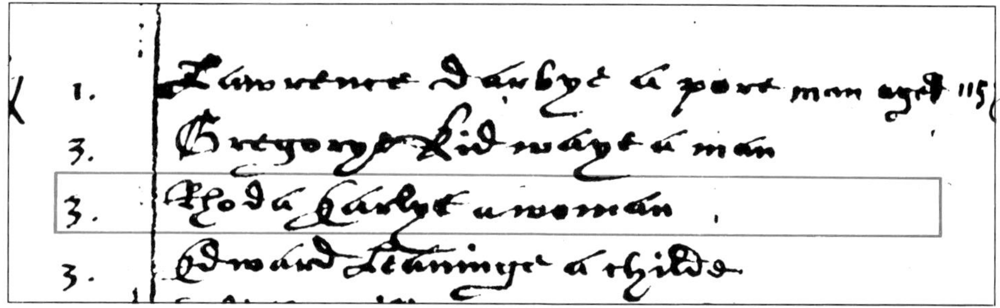

and few originals have survived. It is estimated that from more than 11,000 ancient parishes less than seven hundred have registers that go back to 1538. The remainder have registers that begin at various dates between then and 1597, and some even later than that. It was in 1597 that, for their safer keeping, parchment registers were ordered to be kept and that the earlier entries in the paper registers should be copied into them. Unfortunately the wording of the Act which referred to the copying of the earlier registers included the phrase 'but especially since the first year of Her Majesty's reign' (1558). This provided a loophole for the lazy who were looking for an excuse to limit copying to forty rather than sixty years. The Act also provided for transcripts to be made from the registers within a month after Easter for the previous year for submission to the bishop's registrar. These transcripts are generally known as Bishop's

Abigal wife of John Landemore was buried June 4
Elizabeth wife of Robert Plummer was buried July 30
Richard Stevens an Infant was buried August 13
Sibillia Major Infant buried Aug 30
John Bradly was buried Sept. 14
Elizabth wife of George Baker buri: Sep 16
Elizabth wife of William Alderton was buried Sept. 21
Richd Carrol, buried, October 3
William Brundwood buried Octo: 9
Richd Cobbin, buried, October 13
Ann Bradley buried October 13
Elizabth wife of Abraham Lansdell was buried October 15
Mary Goldsmith an Infant was buried November 1st
Wm Doe, Infant buried Nov 28
Robt. Arthur, buried Jan: 23
George Dale buried Feb. 9th

William Pawlett Curate
Abra: Wetherell } Church
Robt Butler }

Anno Dni 1722

Elizabth Swan Wid buried April 7
John Bumpstead, an Infant was buried April 21
John Newman an Infant was buried May 1st
John Merriol was buried July 16
John Nichols was buried July 19
William Grant, an Infant was buried July 26
Maynard Doe a base begotten Child was buried August 18
John Robinson buried Jan: 26

Abrahã Lansdell buried October 4
Dinah Bennett an Infant bur: Octo: 28
Francis Goldsmith buried October 29
Elizab Lansdell an Infant buried Nov 8
John Walter Gibson an Infant buried ~~Janu~~ february 14
Stephen Rew, Infant, buried Feb: 17
Alice Hammond an Infant was buried February 21

Chr: Grove Curate
Abraham Wetherell } Church
Robert Butler }

1723

Sarah Goldsmith buried May 28
Mary Randell was buried June 26
Sarah Smith was buried July 19
Bridgett Dexter of Stanton was bried August 17
Ann Parker Infant bur: Augst 25
Charles Medcalfe buried Sept. 20
Susan Landemore buried Sept 22
Barbara the wife of Samuel Alderton was ~~Sept.~~ buried October 5
Margt Ireland buried November 4
John Gaught an Infant buri: Nov: 10
John Clarke buried November 22
Johath Bennit an Infant was buried January 12
Ann Newman buried Jan: 30
Wm Crick an Infant was buried March 6
Wm Chambers was buried March 17
Elizab Crack an Infant buried March 17
Richd Bennitt an Infant was buried March 25

Chr: Grove Curate
Abra: Wetherell } Church
Robt Butler }

Transcripts and are usually deposited in the Diocesan Record Office. The original Parish Registers come in a great variety of shapes and sizes, but of more interest is the way in which they were written up. Most of the details of an event would be made in a notebook or on slips of paper by the incumbent or parish clerk and according to the size of the parish, entered into the register later at various intervals, when they remembered. It does not, therefore, need much imagination to see that as a result of this custom, some events were either lost, written up from memory, or entered in the register out of chronological sequence. This, together with the fact that some registers were divided into three sections—baptisms, marriages, burials—others in chronological order with the events mixed according to the sequence in which they happened, and yet others used three separate registers, means that very thorough and careful checks must be made during research, unless the registers have been completely transcribed and indexed.

During the Commonwealth (1648–1660) many clergymen were forced to leave their parishes, especially if they were Royalists. Some took their registers with them, some buried them for safety with the result that many were lost or irreparably damaged, and other registers were destroyed when Cromwellian soldiers plundered the churches. From September 1653 until the Restoration, Parish Registers (i.e. registrars) were appointed to record births, marriages and deaths with the Justice of the Peace to perform civil marriages. In some parishes the registers were well maintained, some to an even better standard than under the old system. In the majority of parishes, however, the standard deteriorated drastically and there are many instances where no records were kept at all during the whole period.

Due to the serious decline of the English wool trade, an Act was passed in 1678 that all the dead were to be buried in wool with a fine being imposed for non-compliance and an affidavit was made by a relative or associate of the deceased. Consequently 'Affid' or 'Affdt' can often be seen after a burial entry in the register. The Act was repealed in 1814, but had ceased to be enforced long before that date.

In 1694 'for carrying on the war against France' a duty was levied on a sliding scale for non-paupers of 2*s*. for a baptism or birth, 2*s*. 6*d*. for a marriage, and 4*s*. for a burial, rising to the considerable sum of £30 for the baptism of a Duke's eldest son, and £50 for a Duke's marriage or burial. The duty was abolished a few years later as it proved to be unenforceable.

During the eighteenth century both the Church and the State were concerned

LEFT
A typical eighteenth-century country parish register from Ickworth, Suffolk showing burials for part of the period 1721–1723. Later in the century special printed registers were produced in which particulars were recorded uniformly throughout England and Wales.

Sampson Lloyd of Birmingham in the County of Warwick Ironmonger and Sarah Parks Daughter of Richard Parks of Birmingham aforesaid Ironmonger Having declared their Intentions of taking each other in Marriage before several Publick Meetings of the People of God called Quakers in Warwickshire according to the Good Order used among them whose Proceedings therein after a deliberate Consideration thereof (with regard unto the Righteous Law of God and Example of his People Recorded in the Scriptures of Truth in that Case) were approved by the said Meetings they appearing clear of all others and having Consent of Parents and Relations concerned

Now these are to certifie all whom it may concern That for the full accomplishing of their said Intentions this Twenty Ninth Day of the Ninth Month called November in the Year according to the English Account One Thousand Seven Hundred and Twenty Seven They the said Sampson Lloyd and Sarah Parks appeared in a Publick Assembly of the aforesaid People and others met together for that end and purpose in their Publick Meeting Place at Birmingham aforesaid and in a solemn Manner he the said Sampson Lloyd taking the said Sarah Parks by the Hand did openly declare as followeth Friends in the Presence of God and this Assembly I take this my Friend Sarah Parks to be my Wife promising with Gods Assistance to be unto Her a loving and faithfull Husband till Death shall seperate us And then and there in the said Assembly the said Sarah Parks did in like manner declare as followeth Friends in the Presence of God and this Assembly I take this my Friend Sampson Lloyd to be my Husband promising with Gods Assistance to be unto him a loving and faithfull Wife till Death shall seperate us and the said Sampson Lloyd and Sarah Parks as a further Confirmation thereof did then and there to these Presents set their Hands and we whose Names are hereunto subscribed being present among others at the Solemnizing of their said Marriage and Subscription in manner aforesaid as Witnesses hereunto have also to these Presents Subscribed our Names the Day and Year above written

This Quaker marriage certificate of 1727 gives more information than is found on Church of England marriage entries of the same date. Note that the names of the witnesses, many of whom could be related to the bride or groom, are given.

about the increasing laxity in performing marriages by clergymen who had been conducting ceremonies with scant regard to the status of both brides and grooms. This state of affairs was resolved in 1754 by Lord Hardwicke's Marriage Act which introduced separate marriage registers on printed forms which required the entries to be signed by the officiating minister, the bride and groom and two witnesses. The Act also reinforced the requirement that all marriages must be preceded by the calling of banns, for three successive weeks, unless a licence was granted, and marriages were only to be solemnized in a Parish Church.

The only exceptions to this rule were marriages of Quakers and Jews, since their records were considered satisfactory, and they were therefore allowed to continue conducting their own marriage ceremonies.

Hardwicke's Marriage Act did not eliminate clandestine marriages. Determined couples made for Gretna Green and other places across the Scottish border and for the Channel Islands, where the regulations were less stringent than in England.

Marriage licences and banns are a subject of importance. The great majority of British marriages were by banns (or 'proclamation'). The couple's intention to marry was announced on three Sundays in their parish churches—or between 1653 and 1660, it could be proclaimed in the nearest market-place on three market-days—to allow anyone knowing of any 'just impediment' to declare it.

Licences, however, were issued by the Church authorities, and these enabled people to marry immediately without banns. Apart from the obvious human need for a hasty marriage those who used them were the prosperous, who wanted to avoid publicity; soldiers and sailors who might be called away at short notice and had no home parish anyway where banns could be called; anyone whose freedom to marry needed to be clarified or (before about 1700) who wanted to marry at the religious seasons of prohibition (Lent, Advent, etc.).

The records (if they exist) of a marriage licence were the 'allegation', a declaration on oath by the bride and bridegroom of their freedom to marry; the 'bond', a record of security given by, usually, a close friend or relation of the truth of this; the 'licence', a document authorizing marriage, often at a stipulated church; finally there was often a register kept of the licences issued.

Licences were normally issued by bishops and archdeacons, or their officials, and the records are among the other archives of those dignitaries. However, where the parties to be married lived in different bishoprics, then strictly the licence should have been issued by the archbishop, although this rule was often broken.

The Stamp Act of 1783 imposed a duty of 3*d.* on all entries in Parish Registers, which was extended two years later to cover Nonconformists. As paupers were exempt, an increasing number of ordinary citizens declared themselves as such in order to avoid the duty. Once more, many poor people failed to have their children baptised. As before, this second attempt to raise revenues through the Parish Registers failed, and the Act was repealed in 1794.

The final piece of legislation of importance regarding Parish Registers is Sir George Rose's Act of 1812 which provided printed form registers for baptisms, marriages and burials that remained the standard form of registration until the introduction of Civil Registration in England and Wales in 1837. As the three principal Church ceremonies continue to the present day, it is of course possible to extend research in the Parish Registers beyond 1837. In fact, as previously stated, during the early years of Civil Registration by no means everyone obeyed the law, and it may be that recourse to the registers will solve an otherwise insuperable problem.

As a result of the Parochial Registers and Records Measure of 1978 a large number of original parish registers have now been deposited in County Record Offices and Diocesan Record Offices where many are being transcribed and indexed. In 1974 Local Population Studies, in association with the Cambridge Group for the History of Population and Social Structure, published the first of its handbooks entitled *Original Parish Registers*. This, together with its three supplements, the most recent of which was published in 1980, is a list of original

A Fleet marriage (*c* 1747). These were clandestine ceremonies which were performed near the Fleet prison in London, and from which they took their name. After the Marriage Act of 1754 all marriages had to be witnessed and registered which in theory made bigamy and the marriage of minors impossible.

parish registers which have been deposited in Record Offices, Libraries and other institutions in England and Wales. The list is arranged alphabetically by county, and alphabetically by parish within each county. It includes original parish registers, rough books of register entries, duplicate books made simultaneously with the registers, and early replacement copies such as those ordained in 1598. It excludes original parish registers still in the possession of incumbents, later copies and all non-Anglican registers. Another useful guide to parish registers is Frank Smith's *A Genealogical Gazetteer of England*, an alphabetical dictionary of places with their location, ecclesiastical jurisdiction, population and date of the earliest entry in the register of every ancient parish. The Gazetteer, be it noted, does not include Wales, Scotland or Ireland.

In the Isle of Man, the earliest records of the Church of England date from 1611 for baptisms, 1629 for marriages and 1610 for burials. All enquiries to the General Registry, Douglas. Information about Channel Island Registers can be obtained from the addresses given in the Appendix.

Religious toleration in England was unknown before the Declaration of Indulgence in 1672 under which Protestant dissenters secured licences for the conduct of worship according to their own consciences in their own meeting houses. They had met together for many years, of course, and a few had kept registers, but these were of baptisms apart from the Society of Friends (Quakers), who had no ceremony of baptism and recorded birth instead. Following Lord Hardwicke's Act of 1753, valid marriages could only be performed by the clergy of the Church of England and by Quakers and Jews, and this remained the law until the introduction of Civil Registration in 1837. Even then, Nonconformist ministers were not allowed to perform burial rites in parish churchyards until 1880.

A Royal Commission was appointed in 1836 to enquire into the state, custody and authenticity of the 'non-parochial' registers, and to recommend means for their collection and arrangement, legal use and availability. The registers were collected following the Non-Parochial Registers Act of 1836, mainly from most but not all Baptists, Congregationalists, Presbyterians, Methodists, and eventually from the Quakers and some other denominations. The Jews and the majority of Roman Catholics refused to part with their registers which remained in their own custody. The registers were transferred to the Public Record Office in 1961 and comprised 7,000 volumes and files. Before the Quakers surrendered their registers, indexed digests were made. One copy was deposited with the local Quarterly Meeting, and another at the Library of the Society of Friends in London. Also included in this category of records at the Public Record Office are unauthenticated registers of baptisms and marriages performed at the Fleet and Kings Bench Prison, at May Fair and at the Mint at Southwark, which had been deposited in the Bishop of London's Registry in 1821. With one exception—the register of the Independent Church at St Petersburg in Russia—the deposited registers relate solely to England and Wales, but include several registers of Huguenot and other foreign Protestant churches.

A *ketubah* (a Jewish marriage contract) is written in Hebrew so it is necessary for it to be translated and interpreted by someone with a knowledge of the language. This *ketubah* dates from 1524 and comes from Venice.

This Dutch print of a Jewish wedding dates from 1721.

In addition there are the headquarters, libraries and museums of various Nonconformist communities which contain extensive records for research. The Baptist Union Library; United Reformed Church Historical Society, which covers Congregational and Presbyterian records; Independent Congregational Library; Huguenot Library; Methodist Archives and Research Centre; and Unitarian Church Headquarters. Enquiries relating to Roman Catholic records should be made to the Archbishop's House in London, or at the local diocesan archives. Jewish records are housed at the Jewish Museum in London and at local synagogues.

Entries relating to Nonconformists often occur in Anglican parish registers; marriages occur as an inevitable consequence of the legislation already mentioned; burials often occur as a practical necessity as many Nonconformists had no burial ground of their own; baptisms are particularly found for the various Methodist divisions, as they originally saw themselves as members of the Church of England,

ACTS OF THE APOSTLES
IN MEMORY OF
JOHN WINTHROP
LORD OF THE MANOR OF
GROTON
FIRST GOVERNOR OF
ASSACHUSETTS AND FOUNDER
BOSTON IN NEW ENGLAND
AMERICAN DESCENDANT

OPPOSITE
This window at Groton Church is dedicated to John Winthrop, founder of Massachusetts, and was presented in his memory by the State of Massachusetts.

A memorial tablet which demonstrates one of the hazards of genealogical research—it is hard to believe that anyone lived as long as 113 years or that at that age, their death could be 'hastened'. At a period when the average expectation of life was less than 60 years, records of people dying at such a great age must be supported by contemporary evidence such as this tablet. If such evidence does not exist, then the records must be treated with suspicion.

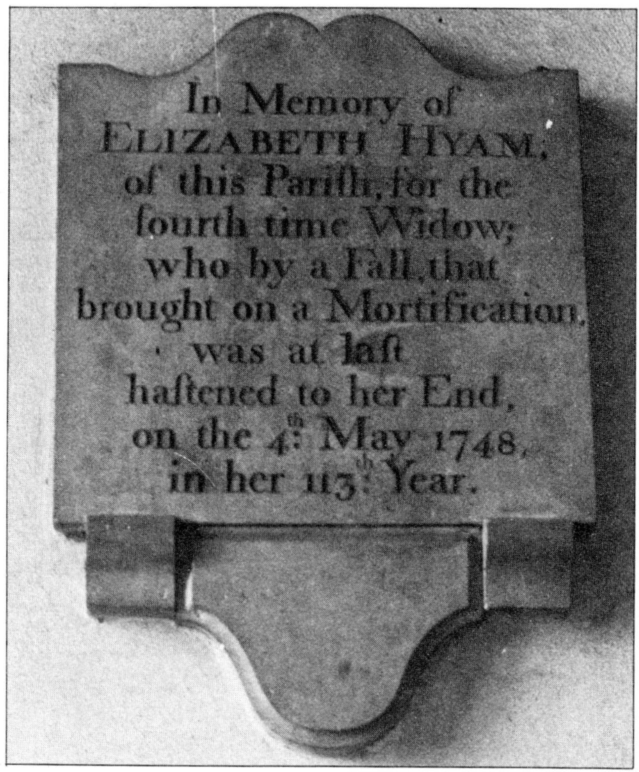

and not dissenters. Also, for some years after 1696, Anglican clergymen were obliged to record births of Nonconformists.

In recent times various classes of Nonconformist records have come to light and have been deposited at the appropriate County Record Office, where it is always advisable to make enquiries.

In many parish churches, monumental inscriptions and tombstones supplement information derived from the registers. Consideration should be given to the parish churchyards, Nonconformist burial grounds and cemeteries authorized by the Act of 1853, which also allowed many cities and boroughs not only to open public cemeteries but also enabled the church and chapel yards to be closed when they were full. There were also private cemeteries which had opened prior to the Act and many more since. Some inscriptions have been transcribed and

IN MEMORY OF

The Fettiplace monuments in the Church of St Mary, Swinbrook, Oxfordshire (*opposite*) and a monument in Essex (*below*) to Richard Cutte and his wife Mary, showing the line of inheritance through the families.

copies are deposited at the Society of Genealogists, the appropriate County Record Office or library, or the British Library. There is also considerable work being undertaken by local Societies to record as much as possible before natural wear and tear, churchyard clearance schemes and vandalism destroy them forever. Registers of local cemeteries are usually kept by the local government authority. If you are able to locate an ancestor's memorial the inscription, including the verse, can contain clues to occupation and career and should be recorded in full and when practicable, photographed. It is also advisable to look for related burials in the surrounding area as many families wish to be buried close to each other. If it is hard to find out where a burial took place, a search in the British Library, Newspaper Library or the County Library in local newspapers for obituary notices may help.

Possibly the greatest contribution made by the Church of Jesus Christ of Latter Day Saints is the recording of parish register entries by births (baptisms) and marriages on computer files. The Computer File Index as it is called, consists of many millions of entries from the parish records of many countries. These are available for examination on microfiches and are of the greatest value in establishing the distribution of surnames at any particular period from the sixteenth to nineteenth centuries. A word of warning must, however, be given about the use of the CFI. Much of the information fed into the computer comes from printed or manuscript transcripts of the original registers, and while every effort is made to see that all the entries are accurate, mistakes do occur. For example, when investigating the Bickley family recently it was discovered that many names were listed under the name Buckley. These entries were taken from the parish of St Leonard, Shoreditch, which when the original registers were

examined showed clearly how the mistakes had arisen. Furthermore, since only identified infant burials are included in the CFI it may turn out that the individual for whom one is searching and whose name one discovers at about the right time and in the right parish in fact died. This would not show up in the CFI, and one could be led badly astray if one were to rely solely on it. Also some areas are less well covered than others.

The mountain vaults of the Church of Jesus Christ of Latter Day Saints in Salt Lake City, Utah, which house microfilm and other records assembled by the Church from all over the world. The vaults are designed to withstand a nuclear attack and the records they contain form one of the most valuable documentary collections of this kind in the world.

The Genealogical Library, Salt Lake City, is open to researchers of all religions. It contains microfilm, printed and manuscript sources from all parts of the world, and is the largest library of its kind in the world.

Other Parochial Records

Until comparatively recently many social services now undertaken by the State or the Local Authority were the responsibility of the parishes. It is consequently necessary to take account of how the parish was administered, and the type of records this produced.

The administration of the parish was vested in the clergymen and church wardens, of which there were usually two. Primarily their duties were to ensure that the fabric of the church was maintained, and to administer the property and money for which they were responsible. The records they left are usually called the Vestry Minutes and Churchwardens' Accounts, both of which can contain evidence of value to the family historian as they mention persons to whom payments were made, or from whom money was received for the upkeep of the buildings, purchases of commodities, payment of rates, and other business that will establish informative facts about particular parishioners. In addition, they provide historical material that is of exclusive interest to that particular parish in question.

However, the records of major importance for genealogical research are those of the overseers of the poor. In the sixteenth century, the problem of the poor was acute and vagrancy was widespread due to the dissolution of the monasteries and the increase of enclosures.

By legislation culminating in the Great Poor Law Act of 1601 normally two substantial householders were nominated each year to be Overseers of the Poor, with the duty of maintaining the poor and setting them to work, the funds being provided by parish rates. Further Acts required that Houses of Correction should be built for 'rogues, vagrants, lewd women who have bastards, and parents leaving their children chargeable to the parish who shall be brought before the Justices for committal'.

Later legislation established the law of settlement and removal which contained the provision that any strangers settling in a parish might be removed by the Justices unless they rented a tenement of not less than £10 annual value or found security to discharge the parish of their adoption from all expenses that may be incurred upon their behalf, or they brought a 'settlement certificate' from their own parish accepting liability for any charges. The Act also authorized the Justices to transport to the plantations in the colonies incorrigible rogues, vagabonds and sturdy beggars. Further legislation provided that serving a parish office, paying a parish rate, residing in the parish, being bound apprentice by indenture to a parishioner, or, if unmarried, serving a year in the service of the parish established settlement.

There was also concern about the prevention of vagrancy, and in 1743/4 a reward of 5*s*. was introduced for the apprehension of any vagrant and removal, after whipping or confinement, to their place of settlement. Incorrigible rogues were treated more harshly. After six month's imprisonment, with whipping at the Justices' discretion, they were either sent home or impressed into naval or military service. Persons sheltering vagabonds were fined a sum of from 10*s*. to 40*s*. Vagrants' children could be apprenticed by the Justices, and bastard children of vagrant women were not to gain a settlement in the parish of their birth. They were in fact hastened from one parish to another to make sure that the baby was born under someone else's haystack. This treatment caused a scandal, as a high proportion of mothers and babies died as a result of this policy.

Throughout the eighteenth century there was considerable litigation between parishes. A parish would claim that someone was settled elsewhere; the individual concerned would then be examined before a Justice, reciting his life history in a document of fascinating detail; his legal place of settlement would be determined and he would be sent there; if the receiving parish had doubts about the legal settlement, a re-examination would be ordered. All efforts were concentrated on avoiding one's own parish having to pay relief. The consequent proceedings, of course, are of great genealogical value.

In 1781/2, because of the 'incapacity, negligence or misconduct' of Overseers, and the 'sufferings and distresses of the poor being most grievous', provisions were made for the inspection of workhouses, and no poor were to be sent into a workhouse more than 10 miles from their own parish, also no persons except the indigent were to be sent to the workhouse, and no children under the age of seven years were to be forcibly separated from their parents.

A further Act in 1792 dealt with the abuses of the removal of vagrants. In future, no reward was to be paid for their apprehension until they had been punished, and no female vagrant was to be whipped for any reason whatsoever. In 1794/5 no person was to be removed until they were actually chargeable, and the Justices were authorized to suspend at their discretion orders of removal upon sick and infirm people. It was also in 1795 that the meeting of Berkshire Justices at the George and Pelican Inn at Speenhamland took place. This gave its name to the ill-advised Speenhamland System under which a scale of relief, based on the size of the family and the price of bread was devised. It never received statutory recognition, but the example was followed throughout the country, and tables showing the 'Speenhamland Act of Parliament' were displayed in ale houses for the edification of their clientele.

Following a Royal Commission of Inquiry, which reported scathingly on the whole system of parochial poor relief, the Poor Law Reform Act of 1834 was passed. Under this Act, the responsibility was transferred from individual parishes to groups of them in Poor Law Unions. The major events in the subsequent history of the Poor Law were the transfer of its administration from the Unions to the County Councils in 1929, and, finally, the assumption by the Central Government in 1948 and 1966 of responsibility, not only for the broad lines of 'public assistance' and 'social security', but also for much the greater part of its detailed administration.

It may come as a surprise to learn that in the sixteenth century the birth of illegitimate children seems to have been an unusual event. Such an occurence was becoming more common in the seventeenth century, and so common as to create little surprise from about 1750 onwards.

The concern shown in this matter by the parish was not solely a moral one, as there was also the more material problem of maintenance on the parish rates. Therefore, if the father could be identified, he was made responsible for the maintenance of the child. If, therefore, the parish register only gives the mother's name, a record of the father's may be found elsewhere among parochial records.

Most poor children were bound apprentices at an early age. By the eighteenth century the old rules governing apprenticeships were disappearing, and they were often used as a convenient way of providing for a pauper child. Most were indentured to learn husbandry or housewifery in their own parish, and this usually resulted in them being used as agricultural labourers or female servants. Those apprenticed elsewhere were indentured to a variety of trades, rarely skilled ones. However, there were abuses of pauper apprenticeship. For the worst, one must consult the records of the mills in manufacturing towns and villages which imported pauper children by the wagon-load from London, contracting to take 'one idiot in every twenty', where the conditions were indescribably horrible, and where the graveyards hold scores of the small bodies of these unfortunates who were literally worked to death.

The Parish Constable was chosen annually from the residents of the parish, and men usually served in rotation. The Constable was appointed by the Justices of the Peace of the county, and was responsible for maintaining law and order, caring for the stocks and whipping post; the apprehension of rogues, vagabonds and others, and bringing them before the Magistrates; the arrest of those ordered to appear in Court; administering punishments to convicted offenders; accompanying vagrants and others to the House of Correction; and various other relevant duties as required. By 1856 the office of Parish Constable had been superseded by the county and town Police Force or Constabulary. The records of the Constables throw much light on the activities of parishioners.

Overseers of the Highways, or Waywardens, looked after the roads and bridges in the parish. They had to pay for the upkeep of roads, which resulted in taxes being levied in the parish. The accounts of the Overseers, where they survive, show who owned property and paid taxes, and also show payments to contractors and individuals who did the work required, and are therefore useful as background material.

The Parish Clerk kept the minutes of the Vestry Meetings, cared for the parish registers and Banns Book, and sometimes led the singing in church. Other duties may have included being the sexton (gravedigger) and caretaker of the church and churchyard. The Sexton's Book, if available, gives details of burials, and often contains far more information than the burial entries in the parish register.

Each county and borough had its Court of Quarter Sessions, and it not only dealt with criminal cases, but also performed the duties of local government before County Councils existed. Typical of such matters are those ensuring that the major highways were kept in good repair; paying coroners for their inquisitions; committing vagrants and others to the House of Correction; committal and release of debtors from gaol; payment for burial of those who died whilst passing through the county; inspection of workhouses and, if warranted, bringing the parish officers to court for orders to be made against them; body-snatching cases; poaching; and instructions and orders to the Parish Constables.

Finally there are the Charity records. Charities of early medieval foundation still exist, and in early times they were almost invariably entrusted for administration to the parish clergymen and churchwardens. Some typical charities concerned themselves with food, education, loans, clothing, skilled apprenticeships for poor children, and coal and fuel.

In all the Parish Records we have mentioned it is almost certain that somewhere you will find a mention of your ancestors, no matter what their status within the community. Apart from providing valuable evidence of their existence, these records give a fascinating insight into the type of persons they were, and create a picture of the environment in which they lived.

The great majority of these records are now deposited at County Record Offices and it is always there that you should first enquire.

The Problem of Dates Before 1752

The generally known basic fact, and for many purposes all that need be considered, is that before 1752 the official English calendar reckoned the year as beginning on 25 March ('old style' or O.S.) and from 1752 the year was reckoned from 1 January ('new style' or N.S.), and that it is customary to show the year by double indication for dates between 1 January and 24 March; thus for example 24 March 1715 should be written 24 March 1715/16, and the following day would be 25 March 1716. The double indication can be found in some registers before 1752.

This much is quite well known, but there were complications which affect Church registers. The fact that both were changed in one year by the New Style Calendar Act has obscured the point that there were two quite separate factors involved: (a) the 25 March new year was English practice from the twelfth century until 1751; (b) England used until 1752 the Julian calendar which incorporated a miscalculation of leap years; this had been amended by Pope Gregory XIII to produce the Gregorian calendar in 1582; this was promptly adopted in Catholic countries, but, as a 'popish invention', less readily so by Protestant countries. Most of Europe had been using the 1 January new year before 1582. The New Style Calendar Act made two changes in the official calendar: (a) with effect from 1 January 1752, the calendar year was reckoned from 1 January and (b) eleven days 3–13 September 1752 were omitted to adjust to the Gregorian calendar, with adjusted calculation of leap years thereafter.

The English colonies including North America used the official English calendar; Scotland, however, adopted a 1 January New Year in 1600, although retaining the Julian calendar; Britain and its colonies were, therefore, ten days (1582–1700) or eleven days (1700–1752) out of phase with the calendar used in much of western Europe.

In the first place, and although surprisingly the fact seems to have failed to be noticed in any standard reference sources, it seems to have been quite widespread practice for a 1 January calendar year to have been used in earlier sixteenth-century registers. A few examples survive, but it seems that many registers were altered to a 25 March year when they were transcribed onto parchment in about 1600; the registers of Chudleigh, Devon, and Fareham, Hampshire, show that the transcribers got into a muddle when changing the dates. Some modern transcribers of registers have also adjusted the dating of their work to a 1 January year basis, rather than preserving the text of the original document, which can cause confusion.

The earlier Presbyterians also had a tendency to use a 1 January new year basis before 1752; for example Tavistock Abbey Chapel registers record in 1693 'N.B. the year is supposed to begin from that we commonly call New Year's Day' and date the records accordingly. This may be in part attributable to a significant number of ministers with Scottish names, presumably used to the Scottish calendar. Similar tendencies can be found among denominations with continental European links; Catholics, Huguenots and Moravians in particular. (One register of a Moravian congregation in London goes so far as to date entries before 1752 by both the Julian and Gregorian calendars.)

The Society of Friends used official English reckoning for the year but objected to months and days of the week named after heathen gods. They used a numerical system, Sunday being 'first-day' and Saturday 'seventh-day'; months before 1752 were March, 'first month' round to February, 'twelfth month'; thus the calendar year started on the 25th of the first month. (The months September to December, being Latin numeration concurring with Friends' numeration, were acceptable.) From 1752, this was changed, January being 'first month' and December 'twelfth month', and this was specified by a printed notice circulated in September 1751 to all meetings in Great Britain, Ireland and America, from the London Meeting for Sufferings.

The Jewish calendar is an extremely complicated subject, outside the scope of this book beyond stating that the Jewish epoch dates (by Christian reckoning) from 1 October 3761 BC, and the year varies between 353 and 385 days in twelve or thirteen months. A detailed account can be found in the *Encyclopaedia Judaica*.

CHAPTER SEVEN

Wills, Administrations and Inventories

Wills and their associated documents are a particularly important record for the family historian. Often they are the only truly personal document a person has left, and the only clue we have to them as people rather than names on a piece of paper or parchment. But, as you will see, they are a complicated subject.

Much of the text of a will is of less relevance to genealogists and so the text can often be summarized. It was customary, for example, to start the will with the set-piece declaration of faith; for example,

> In the name of God, Amen. The sixth day of December in the year of our Lord God one thousand six hundred fifty and fower I, William Currer of Middleton in the parish of Ilkley and county of Yorke, yeoman sick of body but of perfect memory (praysed be God for it) doe ordaine and make this my last will and testament in manner and forme following: First I commend my soule into the hands of Almighty God my Creator who gave it trustinge by the onlie merritts and mediacion of his sonne and blessed Saviour Jesus Christ . . . And my body to the earthe to be buried in the parish church of Ilkley aforesayd at the stall-head where I had my seat formerly at the discretion of my friends And for my worldly goods that God hath beene pleased to bestow upon mee my will and mynde is that they shalbe to 'such and such uses' as hereafter shalbe expressed.

The whole of this lengthy preamble and committal can be summarized as follows: 'William Currer of Middleton, Ilkley, Yorks, yeoman. Will made 6 December 1654. To be buried in the parish church of Ilkley. Usual committal.' The will continues as follows:

> Item I give unto Dorothy my wife the third part as the law doth require of all the remainder of my goods.
> Item I give unto my sonne Henry Currer twenty pounds as a legacie to be paid within one year next after my decease to be put forth for his use.
> Item I give unto my five children Henry Currer my sayd sonne Alice Currer, Jane Currer, Mary Currer and Anne Currer my daughters.

OPPOSITE
The Will of Henry Currer of Kildwick, Yorkshire, 1652. This is part of the register copy in the Prerogative Court of Canterbury. Notice the preamble in which the testator states that he is of sound mind and in which he commends his soul to God and his body to Christian burial. Since wills were a matter that the Church courts dealt with, these were obligatory requirements and do not indicate any particular religious scruples on the part of the testator.

and my bodie to be buried in the parish Churchyarde of Thurstom and for my worldly goods I dispose as followeth. Item I give unto Lawrence Crumpe my yongest sonne three pounds. Item I give unto William Denny my first wifes sonne one Ewe and her lambe. Item I give unto James Crumpe my sonne two pounds and one Ewe and her lambe. Item I give unto Mary James daughter to William James tenn shillings. Item I give to the three poore widdowes releeved in the Collection every one of them one peck of wheate and Rye. The rest of my goods not disposed of, my debts being paid, my funerall expences discharged, I make and ordayne Alice my wife, James and Lawrence my sonnes full Executors of this my last will and Testament. These being witnesses Peter Burnham Wilfrede Cooke James Crump his marke.

The second day of November in the yeare of our Lord God one thousand six hundred fifty foure there issued forth letters of Administration unto Lawrence Crumpe the Grandfather of James and Lawrence Crumpe minors the sonnes and surviving Executors named in the will of the sayd deceased according to the tenor and effect of the sayd will during the minority and to the use of the sayd Minors hee being by virtue of a Commission in that behalfe issued forth first sworne truly to Administer the same.

In the name of God Amen the first day of March in the yeare of our Lord God according to the Computation of the Church of England one thousand six hundredth fiftie and two I Henry Currer of Kildwicke in Craven in the County of Yorke yeoman being of sounde and perfect memory and understanding and considering and well weighing the frayltie and instability of this present life doe make and ordayne this my last will and Testament in manner and forme following That is to saye ffirst and principally I committ my soule into the hands of Allmighty God my maker assuredly trusting in and through the merritts of our Lord and Saviour Jesus Christ to be one of that blessed Company to whome this joyfull sentence (Come ye blessed of my father receive the kingdome prepared for you) shalbee pronounced. And my bodie I committ to Christian buriall at the discretion of my kindred freinds and children. And as touching the disposition of my temporall Estate which God of his goodnesse hath lent unto me and for the avoiding of all differences that might after my decease arise about the same my will and mynde is as followeth ffirst whereas I have allready given and bestowed upon Henry Currer and John Currer my two yonger sonnes the summe of fower hundreth pounds a peece in lieu recompence and full satisfaction of their childs parts and portions as appeares by a generall release under their hands bearing date the first day of October one thousand six hundred forty and eight 1648 To whome also since I have given either of them one hundred pounds of Currant English money to better and increase their sayd childs parts and portions, And whereas I have also given a debt of two hundred pounds owing to mee by Hugh Currer my sonne and heyre apparent unto Mary Currer my daughter in lieu of her childs parte and portion for which sayd debt the sayd Hugh Currer hath sealed and executed two severall bonds or writings obligatorie for the payment thereof accordingly, And whereas I have allready given and bestowed upon Anne Watson my daughter the summe of two hundred and fifty pounds in lieu recompence and full satisfaction of her childs part and portion as by a generall release dated the last day of January in the yeare of our Lord God one thousand six hundred fforty and nyne sealed and delivered unto me by William Watson her husband more fully appeareth, And whereas I have likewise given and bestowed upon Martha Bawdwen my daughter the summe of five hundred pounds sterling in lieu recompence and full satisfaction of her childs part and portion as by a generall release sealed and delivered unto me by Edmund Bawdwen her husband bearing date the eight day of July in the yeare of our Lord God one thousand six hundred and fifty more fully may appeare Now therefore my will and mynde is that all such debts as I shall owe at my death bee paid and discharged out of my whole personall Estate And after payment thereof my will and mynde is And I doe hereby give and bequeath unto the aforenamed Mary Currer my daughter the summe of three hundred

Test: Henrici Currer.

and so on in greater or less complexity, and often including long complicated legal provisions governing the descent of property and the management of the estates of children who were under age. This particular will ends thus:

> Item I make Dorothy Currer my sayd wife and Henry my aforesayd sonne sole executors of this my last will and testament Sealed with my seale and signed the day and yeare abovewritten: William Currer. Sealed and signed in the sight and presence of us Thomas Ferrand Agnes Ferrand Thomas Guyland.

At the end of the will there will be the probate act, in this case in English because the will was made during the Commonwealth, when, from 1653 to 1660 all wills were proved centrally in London. Usually the probate is in Latin, but the form is very much the same, except that the name of the ecclesiastical court is given.

> This will was proved at London the sixth day of February in the year of our Lord God according to the computation of the Church of England one thousand six hundred fifty and five before the Judges for probate of wills and granting administrations lawfully authorized by the oathes of Dorothy Currer the relict and Henry Currer the naturall and lawfull sonne of the sayd deceased joynt executors named in this last will and testament of the deceased to whom was committed administration of all and singular the goods chattels and debts of the sayd deceased they beinge first sworne by vertue of a Commission well and truly to administer the same.

The researcher can abbreviate the will and probate as follows:

> will proved 6th February 1655/6 at London by exors. Wife Dorothy Currer and son, Henry Currer. Witnesses: Thomas Ferrand, Agnes Ferrand, Thomas Guyland. Supervisors—none. Bequests to the Poor—none. Legatees: Wife, Dorothy Currer one third of estate. Son, Henry Currer, £20 to be paid within one year of death. To daughters Alice, Jane, Mary and Anne Currer (all under 21) remainder of goods equally divided. Wife, Dorothy to have education of son, Henry (under 21) and youngest daughter, Anne. Each child to be the others' heir. Property. Tenantright of farm at Middleton, Ilkley and land called Hard Inges. Profits of whole to Dorothy till son reaches 21, thereafter Dorothy to have half for life, but if she remarry, she to have Hard Inges only for life. If son dies before 21 daughters to inherit.

Since January 1858 wills in England and Wales have been proved centrally at the Principal Probate Registry at Somerset House in London, and in Ireland at the Principal Probate Registries in Dublin, and, since 1922, Belfast. The law governing wills in Scotland is different from that in the rest of Britain; testamentary matters in the Channel Islands and in the Isle of Man are still in the jurisdiction of the local courts. Annual indexes of Grants of Probate and Letters of Administration in England and Wales can be consulted at Somerset House free of charge. Copies of wills and administrations may be consulted for a fee.

Before the establishment of the Principal Probate Registry the probate of any

Reading the Will: William Greatbach after Wilkie. Testators sometimes reserve their anger against erring relatives until after they are dead. The expressions on the faces of some of these people suggest that as many of them are displeased with the contents of the will as are happy.

will in England and Wales took place in one of at least three hundred courts depending upon the location of the estate of the deceased. There was a heirarchy of church courts; at the head were the Archbishops' Prerogative Courts of Canterbury and York (PCC and PCY) and the local courts of the Bishops and Archdeacons. There were also areas of 'Peculiar or exempt jurisdiction of Church and other dignitaries' which did not come under the Bishops or Archdeacons' Courts at all.

Probate records of the land-owning classes and the wealthy are most likely to be found in PCC, at the Public Record Office—for which there are printed indexes to 1700 and a consolidated card index 1750–1800 at the Society of Genealogists (in course of publication). The Prerogative Court of York, of which the records are at the Borthwick Institution at York, filled the same role for the northern province (Cheshire, Cumberland, Durham, Lancashire, Northumberland, Nottinghamshire, Westmorland and Yorkshire). Their records were not solely confined to the wealthy, and the indexes and calendars should always be searched in addition to those of local courts.

Details of the exact jurisdiction of each court, the location of their records, and the existence of printed and other indexes, are given in two books: *Wills and their Whereabouts*, by Anthony J. Camp (1974), gives full details of all types of probate records in each diocesan and other record office, and describes the probate procedure fully; *Wills and Where to Find Them*, by J. S. W. Gibson, (1974) is more clearly presented, arranged by (historic) county, with maps to show jurisdictions, and is designed specifically for the inexperienced; either

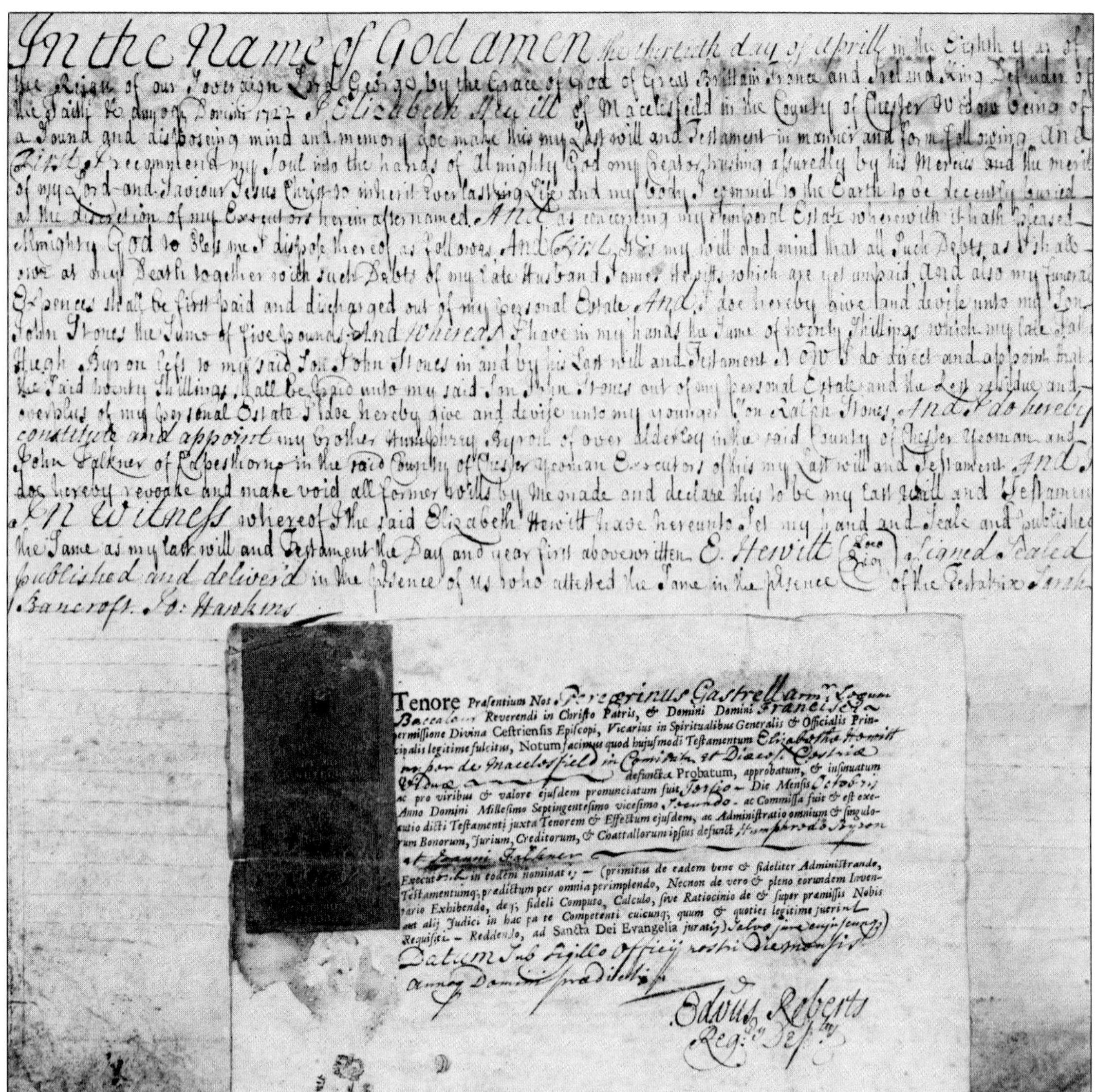

In the Name of God Amen the thirtieth day of Aprill in the Eighth year of the Reign of our Sovereign Lord George by the Grace of God of Great Brittain France and Ireland King Defender of the Faith &c Anno Domini 1722 I Elizabeth Hewitt of Macclesfield in the County of Chester Widow being of a Sound and disposing mind and memory doe make this my Last will and Testament in manner and form following And First I recommend my Soul into the hands of Almighty God my Creator trusting assuredly by his Mercies and the merit of my Lord and Saviour Jesus Christ to inherit Everlasting Life and my Body I commit to the Earth to be decently buried at the discretion of my Executors herein after named And as concerning my Temporal Estate wherewith it hath pleased Almighty God to bless me I dispose thereof as followes And First It is my will and mind that all such Debts as I shall owe at my Death together with such Debts of my Late Husband James Hewitt which are yet unpaid And also my funeral Expences shall be first paid and discharged out of my personal Estate And I doe hereby give and devise unto my Son John Stones the Sume of Five pounds And whereas I have in my hands the Sume of twenty Shillings which my Late Father Hugh Byron left to my said Son John Stones in and by his Last will and Testament I Now do direct and appoint that the said twenty shillings shall be paid unto my said Son John Stones out of my personal Estate and the Rest residue and overplus of my personal Estate I doe hereby give and devise unto my younger Son Ralph Stones And I do hereby constitute and appoint my brother Humphrey Byron of over Alderley in the said County of Chester Yeoman and John Falkner of Capesthorne in the said County of Chester Yeoman Executors of this my Last will and Testament And I doe hereby revoake and make void all former wills by me made and declare this to be my Last will and Testament In Witness whereof I the said Elizabeth Hewitt have hereunto set my hand and seale and published the same as my last will and Testament the Day and year first abovewritten E. Hewitt (Loco Sigi) Signed Sealed published and deliverd in the presence of us who attested the same in the presence of the Testatrix Sarah Bancroft. Jo: Hawkins

Tenore Præsentium Nos Peregrinus Gastrell arm[iger] Legum Baccalau[reus] Reverendi in Christo Patris, & Domini Domini Francisci permissione Divina Cestriensis Episcopi, Vicarius in Spiritualibus Generalis & Officialis Principalis legitime fulcitus, Notum facimus quod hujusmodi Testamentum Elizabethae Hewitt nuper de Macclesfield in Comitatu et Diocesi Cestriae defunctae Probatum, approbatum, & insinuatum ac pro viribus & valore ejusdem pronunciatum fuit, Tertio Die Mensis Octobris Anno Domini Millesimo Septingentesimo vicesimo Secundo. ac Commissa fuit & est executio dicti Testamenti juxta Tenorem & Effectum ejusdem, ac Administratio omnium & singulorum Bonorum, Jurium, Creditorum, & Catallorum ipsius defunct[ae] Humphrido Byron et Joanni Falkner Executoribus in eodem nominat[is] (primitus de eadem bene & fideliter Administrando, Testamentumq; prædictum per omnia perimplendo, Necnon de vero & pleno eorundem Inventario Exhibendo, deq; fideli Computo, Calculo, sive Ratiocinio de & super præmissis Nobis aut alii Judici in hac parte Competenti cuicunq; quum & quoties legitime fuerint Requisiti Reddendo, ad Sancta Dei Evangelia juratis) Salvo jure cujuscunque.

Datum sub sigillo Officii nostri die mensis et Anno Domini prædictis.

Edwus Roberts
Reg[istrarius] Dep[utatus]

The original Will of Elizabeth Hewitt dated 30 April 1722 with Grant of Probate.

will set the searcher for probate records on the right path. These two books also give details of probate records in Scotland, Ireland, and in the Channel Islands and for the Isle of Man (for which probate matters are still dealt with locally). Many testators elsewhere in the British Isles also had property in England and Wales, so their wills also may appear in PCC. Another book which the researcher will find useful is *A Simplified Guide to Probate Jurisdictions* by J. S. W. Gibson published by the Federation of Family History Societies and Gulliver Press.

Properly speaking, a 'will' deals with real estate, though under Scottish law before 1868 and certain Channel Islands law only personal (i.e. movable) property could be bequeathed. A 'testament' deals with the bequest of personal goods such as clothing, furniture, stock, farming implements, trade tools, bonds, book debts or money in any form; hence the phrase 'last will and testament'. In cases of intestacy or where there was a defect in the will the next of kin or a creditor applied for letters of administration. The Administration Act was entered in a book and there was also the Administration Bond whereby the administrator gave security for acting properly. It was usual to submit an inventory of the deceased's goods with the will, and almost invariably with administrations especially before about 1720. Inventories are sometimes found filed with wills and sometimes separately, as in the case of wills and administrations proved in the Prerogative Court of Canterbury, and as they list the deceased's possessions, are a fascinating record for a family historian.

Estate Duty Registers

Legacy or death duty was first introduced in 1796 and was a tax payable on legacies and residues of personal estate of deceased persons. The estate duty registers and their indexes are available for inspection in the Public Record Office in London for England and Wales. The registers begin in 1796 and continue until 1894, but can only be read if they are 125 years old. The indexes, however, can be consulted for the whole period. Before 1812 there are separate indexes for each court, later a single consolidated index.

Estate duty registers can be a valuable aid to the family historian in finding in which court a will was proved or an administration granted. They contain a good deal of useful information which may supplement the will itself. For example, in the will you may find that the testator has stated 'to all my children' or other such persons unnamed as such. In these registers their names are shown together with their relationship to the deceased. Apart from giving names of the legatees and their degrees of consanguinity, these registers also show the name of the deceased, the date of the will, the place and date of probate, the name, address and occupation of the executors, details of the estates, legacies, annuities and the duty paid.

The Irish Public Record Office in Dublin has consolidated indexes of wills and administrations from all Irish courts from October 1829 to 1879 and abstracts from 1829 to 1839, originating in the Inland Revenue Office.

CHAPTER EIGHT

Land Records

Although the number of people who own their own house is greater today than it has ever been, the fact remains that the records attached to land ownership and tenancies generally provide a valuable source of genealogical information.

Records of this cover a large range of sources spanning a thousand years or more of history. Probably the best known of all is the Domesday Book, a survey of his kingdom ordered by William the Conqueror in 1086. The Norman system of land tenure was based upon military service, and to ensure an effective army land was granted in return for knight-service defined in terms of quotas of armed men. The inventory of his kingdom was made so that the King could know not only the number of towns, villages and manors he and his barons possessed, but also their revenue and population. It was carried through with a degree of thoroughness unequalled until modern times, and the feudal system it established endured for several centuries. However, within each estate (called a 'manor') tenancies continued in a way which had begun before the Normans arrived.

Essentially there were two types of manorial tenant, those who were free and those who were villeins or 'bondmen'. In his turn the Lord of the Manor held his land from a higher noble who held his land from the King in return for military service. Free tenants gave military service or paid rent, villeins had the use of land in return for work on the lord's land. In time both the Crown and the lords of the manor found it more convenient to commute both the military and farming services for money and to hire men to do the work required to run their estates or to fight their battles. The villeins' land was held according to the custom of the manor and its transfer from one tenant to another, frequently on the death of a tenant when it would usually pass to his son, was recorded in the Court Rolls of the manor. The tenant's evidence of title was by a copy of this, thus the term 'copyhold' tenure. But the Manor Court did not confine itself to matters to do with the transfers of tenancies only. Such officers as the reeves, tithingmen and haywards were appointed annually by the Manor Courts, which also dealt with the enforcement of the customs of the manor, the punishment of petty misdemeanours, and the settlement of minor disputes between tenants and neighbours. It is obvious, therefore, that if you can identify the manor your ancestors were living on, and if the manorial records have survived, you could discover a wealth of valuable information.

Coming nearer to our own day, title deeds, Land Tax Assessments, mortgages,

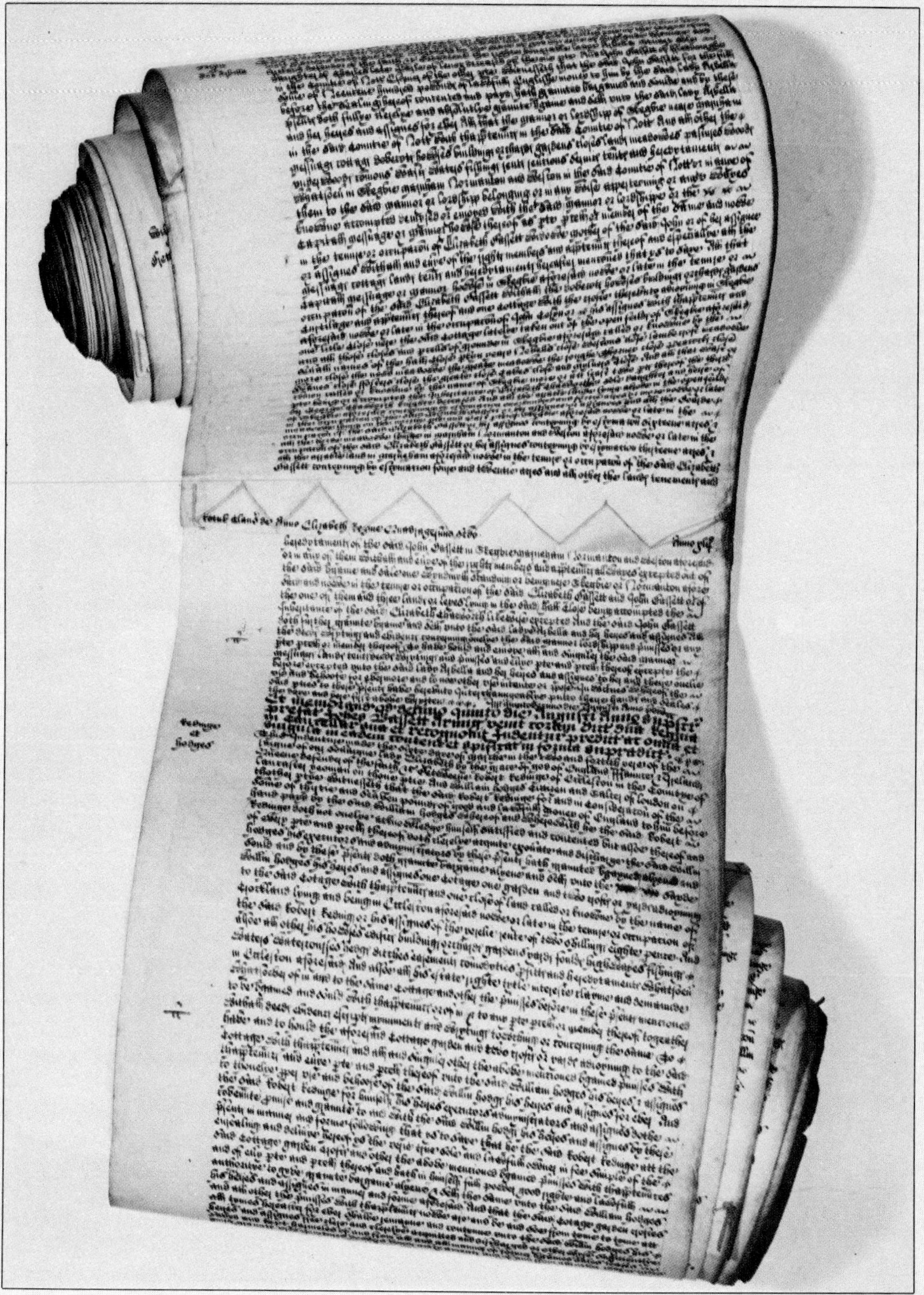

Close Rolls dating from the time of Elizabeth I are written in court hand and relate to the grant of land and privileges to individuals and corporations.

Hearth Tax Returns, Enclosure Awards, tontines and annuities, insurance and tithe records all yield a vast amount of information about all manner of people in all walks of life, and not only the so-called landed gentry.

Similarly connections between families and between different generations of a single family can be deduced from a study of title deeds enrolled on the Close Rolls, which extend back to the twelfth century. These generally concern grants of land and privileges by the Crown to individuals and corporations including monasteries, chantries and charities. In 1599, for example, Peter Page bought land from William Kirkeby of East Hatfield, Yorkshire, yeoman, which had formerly been part of the lands of the Yorkshire Priory of Nunkeeling. Deeds in the Close Rolls showed that this land had formerly belonged to Roger Kirkeby and that it had descended to his son Christopher who had died without issue, and that then it came to William, Christopher's younger brother, then to William's son Roger in 1582.

In the Close Rolls for 1630 a deed is recorded between Martin Button of Bath and Capt. Robert Kirby of Woodbridge in Suffolk on one part and Sir William Withipoll and his son, Francis, on the other. Among the lands included in this transaction, which mainly concerned the estate of Sir William Read of Osterley Park, in Middlesex, were some which formed part of the lands of Nunkeeling Priory.

The common factor between these two transactions was of course Nunkeeling Priory, for there was otherwise nothing to connect Capt. Robert Kirby of Suffolk with William Kirkeby of Yorkshire. However, on closer investigation it was discovered that the Nunkeeling Priory estate was bought at the dissolution of the monasteries by Sir Richard Gresham and John Thynne of Bath. Sir Richard Gresham's great-niece was Lady Rebecca Seckford, whose granddaughter was the wife of Robert Kirby of Woodbridge. Robert Kirby's great-grandfather, Andrew Kirby, according to heraldic evidence, came from a family settled since the tenth century in Lancashire, whose branches extended into Yorkshire.

Land records, therefore, can be invaluable in providing information about families from which much additional information can be deduced. They can also tell us much about the day-to-day lives of our ancestors, and especially about fluctuations in their fortunes. Most of these records were written in Latin up to 1732, which can be a problem for the amateur researcher. Many Manorial Rolls are in County Record offices (not always in the obvious county), in the Public Record Office, in the British Museum and in private hands. A list of known Manorial records and their whereabouts can be seen at the National Register of Archives.

While it is possible to use Title Deeds as genealogical sources without knowing much or anything about the law of real property, it is, all the same, advisable to have a passing acquaintance with the law. It must be realized, for example, that fines and recoveries represent fictitious transactions aimed at circumventing certain statutory prohibitions on the transfer of title. Similarly, a conveyance by lease and release was devised for a specific purpose. A useful brief introduction

Know all Men by these Presents That We William Trefusis Reichenberg of Devereux Court in the Parish of Saint Clement's Danes London Esquire and John Rodolphus Reichenberg of Trevidar in the Parish of Saint Buryan in the County of Cornwall Esquire are held and firmly bound to Miss Elizabeth Trefusis of Stafford Row in the Parish of Saint George Hanover Square London in the penal Sum of One thousand two hundred pounds of good and lawful Money of Great Britain To be paid to the said Miss Elizabeth Trefusis or her certain Attorney Executors Administrators or Assigns For which Payment to be well and faithfully made We bind ourselves our and each of our Heirs Executors and Administrators jointly and severally firmly by these Presents Sealed with our Seals Dated this fourteenth day of June in the thirty sixth year of the Reign of our Sovereign Lord George the Third by the Grace of God of Great Britain France and Ireland King Defender of the Faith and so forth And in the Year of our Lord One Thousand seven hundred and ninety six

The Condition of this Obligation is such That if the above bounden William Trefusis Reichenberg and John Rodolphus Reichenberg or either of them their or either of their Heirs Executors or Administrators shall and do well and truly pay or cause to be paid unto the above named Miss Elizabeth Trefusis her Executors Administrators or Assigns the full Sum of Six hundred pounds of lawfull Money of Great Britain on the twenty ninth day of September next with lawful Interest for the same after the Rate of Five Pounds per cent per annum Then this Obligation to be Void or else to be and remain in full force and Virtue

Sealed and delivered by the above named William Trefusis Reichenberg being first duly stampt in the presence of
Henry St John

William Trefusis Reichenberg
J. R. Reichenberg

Sealed and Delivered by the above named John Rodolphus Reichenberg in the presence of
John Trewe[illegible]k

An eighteenth-century land-purchase bond in which William Trefusis Reichenberg of Devereux Court, St Clement Danes, London, and John Rodolphus Reichenberg of St Buryan, Cornwall, are bound to Elizabeth Trefusis to pay her £600. The penalty for failure to pay is £1200.

to the significance of title deeds is Pamphlet no. H 72, published in 1968 by the Historical Association of Great Britain, entitled *Title Deeds 13th–19th Centuries*, by A. A. Dibben.

Basically, a conveyance of land is between two parties, a party in this context being one or more individuals. A deed may be a simple conveyance of a freehold interest in land from A to B or a lease for a term of years from C to D, or be increasingly complex in conveying extensive estates, creating trusts, remainders and entails for generations to come. The more complex the conveyance the greater the chances of finding genealogical information, for earlier deeds and transactions will be recited and set out, and relationships may be traceable backward for several generations. A series of deeds, both simple and complex, dealing with the same property over a number of years can give a very great deal of information about a family if the property remained in its hands throughout the period. Since it was not uncommon in Britain for families to own property for two or more centuries, the accumulation of deeds and conveyances over this period, even for quite minor families, can be extremely large.

The series of documents known as Feet of Fines not only cover an unbroken period of more than six centuries, but have no parallel in the records of any other country except perhaps some archives in Edinburgh. Beginning at the end of the twelfth century, they continue into the nineteenth. These were records of fictional law-suits over possession of land to obtain the judgement of the Court as to ownership, which was a 'watertight' title. Fines were written in triplicate on parchment. The 'foot', which is the official copy of the document, was retained in the court records and still survives. A typical example, in translation, might read as follows:

> This is the final agreement made in the Court of our Lord the King at Westminster in the quindene of Easter in the 7th year of the reign of King Henry VII before A.B, C.D, E.F, Justices of our Lord the King and others there present, etc. between W.X the demandant and Y.Z the deforciant of 8 acres of land and 2 acres of meadow with their appurtenances in Waxham concerning which an assize of mort d'auncestor was summoned between them in the aforesaid Court. Namely that the said Y.Z granted to the said W.X and his heirs all the aforesaid land. To hold to him and his heirs paying therefore yearly 6*d*. for all service.
>
> And the said W.X for this grant gives the said Y.Z three shillings.

Similar records useful in medieval genealogy are the Curia Regis Rolls, De Banco Rolls, and Docket Books of the Exchequer. Another extremely valuable type of enquiry was that which was conducted after the death of many landowners, known as an Inquisition Post Mortem (IPM). On the death of such a man, an enquiry was held to determine the extent and location of his land, and the terms under which he held it. This usually elicits the date of the tenant's death and the name, age and relationship of the next heir. Unfortunately these enquiries ceased in 1645 and were not renewed at the Restoration.

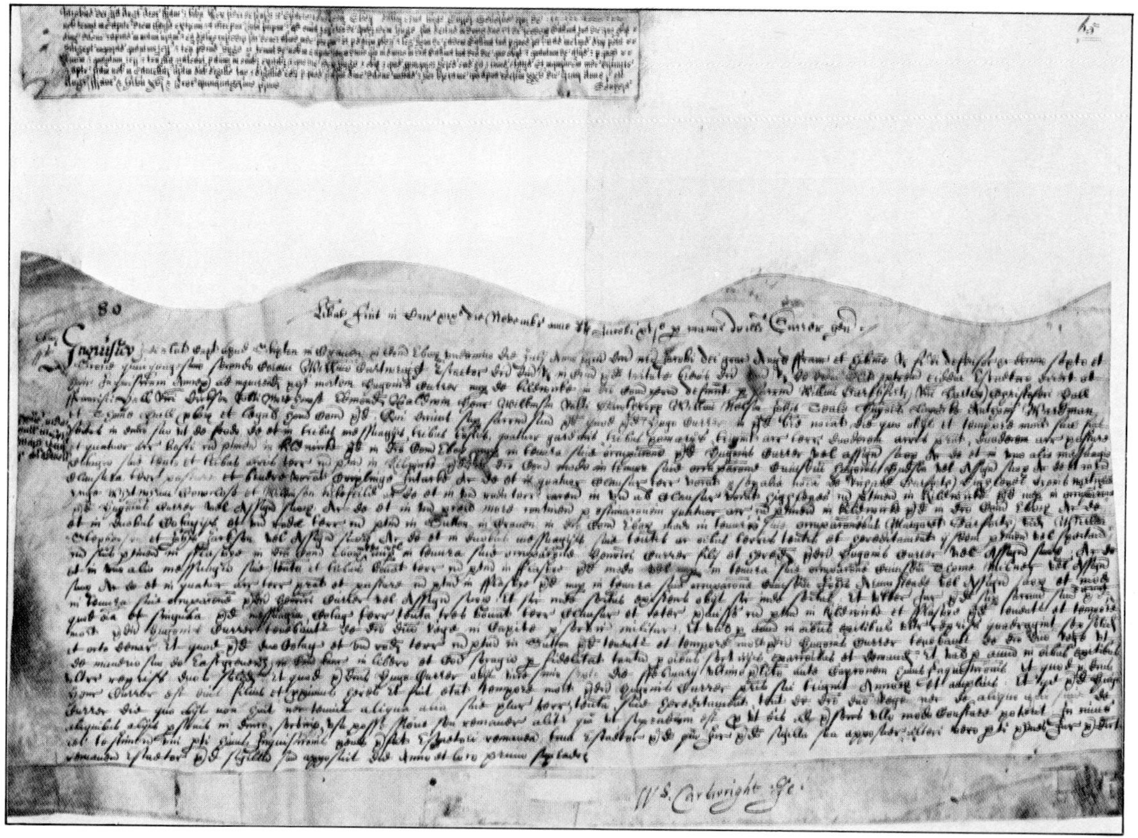

This inquisition post mortem on Hugh Currer of Kildwick is written in Latin in secretary hand (*below*). The writ, which is also in Latin, is written in court hand (*above*). The document sets out the terms on which Hugh Currer held his land and gives the name and age of his heir.

During the English Civil War, landowners who supported the King against the victorious Commonwealth had their lands confiscated by order of committees appointed to investigate the actions of the owners. Having 'confessed their delinquency' and given a pledge to adhere to the Commonwealth, they had to give a full account of their possessions and were then allowed to 'compound' by surrendering a portion of their estate, which varied according to their 'guilt'. The records of these committees (PRO Class SP/23) give a lot of information about the condition of such individuals, often mentioning their heirs and other members of their family. They are known as Composition Papers.

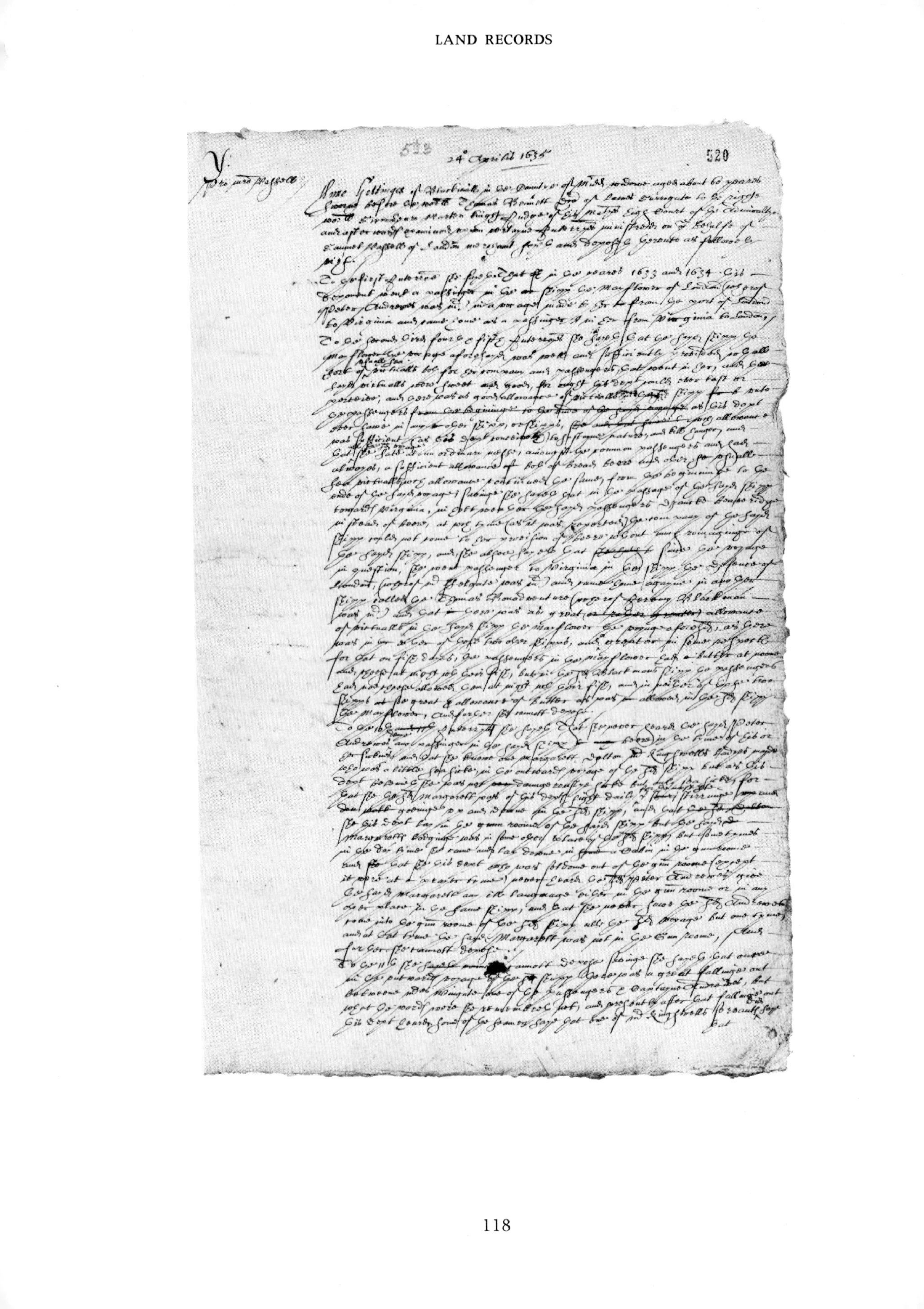

24° Aprilis 1635 520

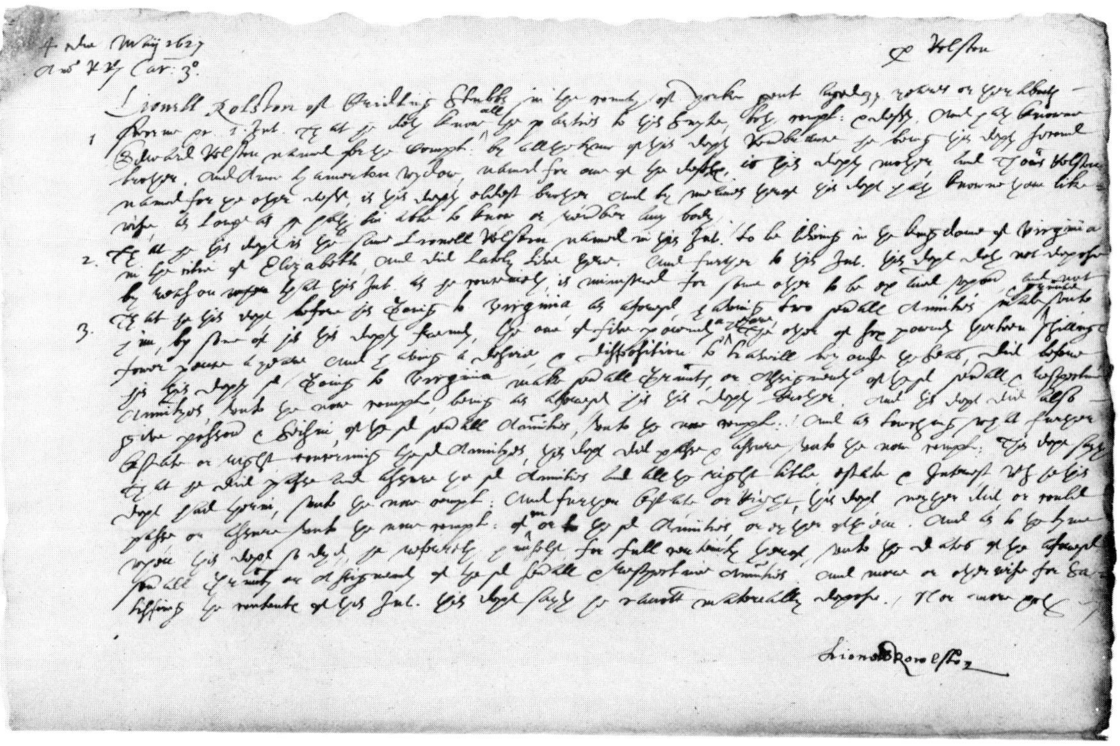

Above: The deposition of a witness in a case brought before the Chancery Court on 4 May 1627. Lionel Rolston describes how he was living in Virginia and how, before he went, he received certain annuities from his friends. He gives his age as 37. (Class C. 24)

Opposite: The deposition of a witness in a case brought before the High Court of Admiralty in 1635. The witness, Anne Gittings of Blackwall, Middlesex is a widow, aged 'about 60 years' and describes living conditions aboard the *Mayflower* (Capt. Peter Andrews) on a voyage to America in 1633 and 1634. (Class HCA 13)

Exchequer Class E 179, at the Public Record Office, London, are records of tax assessments. Among these, the 'Lay Subsidies' are useful because they give the names of taxpayers at the level of wealth taxed that year. They are listed by years and 'hundred' divisions of counties. Also in this class of document are the Hearth Tax returns of Charles II's reign, many of which have been published by local historical societies, and other lists of taxpayers such as some Poll Tax returns. The lists include not only those who paid the tax, but also those who were exempted from paying on account of poverty. This is the only comprehensive list of householders in the late seventeenth century. Unfortunately not all assessments have survived, but these returns are a primary source well worth consulting.

A particularly useful adjunct to subsidy records is in the class E 115 at the Public Record Office; these are certificates of residence for subsidy, and their main value is in effect as a record of 'change of address' where a taxpayer moves away.

CHAPTER NINE

Records of the Services and Professions

Naval Records

Seamen's lives are often depicted as adventurous, daring and exciting. However, underneath the glamour there was another side. There were people who chose the Navy as their career voluntarily, but there were many more who were literally pressed into the 'King's Navy' for what would seem to us a pittance. Conditions were harsh. This was particularly true for those who were below deck. For those above, life was not absolutely cosy either.

The abundance of records that exist shed a great deal of light on these men's lives. Some records give such personal details as what they looked like and even what they ate! This chapter gives a brief summary of those records of particular genealogical interest which are available.

For men serving before the Restoration (1660) no systematic records survive but mentions of individuals on ships are to be found in printed *Calendars of State Papers, Domestic*.

Commissioned Officers

Histories of sea officers' careers can be found in printed books as well as manuscript sources. Taking printed sources one must mention Charnock's *Biographia Navalis* (1794–98), Marshall's *Royal Naval Biography* (1823–30) and O'Byrne's *A Naval Biographical Dictionary* (1849) describing all officers serving in the Navy in 1834. There is also the *Commissioned Sea Officers of the Royal Navy (1660–1815)* published by the National Maritime Museum which presents the dates when officers joined certain ranks. The first manuscript record to look for is the Lieutenant's passing certificate which, depending where you find it, gives you a copy of his baptismal certificate and summarizes his previous training and career.

If you are unlucky enough not to find your man here try and find his Record of Service which will give the dates when he served on a particular ship. From this you can look up the ships' Muster Rolls when he was serving as a Midshipman or as an Able Seaman to seek his place of birth.

Warrant Officers

This term means that they were seamen but were under receipt of warrants. Up to some point in the nineteenth century the commissioned officers were not men who actually navigated ships; this was left to those who were known as the

Bounty Paid	Nº	Entry.	Year	Appearance.	Whence and whether Prest or not.	Place and County where Born.	Age at Time of Entry in this Ship	Nº and Letter of Tickets.	MENS NAMES.	Qualities.	D D.D. or R.	Time of Discharge
£ 1	61	10th May	1803	May 18th	Vol	Stratford	22		David Conn	LM		
					Prest	London	20		Jos Button	LM	R	14th Jun
		O: Nº 11th d. 18 Mar		11th	HMS Utrecht Vol.	Holland	23		John Recain	LM		
						London	26	K.C 258	Steph.n Lennard	AB	D	17th April
	5					Leeds Kent	22		Jn.o Highland	LM		
		20th				London	27		Jn.o Edmund alias Kenman	Ord.		

Year	Whither or for what Reason.	Stragling or Neglect.	Slop Cloaths Supplied by Navy.	Cloaths in Sick Quarters.	Beds.	Dead Mens Cloaths.	Tobacco.	Date of the Parties Order for allotting Monthly Pay.	Wages remitted from Abroad.	Two Months Advance	Neceffaries fupplied Marines on Shore.	To whom the Tickets were delivered	When Muftered Month August Days 4 11 21 29
			4.14.11		16/		19/			2.2.0			n o a b
1803	Gibraltar		0.5.0		13/								
			3.9.6		13/		10.7						n o a b
1804	HM Brig Camelion per Order of Lord Nelson K.B.		3.18.7		13/		19/						
			5.3.1				1.10.1						n o a b
			5.1.3				1.3.9			2.2.0			n o a b

The ship's muster roll of the Victory (1805).

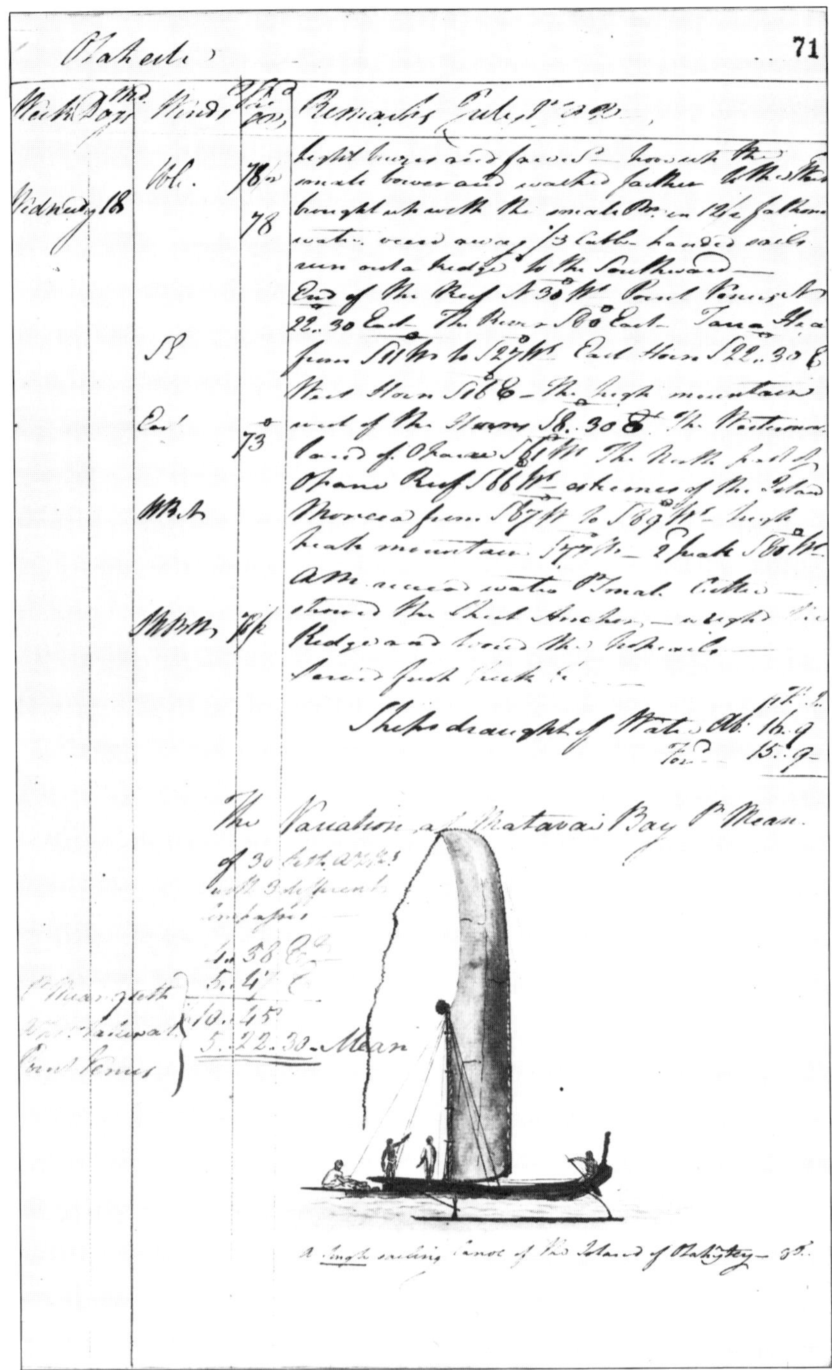

Part of an eighteenth-century ship's log. Ships' logs occasionally contain information relating to births, marriages and deaths at sea, but more often they are of general interest.

Masters and their Mates. Formally they were only classed as Warrant officers together with pursers, gunners, engineers, carpenters and boatswains, more commonly known as bosuns. There should be some record for all of these although not all have survived.

Ratings

Before the mid-nineteenth century, generally speaking, it is necessary to know in what ship a man was serving at a particular time. You then use the Muster Rolls which will give details as previously described as well as the ship in which he last served and the date he was discharged from that ship.

From 1853 'Continuous Service Engagement' was introduced. Seamen were given numbers and thus a record of services followed which gives the date and place of birth as well as a physical description and a list of the ships in which he served. For the really ardent researcher there is no end to the length to which he can pursue his studies, like looking up the ships' logs and learning of every single event that occurred in this particular ship. Some of the details may be repetitive like the exact geographical situation of the ship at a particular time of day and the climate, but these logs also record such happenings as 'Seaman Bloggs was insubordinate to an officer, received a hundred lashes on the deck and was sent below'.

These records of services continue up to 1891 and are compiled from when seamen actually joined the Navy. For any records of service of seamen who joined after that date, direct descendants can write to the Naval and Army Records Centre.

The Marines

By an Order-in-Council in 1664 what is now known as the Royal Marines was founded. They were men who not only sailed in ships but also fought on land and therefore were responsible to both the Navy and the Army. Officers' records are in the Admiralty Series. For other ranks you can find your man according to which division he was stationed in; these were at Chatham, Woolwich, Portsmouth and Plymouth. You begin by searching the Description Books and from these you can go on to look for a record of service.

Coastguards

Basically Coastguards were men drafted from the Navy beginning about 1816. Here all you need know to begin your research is which station a man was serving at a particular time. From there you can trace all kinds of records from his last ship in the Royal Navy to his date of discharge. Coastguards were administered by the Navy but paid for by the Customs. Therefore, a word of warning: sometimes a man will be described on marriage certificates as a Customs officer when he in fact was a Coastguard.

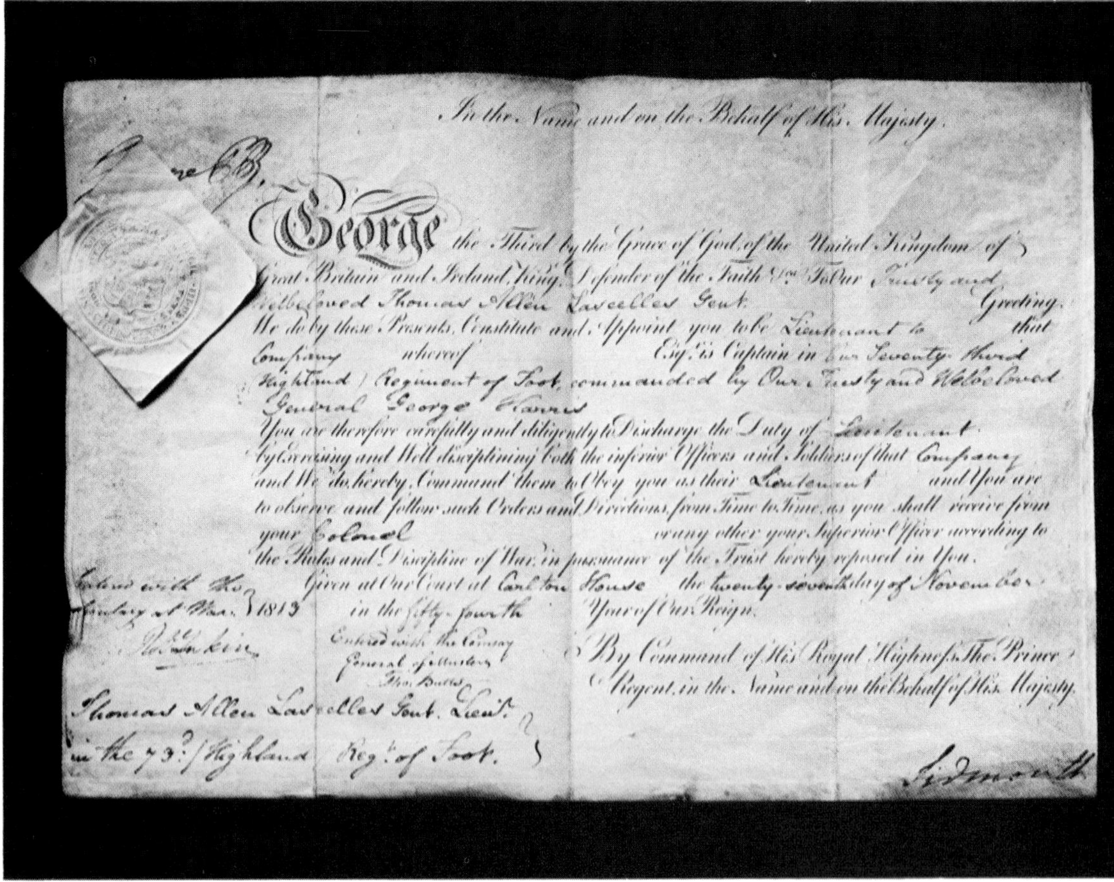
In the Name and on the Behalf of His Majesty.

George the Third by the Grace of God, of the United Kingdom of Great Britain and Ireland, King, Defender of the Faith &c. To Our Trusty and Well beloved Thomas Allen Lascelles Gent. Greeting. We do by these Presents, Constitute and Appoint you to be Lieutenant to that Company whereof Esq. is Captain in Our Seventy third Highland Regiment of Foot, commanded by Our Trusty and Well beloved General George Harris. You are therefore carefully and diligently to Discharge the Duty of Lieutenant by Exercising and Well disciplining both the inferior Officers and Soldiers of that Company and We do hereby Command them to Obey you as their Lieutenant and you are to observe and follow such Orders and Directions, from Time to Time, as you shall receive from your Colonel or any other your Superior Officer according to the Rules and Discipline of War, in pursuance of the Trust hereby reposed in You. Given at Our Court at Carlton House the twenty-seventh day of November 1813 in the fifty-fourth Year of Our Reign.

By Command of His Royal Highness The Prince Regent, in the Name and on the Behalf of His Majesty.

Sidmouth

Entered with the Secretary at War 1813

Entered with the Commissary General of Musters

Thomas Allen Lascelles Gent. Lieut. in the 73rd Highland Reg. of Foot.

A lieutenant's commission in the 73rd Highland Regiment of Foot (*c* 1813). A researcher finding such a document in the course of investigations should go on to examine the appropriate regimental records from which much information about the officer concerned could be found.

Military Records

Before the Civil Wars (1642–49) there was no regular standing army in England. Regiments were raised to meet a particular requirement and were known by the name of the Colonels who formed them. No systematic records of such regiments survive though references to individual officers and soldiers can be found in State Papers Domestic, Foreign, and other records at the Public Record Office and the manuscript department of the British Library.

After the Restoration (1660) records became more abundant but do not really contain much biographical information of officers and men which is of use to the researcher until the nineteenth century.

Officers

Service records of commissioned officers of the British Army can be traced with only approximate completeness from the year 1660. From the mid-eighteenth century preliminary details can be obtained from Army Lists but family details can be found to be only satisfactory if the officer was serving after 1829. There are the Commander-in-Chief's memorandum papers which begin in 1793. Frankly this is over-emphasized as a useful source. Sometimes you can find a letter of recommendation containing family background but experience shows this is the exception rather than the rule. There are Returns of officers' service 1808–10, but these give no personal details and only include the ranks of General down to Major.

In 1829 systematic records of services were introduced which were arranged by regiments and these unfortunate officers, of which there were many, were placed on half pay. Both they and their counterparts in the Royal Navy suffered because of the vast reduction of the armed services after the Napoleonic Wars. These records contain place of birth, details of service career, details of marriage, spouse and children, if any, with their dates of birth. You should be able to find such records up to about 1870. Thereafter one has to rely on Army Lists.

Other Ranks

Here you can be more hopeful. The first source one recommends are the soldier discharge papers which cover the years from 1756 to 1913. These are useful only if your man was discharged on a pension, not if he died on active service or if he deserted. Equally it is necessary to know the name of the regiment in which he served until 1873. From then until 1883 the papers are arranged separately for the cavalry, infantry, artillery, and so on. It is only from then onwards you find all discharge certificates, except for those who died, in one long alphabetical series for the whole Army.

These papers contain much information: the place of birth, the age of the soldier when he enlisted, his physical description, previous occupation and intended place of residence on discharge. They also give details of his career and conduct. Furthermore, some show medical details which can be very illuminating especially if he was somewhat intemperate or committed an indiscretion and suffered accordingly. Some of the later papers go even further by giving traces of next of kin, of marriage and of children.

Other series which give you vital information are the Regimental Description Books, whose survival is somewhat precarious, and the Casualty Returns. If all else fails you can search the Muster Rolls and trace a man's activities month by month. Sometimes here you can find personal details. For example, a search was made to find one James Ashley in a certain infantry regiment. There was no Record of Service for him and the Description Book was missing. After a fifteen-year search in the Muster Rolls it was discovered that he and his wife died in a yellow fever epidemic in Bermuda. This disaster occurred as the disease spread from a prison hulk moored off the Island where it began and thereupon it raged

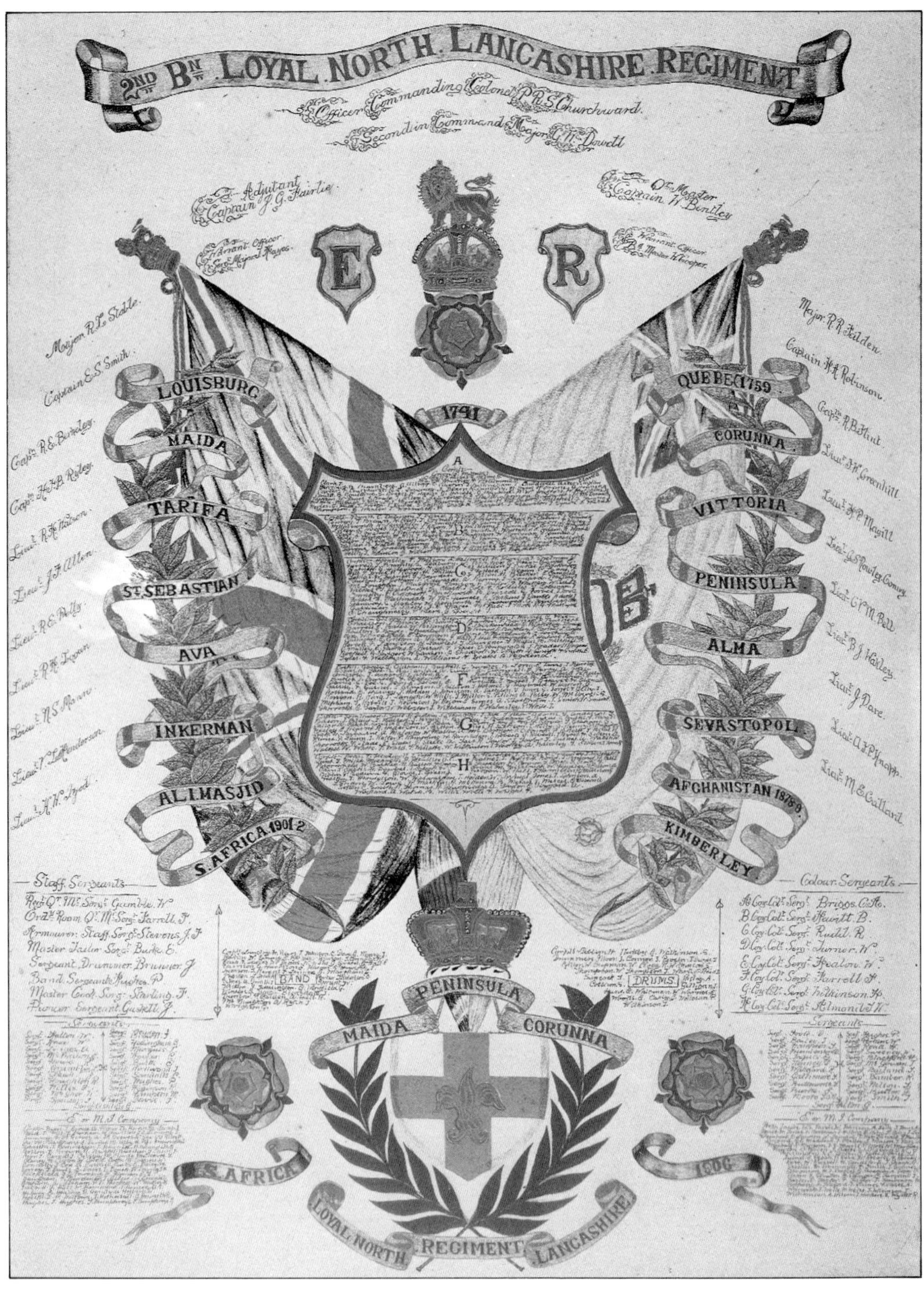

A commemorative regimental roll dated 1906 and showing the names of all officers and men. This is not an official document, but is no less useful for that. Such rolls were usually privately produced to celebrate some special regimental occasion.

all around. His two orphans were sent back to England and put into the Duke of York's Military School. Thcy stayed there for just over a year before they were sent to a maternal uncle in Australia. The reader will be left in no doubt that to find this information was a triumph.

Militia

This ancient body is best described as a part-time army raiscd when needed. Today it is best known as the Territorial Army. The first series of Muster Rolls dates from 1522–1640. Some of these records are to be found in the Public Record Office, others in private muniments, others still in County Record offices. You are likely to get information on names only but even that is helpful in this period. A number of these Muster Rolls have been published by local record societies.

The Militia was very active during the Napoleonic Wars when a large part of the regular army was abroad. Most recent records that have survived are in the form of Muster Rolls as described above, but there are some records of service for other ranks.

Mercantile Marine

The whole of the merchant service was controlled by the Department of the Board of Trade and under this body was the Registrar General of Shipping and Seamen whose records we are concerned with. Those of genealogical interest begin for seamen who served after 1835. Although from 1747 Masters or owners of ships were obliged to keep Muster Rolls of each voyage made, in which were entered the names of officers and seamen, only a few of these survive up to 1835 when a new system known as 'The Agreements and Crew Lists' was introduced. In the first series, 1835–1844, you can find details of age and place of birth only. The next series, 1845–1853, when the system of seamen's tickets was introduced, is the only one of real value. Here you find place and date of birth, with physical descriptions and the nicety as to whether the seaman could read or write together with his shore residence.

The ticketing system proved so unpopular with seamen and the administration involved outweighed the information gained so it was abolished in October 1853. Thus a new register was introduced, but in 1856 the department was satisfied that the Crew Lists sufficed and that, too, was abolished. Thereafter, unless you know a man's ship together with its port of origin, you will have a difficult task in tracing him.

For Master Mariners and Mates, Certificates of Competency were issued as a result of the Merchant Ship Act of 1850. These registers contain the place and date of birth and the port where the certificate was issued. You should find your man here if he was certificated before 1900.

Customs and Excise

The Boards of Customs and Excise were not amalgamated until 1910. The Customs were responsible for controlling the revenue at ports and the Excise men were responsible for seeing duties were paid.

Some personal details of Customs officers can be found, but records for many at the ports of London and Liverpool have been destroyed.

For Excise men there is a magnificent collection of Board Minute Books dating from 1688 that continue up to the late nineteenth century. From these we can trace a man's career from when he started as a supernumerary until his discharge or death. Often we find that a man followed in his father's footsteps and his own sons followed suit. There are also some entry papers which give personal details of men who joined the services after 1820.

Railwaymen

A railway enthusiast can have a beanfeast at the Public Record Office where he can find a multitude of original records together with many printed histories and periodicals. This mass of stuff deals with every aspect of railway organization which varied from company to company, particularly when it comes to staff records. Regarding the staff records, their usefulness varies and to search them can be frustrating. One only has to use them when you lose a railwayman in records like the Census Returns. Railwaymen obviously were moved about. Often if you are looking for an engine driver in one company you find only the station staff records have survived or vice versa. However, do not be daunted by this and have a go at them if you feel fit to do so. With these records you will also find some for the Inland Waterways. Bargemen and their families are usually elusive to say the least.

The General Post Office

Anyone who is looking for a postmaster or letter carrier, which a postman was formerly known as, can go to the General Post Office record room in London to see what he can find. There are registers of correspondence to look at as well as other material which is interesting, if not biographical. Often you can find reference to a particular person in one form or another. However, searching in this area is not particularly productive.

All the service records listed above, apart from those to do with the Postal services who retain their own records, are housed in the Public Record Office at Kew.

OPPOSITE

An Oxford Degree Ceremony, 1842: records of all students at Oxford and Cambridge, as well as of other schools and universities, are of great importance for the genealogist and the family historian as they can often shed light on the career of the ancestor concerned.

Professions and Trades

If your ancestor did belong to one of the professions or trades, it does not necessarily mean that you are going to have an easy path in tracing him, though it is worth taking up the challenge. Before describing the cross-section, it is recommended that you make one or two reference checks in printed sources. The first of these is to consult The University Alumni. Most ancient Universities have published details of their former students back to the sixteenth century. In England there are two publications, namely the Oxford and Cambridge Alumni. The details you will find in these records are the names of the father, his rank and occupation, where the student lived, his college and his later career if known.

If you fail here you can try the Dublin Alumni, and following this, the printed books of the four old Scottish Universities. Sometimes one can be very lucky in one's searches of these records and find whole generations of families.

Many public schools, too, have published records which can be consulted.

Clergy

Practically all clergy of the Church of England in former years went to either Oxford or Cambridge. The famous *Crockford's* was first published in 1848. Before this date there were Clergy Lists as well as ordination papers which are kept in the diocesan office of the See in which the priest was ordained.

You will find records of the Nonconformist clergymen among the records of

During a young man's apprenticeship, which could last from five to seven years depending on circumstances, he would receive his tuition, food and lodging from his master in return for a fee. He was not free to marry until he had completed his apprenticeship. These four engravings show the types of trades to which young men might be apprenticed.

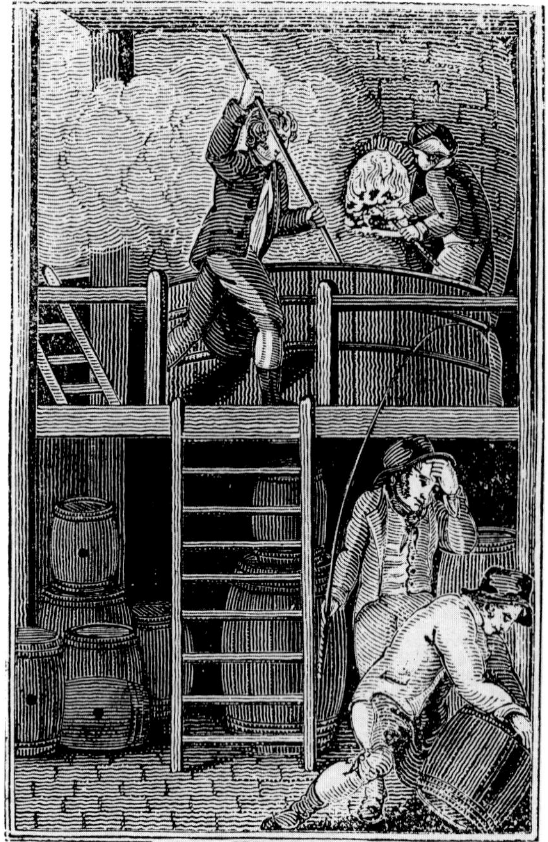

The brewer

The cooper

their particular denominations. However, the best place to start is to look at a card index in the Dr Williams Library in London which gives you details of mainly Independent and Congregational clergymen. These usually give some details of their background and you can sometimes find their photograph and references to their funeral sermons as well. Similarly for a Baptist minister you go to the Baptist Union where again they have their own card index. For Methodists and others there are details at the John Rylands Library in Manchester.

Medical Profession

Early material concerning doctors is really rather sketchy. There are a few records at the libraries of the Royal Colleges of Physicians and Surgeons. Curiously enough few doctors went to English universities. They were trained either in Edinburgh or at Leyden in Holland.

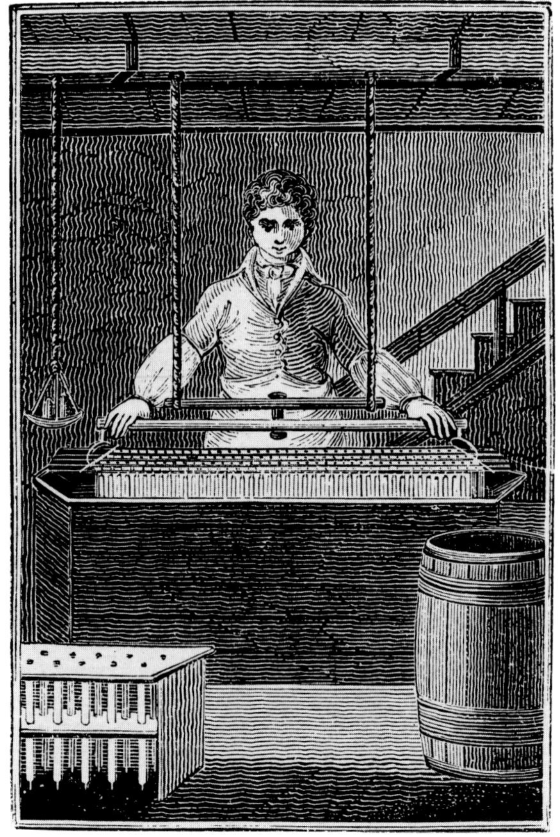
The tallow chandler

The printer

The first medical directory was published in 1847 and in 1849 a system of medical registration was set up. The entries show their qualifications and the place where they were practising. They may have been members of the Barber Surgeons' Company or members of the Society of Apothecaries. In 1815 licenciates of the latter society were introduced which cover apothecaries all over the country. Today we think of apothecaries as pharmacists or chemists but at that time pratically all doctors would have had that qualification. Looking at the records you will see that the courses they attended covered a much wider area than basic chemistry.

Legal Professions

Barristers when called to the Bar became members of one of the four Inns of Court. They all have published records of their members. If you want further

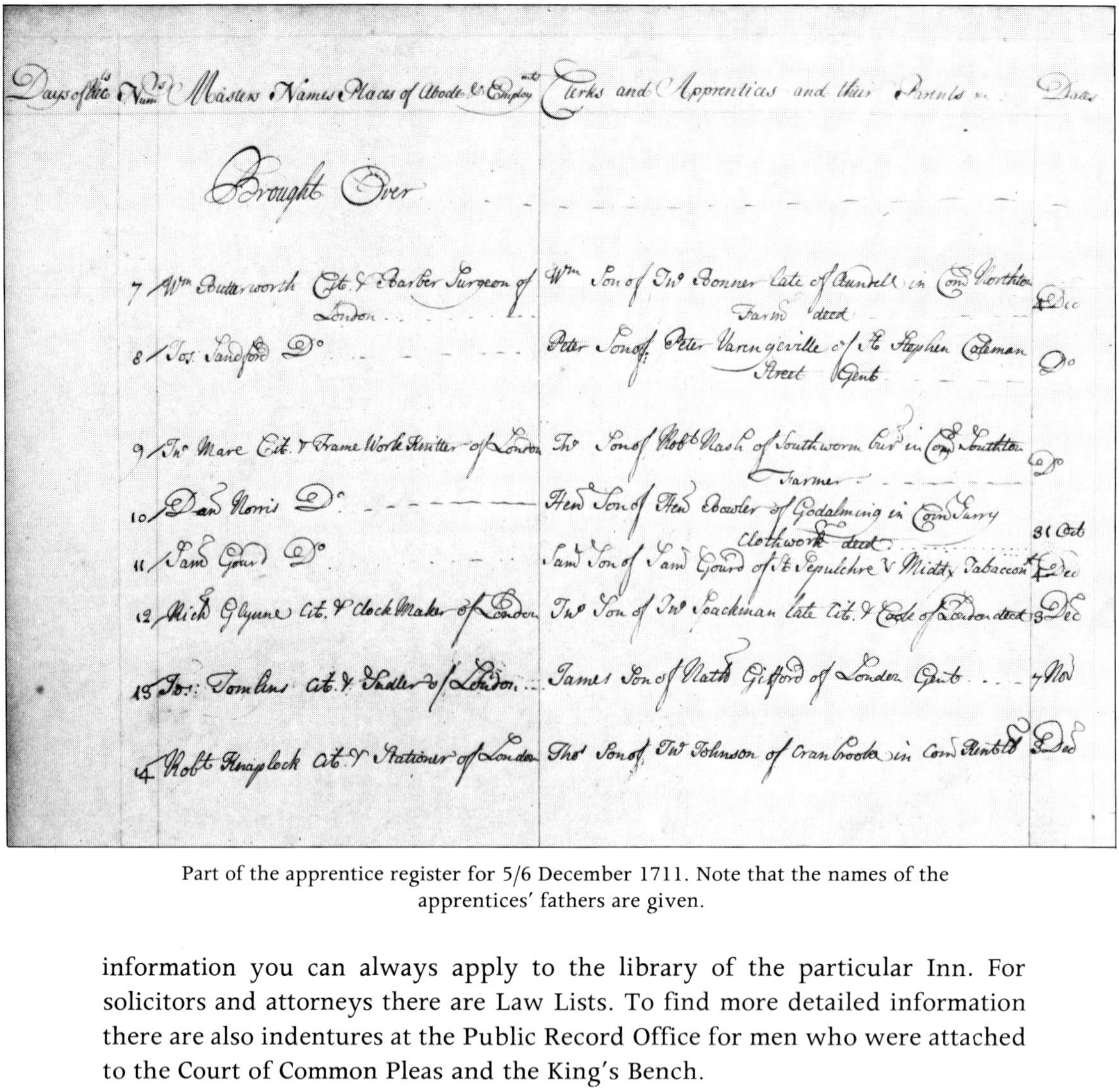
Days of the Month | Numbers | Masters Names Places of Abode & Employ | Clerks and Apprentices and their Parents | Date

Brought Over

7 Wm Butterworth Cit. & Barber Surgeon of London | Wm Son of Jno Bonner late of Aundell in Com Northton Farm deed | Dec

8 Jos. Sandford Do | Peter Son of Peter Vanngeville of St Stephen Coleman Street Gent | Do

9 Jno Mare Cit. & Frame Work Knitter of London | Jno Son of Robt Nash of Southworm Bur in Com Southton Farmer | Do

10 Dan Norris Do | Hen Son of Hen Bowler of Godalming in Com Surry Clothwork deed | 31 Oct

11 Sam Gourd Do | Sam Son of Sam Gourd of St Sepulchre & Midd Tabacconist | Dec

12 Rich Glynne Cit. & Clock Maker of London | Jno Son of Jno Packman late Cit. & Cook of London deed | 3 Dec

13 Jo: Tomlins Cit. & Sadler of London | James Son of Nath Gifford of London Gent | 7 Nov

14 Robt Knaplock Cit. & Stationer of London | Thos Son of Jno Johnson of Cranbrooke in Com Kent | Dec

Part of the apprentice register for 5/6 December 1711. Note that the names of the apprentices' fathers are given.

information you can always apply to the library of the particular Inn. For solicitors and attorneys there are Law Lists. To find more detailed information there are also indentures at the Public Record Office for men who were attached to the Court of Common Pleas and the King's Bench.

Apprenticeship

Apprenticeship for trades and professions dates back in some cases to the Middle Ages. Livery Companies and Guilds were formed particularly in the city of London and in some of the major trading cities such as Bristol, Exeter, York and Newcastle. They laid down standards of workmanship for their craft. As a result young men were bound to masters of the trade concerned for periods varying from five to nine years after which they became freemen of the company.

Many of these records have survived and for London many have been deposited at the Guildhall Library while others are still in the Halls of the companies concerned, e.g. the Goldsmiths' and Stationers' companies, where you can apply direct for information. Similar records exist for the provincial guilds.

and Memorials of Indentures Articles	Terms of Years	Summs and Values given or contracted for and Duties: £50 or under	6d Duty	Above £50	12d Duty	
		95	2.7.6			£ 26.11.½
Common Ind & Counterpt	8 ys from Date	8	4 —			
Do	7 ys from Date	17	8 6			
Do	Do	5	2 6			
Do	Do	5	2 6			
Do	Do	10	5			
Do	Do	8	4 —			
Articles of Agreemt & Counterpt				140	7 —	
Common Ind & Counterpt	7 ys from Date	50	1.5 —			
		198	4 19	140	7	11 19
					£ 4 19	

The apprentice binding registers usually give the name, address and trade of the apprentice and address of the master. Besides being apprenticed it was possible to become a freeman of a company by redemption which meant that you paid a fee having satisfied the Livery of your capabilities.

If you are not sure to which company your ancestor belonged, you are encouraged to go in person to the City Chamberlain's office to search the freedoms admission register, or failing this, apply in writing.

It is important to note that from the beginning of the nineteenth century a man could belong to a company different from that of his trade, i.e. a fishmonger could belong to the Drapers' Company.

Besides these sources there is an index of details of Apprentices compiled by Perceval Boyd from Inland Revenue records, copies of which are kept at the Society of Genealogists and the Guildhall Library. This is presented in two series, namely 1710–1760 and 1761–1772. Between the latter date and 1809 you can wade through the registers in the Public Record Office which are unindexed. These do not include poor law apprentices which are mentioned in Chapter 4.

The British Resident in India presiding over a musical performance.

Records of the British in India

There is a considerable collection of personal records of the East India Company and later of the Indian Empire at the India Record Office and library. This contains details of the Civil Service and the Army, as well as other personnel living in the subcontinent.

CHAPTER TEN

Celtic Ancestors

The inhabitants of Cornwall and Wales, as well as of Scotland and Ireland, were Celtic rather than Anglo-Saxon. As in the early 1800s half the population of the British Isles lived in these areas it is an important aspect, and family history in these areas has some particular features as a result of the racial background. The first is surnames: all of the Celtic races originally used 'patronymics' rather than surnames, which means that in place of a surname they used their father's and/or their grandfather's christian names.

So for example, a Welshman called 'Evan ap Llewellyn ap Owen' was Evan son of Llewellyn, son of Owen, and Cornishmen would use the same formula, but without the 'ap', so a Cornishman named John Richard William was John son of Richard son of William. In the course of time these became fixed as regular surnames—generally earlier at higher social levels and in the less remote areas, and later among poorer people and in remoter areas. So a squire in Monmouthshire or East Cornwall would have adopted a fixed surname before 1600, but a labourer near Lands End or in Snowdonia could be found using a patronymic name in the 1750s. Mostly these became fixed as surnames simply as Williams, Jones (John), etc. But some Welsh names slurred the 'ap' so that 'ap Richard' became 'Prichard', and similarly Prees or Price, Proger, Bowen and Bevan derive from ap Rhys, ap Roger, ap Owen and ap Evan.

In Scotland and Ireland it worked similarly but the Gaelic language gave them 'Mac' for 'son of' and (only in Ireland) 'Ui' or 'O' for 'grandson of', and so you get the numerous names beginning in 'Mac' and 'O'. But these were further complicated by the clan system so that not only would everyone descending from the original Donald call themselves MacDonald, but others who joined the clan would as well, although not related. The Scots tended to keep their prefix 'Mac', but quite often the Irish have dropped the 'O' in more recent years. For example, President Ronald Reagan's great-grandfather in County Tipperary began his life as Michael O'Regan. The Scots and the Irish began using fixed surnames earlier than the Welsh or Cornish.

As well as the clan system, genealogy was important to the Celts for inheritance of their land. Welshmen for example, inherited land by 'gavelkind', equal shares for each child, and so preserved their genealogies as title deeds to their lands. For many people from kings to abbots and minor chieftains, their position depended upon their kinship as much as it did for small farmers. As a result there is a great deal of genealogy preserved from very early dates; the O'Neills of Ulster have the most ancient documented pedigree in Western Europe, and there is the saying 'as long as a Welsh pedigree'.

Nor should it be thought that these ancient pedigrees are out of reach of ordinary people. A minor Scottish customs official has been traced back to Ailill Olum, King of Munster in Ireland, one and a half millennia before, and President Ronald Reagan is a great-great-grandson of Thomas O'Regan, a poor landless labourer who none the less descends from Raigan, nephew of the great King Brian Boru, a thousand years before.

But all too often, Celtic genealogy gets lost in the confusion of too many people with a single surname, with inadequate records to distinguish who is who, Jones and Davies in Wales, Williams and Thomas in Cornwall, MacDonald and Campbell in Scotland, Murphy and O'Brien in Ireland. There is a glen in the Scottish Highlands where every family was surnamed Ross, and a hundred and thirty-two Ryan families in a single village in Tipperary. Add to this the problem, all too often, of laxity in keeping more recent records, and the common problem of Celtic genealogy is to bridge the gap between nineteenth- and twentieth-century records and the earlier traditional pedigrees.

Some of the paucity of records is due to causes like the Hebrideans who kept no parish registers as firstly, everyone knew everyone's family history anyway, so why write it down? and secondly, few if any of them could read or write. Oral family history is important, for many old people can remember traditions of families, often surprisingly far back. One man's grandmothers, one Irish, one Scottish, gave him a great deal of the story of his ancestors, and the intense interest that Celts have in their own and their neighbours' ancestors is surprising until you remember it is a habit ingrained for a thousand years and more.

It is important to remember that the Celts had their own languages, Irish and Scottish Gaelic, Welsh and (now extinct) Cornish. Only the earlier records are written in these languages, but a trap is when surnames are Anglicized, for example when the Scottish or Irish 'Gowan' and Cornish 'Gof' get translated as Smith. Apart from these aspects the records for more recent Welsh and Cornish research are organized in the English way, as described in earlier chapters. Welsh archives are divided between the National Library of Wales at Aberystwyth, and local county record offices. As the latter are a new development, the National Library remains the key source, and they have there as well a treasure-house of ancient Welsh genealogies.

In Scotland, the archives are ideally organized. The parish registers of the (Presbyterian) Church of Scotland were all called in to the central archives in 1855, and this coincides with the start of Scottish General Registration on 1 January 1855. There are also census records open to the public up to 1891.

Nearly all the Scottish archives a family historian will need are very conveniently in the two adjoining buildings of the Scottish Record Office and the West Register House in Edinburgh. In addition to the usual sources of General Registration, parish registers, wills (called 'testaments' in Scotland) and census records, there is a further vast series of records unique in Europe, which reflect the fact

Detail of a map of Munster (sixteenth century). It is interesting to note that the names of the landowners have been included.

that the Law of Scotland is based upon Roman Law rather than upon the Common Law of England, Ireland and America. These records are legal ones, relating particularly to the ownership, inheritance and acquisition of land, of which the most important are 'Services of Heirs' and 'Sasines'. Since in Scotland, land could not be devised by a will but could only pass by either inheritance or by legal act, a great deal of the genealogy of any owners of land and their relations is recorded

The Record Office, Edinburgh.

in these archives. In general the wealth of material available in Edinburgh means that researching Scottish family history should be a happy task.

Irish research is, however, a subject on its own, but an important one, as in 1801 one-third of the population of the British Isles lived in Ireland. To understand Irish research one needs to understand Irish history. The truly Irish people have ancient roots in their country, and this is the race to whom much of Europe is indebted for a legacy of Christianity and culture.

In the Middle Ages, Anglo-Norman knights invaded Ireland and became assimilated—'more Irish than the Irish themselves'. Burke, for example, is the Norman name de Burgo. Later settlers in Ireland were Protestant, as distinct from the ancient race which was, and has mostly remained, Roman Catholic. From England came the so-called 'Anglo-Irish' landowners, merchants, and the like; from Scotland came Presbyterians who largely settled in the northern Irish province of Ulster—these being usually termed in America the 'Scotch-Irish'. There were other much smaller groups too, such as the Huguenots from France and the Palatines from Germany. In the later seventeenth and for much of the

A thirteenth-century Irish whalebone book cover, showing a coat of arms, warriors and heraldic beasts.

The National Library, Kildare Street, Dublin.

eighteenth centuries, Penal Laws repressed the Catholics, and most power and wealth was represented by the 'Protestant Ascendancy' of the Anglo-Irish. As a result, early Catholic church registers are rare, and they left few other records as they could not, for example, legally own land.

The difficulties of Irish research tend to be exaggerated, because the Public Record Office at the Four Courts in Dublin was burnt down in 1922, and much of what was there was lost. However, it has to be appreciated that only about half the existing Church of Ireland (Protestant Episcopal) parish registers were lost in the fire—and the majority of those were from small rural parishes with few Protestant inhabitants, while seven-eighths of the population were Catholic or Presbyterian, whose parish registers were not in the record office in 1922, and so were not lost. Certainly the original probate court records were also lost, but a great many of these wills survive as copies or in the abstracts. The general question of Irish research is governed by the scattered nature of the records, which is in many ways a blessing as this saved them from loss in 1922.

Northern Ireland, six counties in the province of Ulster, became separate in 1922, and many local records are held there, but as Dublin was the capital of all of Ireland until that date, some important archives relating to the North are still in Dublin. For example, one such treasury of information is at the Registry of Deeds at King's Inn in Dublin where all property deeds and records such as wills relating to property are recorded (much like an American county courthouse, but with all thirty-two counties recorded together) after 1708. And at the Genealogical Office in Dublin Castle there are the recorded pedigrees of many of the Anglo-Irish landowners and their families.

General Registration of births, marriages and deaths in Ireland began on 1 January 1864 (although registration of Protestant marriages began in 1845) and copies of the Dublin registrations relating to the Northern six counties are held in Belfast. Parish registers of all denominations for the six counties, or microfilms of them, are also either held in the Public Record Office of Northern Ireland, Belfast, or are being gathered in.

In the twenty-six counties of the South, the Republic of Ireland, records of General Registration are kept at the Custom House, Dublin. For parish registers it is much more complicated: Catholic registers (which relate to the great majority of the population) are held by the individual parish priests, but microfilms of all of these prior to 1880 are at the National Library in Dublin—although the written permission of the respective priest is necessary before they can be examined. Church of Ireland registers are largely still held by the rectors of each parish, although increasingly the registers, or copies or microfilms of them, are being deposited at the Public Record Office in Dublin. Quaker records are kept at the Friends' Meeting House in Eustace Street, Dublin. Other important archives in Dublin are held by Trinity College, the State Paper Office in Dublin Castle, the Representative Body of the Church of Ireland, and for lawyers, the Library at King's Inn. The period before the suppression of native Irish culture in the seventeenth century is superbly documented in the library of the Royal Irish Academy. Finally, it should be remembered that all of Ireland was governed from London before 1922, and many records are in British archives (particularly of the army, navy and police).

In essence, Irish research is not easy, but the difficulties are often exaggerated, and a great deal can be accomplished with care and application. The reward for success can be connection with some of the oldest documented pedigrees in Western Europe.

CHAPTER ELEVEN

Immigrants

Throughout history the British Isles have played host to people from all over Europe, and more recently from all over the world, who wished to settle here. There are many Britons whose parents or grandparents came here as refugees from tyrannical regimes in Europe, the chief of these being Jews, Poles and Russians.

During the eighteenth and nineteenth centuries a few permanent refugees came to Britain, fleeing the French Revolution, and Germans came in the wake of the Hanoverian Kings. From the family historian's point of view one of the largest groups of immigrants were the Huguenots who came in large numbers during the sixteenth and seventeenth centuries, and it is with them that we propose to concern ourselves in this chapter.

The origins of French Protestantism are to be found in the teachings of Erasmus and Luther. As elsewhere in northern Europe it was the availability of printed bibles almost more than anything else which had such a profound effect on the academic, professional and artisan classes of society. The Church reacted vigorously and the faculty of theology of the Sorbonne obtained from François I an ordinance in 1535 for the suppression of printing. However the demand for bibles grew rapidly, and wherever they were read in the vernacular, the movement for reform grew apace.

The Huguenots had been assured that liberty of conscience would be granted, and showed themselves to be loyal subjects on the accession of Louis XIV, when their rights under the Edict of Nantes were reaffirmed. Once Louis XIV gained his majority, persecution began to increase and rights offered by the Edict of Nantes were eroded until its final revocation in 1685. More than 400 proclamations, edicts and declarations attacking the Huguenots in their households, civil freedom, property and liberty of conscience were promulgated between 1660 and 1685, in the course of which time more than 200,000 Huguenots left France to seek sanctuary in Switzerland, Germany, the Netherlands and England.

Owing to the restrictions placed upon their movements by these Edicts, those from south-east France mainly went to Switzerland, seeking the shortest route. Those in the north-east and some from the north-west went to the Netherlands; most from the north-west and south-west came to England. From Normandy, Picardy and the Pas de Calais they arrived in strength in Kent and Sussex. Those using the Atlantic route from Saintonge and Aunis formed the basis of the French Churches in the west of England. However, it did not mean that all would stay

A trade card for Peter de la Fontaine, a Huguenot goldsmith and silversmith.

at their first port of refuge. Those who eventually settled in Germany travelled via Switzerland, and the American Huguenots mainly descend from those who had at first sought refuge in England. During the last decade of the seventeenth century, when William of Orange was not only Stadtholder of the Netherlands but also King of the United Kingdom, there was a great interchange of refugees between the Netherlands, England and Ireland.

It is always natural that refugees should choose to live near their fellow countrymen, especially where communities exist that have been established as a result of previous migration. Such places in England were London and Canterbury. Some emigrants were close to and used the liturgy of the Church of England, but others were closer to Presbyterian doctrines and were classed as Nonconformists. Between 1681 and 1720 approximately 200,000 Huguenots left France and of these it is thought that some 40,000 came to England and of those, about 15,000 settled in London. This migration, spread over forty years, should be seen in the context of the contemporary population of London in 1700, which was 50,000.

The Huguenots settled in two main London colonies, in Soho and Spitalfields. Spitalfields already had a long tradition of political and religious disaffection, and was a stronghold of nonconformity. The silk weaving industry had already been established there in the first half of the century, so it was a natural rallying point for immigrant Huguenot artisans, particularly those skilled in that industry.

Why Soho became the other great centre is not so clear. It was possibly because the French congregation had settled in that part of Westminster in the 1640s. In 1682, when large scale migration from France began, these refugees were granted a lease of the Greek Chapel in Soho, which no doubt attracted many of them to this quarter of London. It also seems that many who settled in Soho were of bourgeois and aristocratic backgrounds. This is supported by the fact that many of these refugees were goldsmiths or silversmiths, jewellers, engravers, clock and watchmakers, or tapestry weavers, who naturally gravitated to the fashionable residential quarter of London near to the Court.

By the second half of the eighteenth century the specifically Huguenot character of both Soho and Spitalfields had declined greatly. Many of the refugee families had become anglicized through intermarriage and knew nothing of the persecution which had originally brought them from Europe. By 1800 only two Huguenot chapels survived in Soho, but one chapel in Spitalfields was still using the French language in 1840. During this period, the centre of the silk weaving industry moved from Spitalfields to Bethnal Green and this no doubt helped to destroy many of the French influences and ways of life which had been prevalent in Spitalfields. But there remains a French Church in Soho Square to this day.

Huguenot records in France vary according to locality. In the country as a whole there are few which begin before 1660, but those of Caen, La Rochelle, Rouen and Nîmes are very extensive and begin at the end of the sixteenth century and continue up to the Revocation of the Edict of Nantes in 1685. The usefulness of French Protestant records is not confined to English and American families of Huguenot descent. They contain many references to English, Scottish

This print of a Hogarth painting shows the congregation emerging from the Huguenot Church, Soho, French religious refugees settled both in Soho and in Spitalfields where they played an important part in the silk-weaving industry.

A Jewish receipt roll dating from 1533.

and Irish Protestant families resident in France, and especially to merchants trading between British and French ports.

For those who have Huguenot ancestors, membership of the Huguenot Society is of great value. The Society's transactions include transcriptions of many Huguenot Parish Registers as well as naturalization papers and kindred material.

The medieval Jewish communities in England (Jews were prominent in Exeter) were expelled in 1290. Small crypto-Jewish communities existed in London and Bristol in the sixteenth century, but due to contemporary persecution they were outwardly Christian and were recorded in Anglican registers. The official re-admission of Jews dates from 1655, the earliest being Sephardim from Portugal and Spain who settled in London. Later arrivals were Ashkenazim from Germany and Central Europe (some coming via the British colonies in the West Indies and North America) and it is these who are relevant outside London. The oldest surviving Ashkenazi synagogue in the country is that at Plymouth founded in 1768. Their activities were in specialized trades, for example as jewellers or tailors, or in naval victualling, and international commerce. Jews suffered numerous legal disabilities until the nineteenth century, only being allowed to own property from 1728, have British nationality from 1740, vote in elections from 1835, and graduate at universities from 1870. However, their religion did not bar their wills from the Christian Church probate courts.

Jewish records are a specialized subject on their own. Firstly certain of them are in Hebrew or Yiddish, some using the Hebrew alphabet and the Jewish calendar. Secondly, what is recorded is largely distinct from Christian registers; for example birth records are rare, and commonly there are only registers of circumcision of boys (at eight days old); conversely marriage records are particularly good, often including the marriage contract, despite Jewish marriages being exempted from Lord Hardwicke's Marriage Act of 1753; surnames are a particular difficulty, as these were often changed, and secular surnames may not occur in synagogue records where the patronymic (for example Moses ben Jacob) was used. Wills are a particularly valuable source, and due to a good deal of mobility a large proportion were proved in the Prerogative Court of Canterbury, but many other sources are eliminated by legal disabilities; for example Jews did not have a vote before 1835 so they do not appear in earlier voters lists or poll books.

There are extensive collections of material (including many researched pedigrees) at the Jewish Museum, London, and the Mocatta Library, University College, London. The Weiner Library, holding a great deal of German and other continental material (relevant in so far as nearly all British Jews are of immigrant origin) has been transferred to Tel Aviv. Printed material includes a general guide with a good bibliography: Edgar R. Samuel, 'The Jews', *National Index of Parish Registers*, III (Chichester 1974), pp. 957–976. There are extensive references in the *Proceedings of the Jewish Historical Society*, (in progress); and in Cecil Roth's *The Rise of Provincial Jewry* (1950). Since most Jews in England are of immigrant origins, the extensive material on aliens at the Public Record Office, London, particularly in classes HO 1 to HO 4, is invaluable.

CHAPTER TWELVE

Emigration to Australia and America

This is a subject which is of considerable importance as a great deal of the interest in family history in the British Isles is from descendants of emigrants. Tracing the origins of an emigrant can sometimes be exceedingly difficult, and the key to success is very sound 'homework' in the archives of the destination country.

Australia and New Zealand

Here the question of tracing origins back to the British Isles is usually very straightforward, as for all but the earliest settlers, death certificates in both Australia and New Zealand include so much personal detail, including usually the place of birth and the names of both parents, that the research is entirely clear-cut and free from problems.

Many of the earliest settlers were convicts and research into these, while less delightfully clear-cut than it is in later records, is none the less well documented. Australian sources include details of the court where conviction occurred and dates. The British court records then supply a lot of information. It should not

A List

of Persons transported as Criminals to New South Wales in the Earl Cornwallis in the month of August 1800 specifying the term for which each Person was transported and the date and place of the Conviction.

Names	Where convicted	When	Term
Mary Twynham	Berks	Assizes 16 July 1798	7 Years
Ann Copsey			
William Perry	D°. (Reading)	2 Session 17 Jan 1800	7 Years
Dennis Brady	D°.	Assizes 1 March 1800	Life
Thomas Allum			
William Knight			
Thomas Elsley			
Thomas Dowling			
Mary Bawden	D°.	D° 6 March 1800	7 Years
James Howard	Cambridge	D° 12 March 1799	Life
Robert Copps	D°.	D° Session 17 Jan 1800	7 Years
James Oadham	D°. (Ely)	Oyer & Terminer & Gaol Delivery 25 March 1800	7 Years

Part of the list of criminals transported to New South Wales in the *Earl Cornwallis* in August 1800.

OPPOSITE
A group of convicts in a settlement in Tasmania.

Preparing to emigrate: this watercolour by R. Hillingford depicts a family preparing to leave England for South Australia.

be thought that people were always natives of the locality where they were convicted, as, for example, a case was researched recently where a man tried in Scotland was a native of Staffordshire, and the Rector of his native parish was a witness for his good character at the trial.

North America

It is difficult in practice to distinguish, for research, Canada from what is now the United States, as in practical terms of emigration research the boundary between them counted for very little. Many Irish immigrants to America, for example, travelled to Canada, and then up the St Lawrence, and arrived in the United States via the Great Lakes, and immigration to the United States from Canada has always been substantial—quite apart from migration the other way, such as by the Loyalists after the War of Independence.

Nineteenth-century emigration is usually less difficult to research than that of earlier dates. The great bulk of English, Welsh and Scottish migrants can be readily traced through the combination of modern records on either side of the Atlantic. The United States Census of 1900, for example, records the month, year, and place of birth, the year of immigration, the number of years married, and many other details. Earlier census records, death certificates stating the

Tyrolean Lutheran emigrants to Georgia in June 1732.

names of parents, military records of birthplace and naturalization records stating often the actual country of birth, are all of great value. In theory (but regrettably with many omissions) there should be complete passenger lists of all ships arriving in United States ports after 1820 (but without the equivalent for Canadian ports, nor records of immigration from Canada). The great bulk of British emigrants left after civil registration had begun in England and Wales, and the research is normally routine. For Ireland, and to a lesser extent Scotland, the problems of Celtic surnames, of too many people in a locality with common names, and a later start of civil registration, it is less clear-cut, and considerable problems can occur, although it is worth recalling that gravestones often give information about an immigrant's birthplace.

Although United States census records began in 1790, it is only from 1850 that birthplaces were stated and indeed that they named everyone, rather than merely the heads of households. However earlier military records (including those of the Revolutionary War) often state birthplaces.

Colonial Period America

British settlement in America began very simply with various groups settling in the northern half of the east coast—now essentially New England, and the London-based Virginia Company settling the southern half (note that the term

Nineteenth-century emigrants to America.

OPPOSITE

An early nineteenth-century ticket for a voyage from Londonderry to Philadelphia. For £4 the steerage passenger was entitled to ten cubic feet of luggage space and a meagre ration of bread, biscuits and water. No meat or green vegetables were provided and he had to do his own cooking and provide his own utensils.

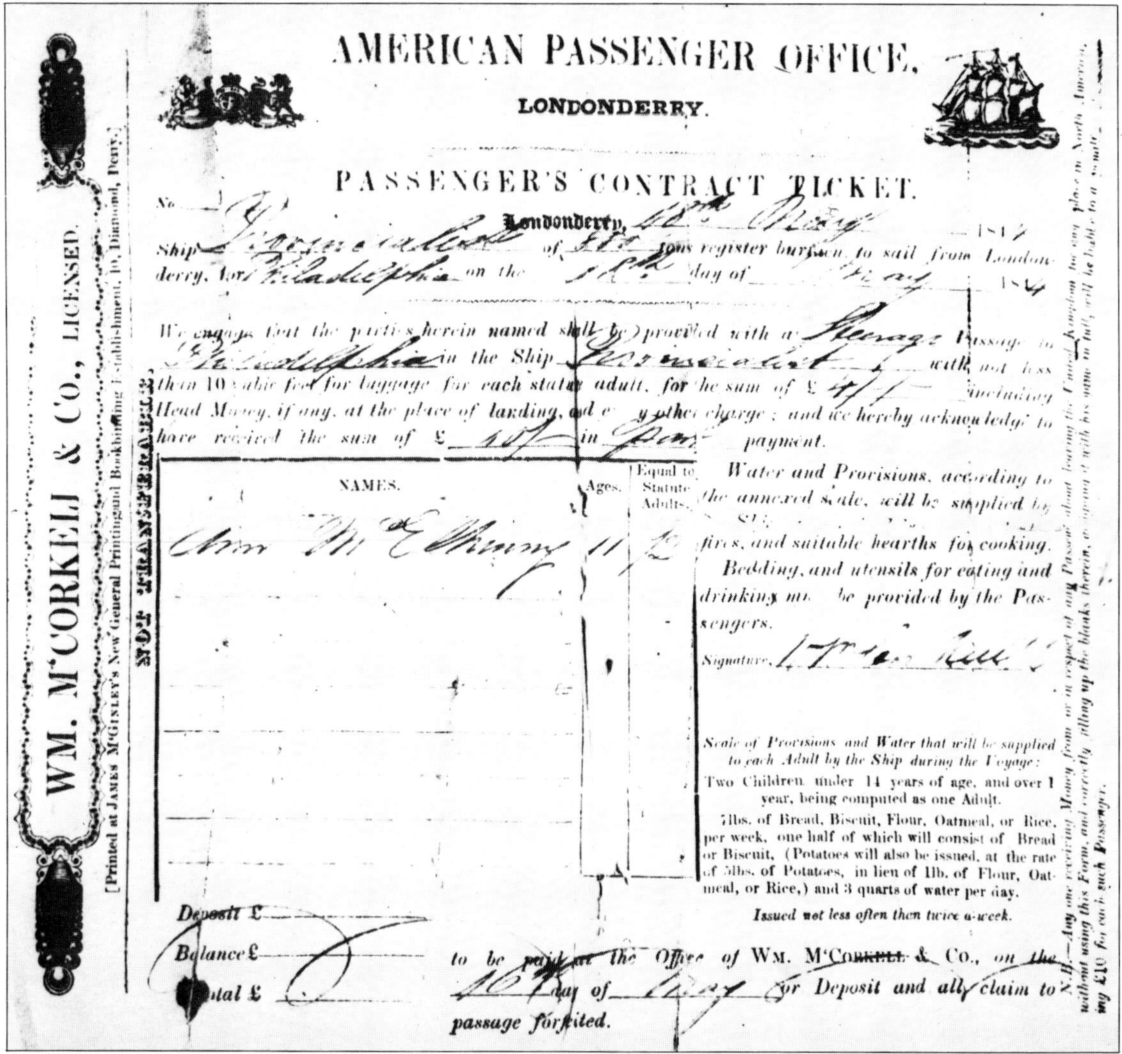

AMERICAN PASSENGER OFFICE,
LONDONDERRY.

PASSENGER'S CONTRACT TICKET.

No. ______

Londonderry, ______ 184__

Ship ______ of ______ tons register burthen, to sail from Londonderry, for Philadelphia on the ______ day of ______ 184__

We engage that the parties herein named shall be provided with a Steerage Passage to Philadelphia in the Ship ______ with not less than 10 cubic feet for luggage for each statute adult, for the sum of £ ______ including Head Money, if any, at the place of landing, and every other charge; and we hereby acknowledge to have received the sum of £ ______ in ______ payment.

NAMES.	Ages.	Equal to Statute Adults.
Ann McElhinny	11	½

Water and Provisions, according to the annexed scale, will be supplied by ______ fires, and suitable hearths for cooking. Bedding, and utensils for eating and drinking must be provided by the Passengers.

Signature, ______

Scale of Provisions and Water that will be supplied to each Adult by the Ship during the Voyage: Two Children under 14 years of age, and over 1 year, being computed as one Adult.

7lbs. of Bread, Biscuit, Flour, Oatmeal, or Rice, per week, one half of which will consist of Bread or Biscuit, (Potatoes will also be issued, at the rate of 5lbs. of Potatoes, in lieu of 1lb. of Flour, Oatmeal, or Rice,) and 3 quarts of water per day.

Issued not less often than twice a-week.

Deposit £ ______
Balance £ ______
Total £ ______ to be paid at the Office of Wm. McCorkell & Co., on the ______ day of ______ or Deposit and all claim to passage forfeited.

WM. McCORKELL & CO., LICENSED.

[Printed at James McGinley's New General Printing and Bookbinding Establishment, 10, Diamond, Derry.]

NOT TRANSFERABLE.

N.B.—Any one receiving Money from or in respect of any Passenger about leaving the United Kingdom for any place in North America, without using this Form, and correctly filling up the blanks therein, ... with his name in full, will be liable to a penalty of £10 for each such Passenger.

'Virginia' covered a far wider area then than the modern state of that name).

There were several elements in New England settlement: a Cambridge-based strongly Puritan group, drawing members from south Yorkshire to Essex and the Thames estuary; groups based on Dorchester, Plymouth, and to a lesser extent Bristol, in south-west England, which were less narrowly religious, and were also attracted by commercial prospects such as the finest cod-fisheries in the world. The origins of many of these settlers can be traced by identifying the groups in which they emigrated, many of the earlier groups of settlers having travelled together from a single area in England.

In Virginia and the other southern states, the main impetus of settlement came from the pressure of primogeniture (whereby the eldest sons inherited the lion's share) upon younger sons of the landed, merchant and professional classes,

Anticipation and disillusionment. Although many emigrants may have longed to return home, only a few of the more successful were able to raise the fare to do so once they had arrived in America.
Outward bound (Dublin)

Homeward bound (New York)

This lithograph, depicting life in rural Ireland, was published by Currier and Ives. It, and others like it, kept alive the memory of life at home for emigrants to America.

seeking their future in the world. There were various emphases; for example Maryland offered religious toleration to the Catholics, but essentially the earliest settlers in the south were rather more rural in background. Much of the earlier labour force came from indentured servants, who went especially from London and (after 1654) from Bristol, where many were recorded with their places of origin. The southern states operated a 'headright' system, whereby anyone who paid the fare of a passenger to people the colony was entitled to a grant of fifty acres of land. This was much abused, even crew members of ships being claimed as headrights, but it also generated lists of persons arriving in the colony, a source of great value if the correct reservations about this evidence are kept in mind.

Family groups are identified in these colonies, for example, groups of intermarried kin from the south Yorkshire group, the Norfolk/Suffolk area, and London, Southampton and Bristol merchants. Identification of the group in which an emigrant travelled, not always a geographical group, but sometimes a scattered kinship group, is the first step, usually, to identifying the British origins.

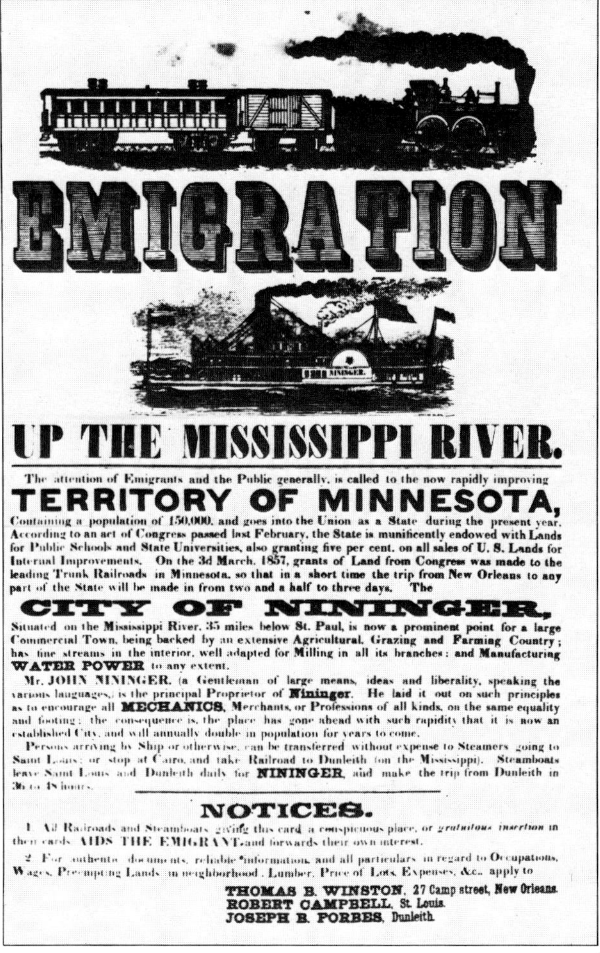

By the middle of the nineteenth century great encouragement was being given to men and women willing to open up the Middle West of North America. Notices such as this were published by the promoters of new towns, in this case John Nininger.

It is obviously impossible to cover the entire subject of the genealogy of colonial American settlers in a single chapter, but two other important groups need to be mentioned.

The Society of Friends (Quakers) settled especially in the later years of the seventeenth century in eastern Pennsylvania and western New Jersey. Quaker records are superb and many settlers brought with them a certificate from their Meeting in England or Wales—which often survives as a record of their origins. It is a point worth noting that many superficially Irish Quakers were in fact English, but had spent a few years in Ireland before moving on yet again to Pennsylvania.

A very important American immigrant group are what are called the 'Scotch-Irish'. These were Presbyterians from northern Ireland, many only two or three generations away from the Scottish settlers in the Plantation of Ulster, who emigrated as a result of social and economic pressures in Ulster. In general they settled inland from the planters in the Tidewater, in effect a screen between the planters and the Indians. It is significant to note that almost all Irish emigrants before the middle decades of the nineteenth century were Protestants from the north. Catholic Irish emigration was very largely during and after the Famine Years of 1845–1849.

Scottish emigration to North America, before that in the nineteenth century era of modern records, was largely to Canada, especially Nova Scotia, although other groups can be found such as the Highlanders who settled in the Cape Fear area of North Carolina.

In any research dealing with emigration, the key to success, and this cannot be repeated or stressed too often, is exhaustive and thorough background research in the country of destination, and also the avoidance of the common trap of assuming research in America has reached the immigrant, when in fact it may well have reached someone who had moved in from the next state or colony, and not an immigrant at all.

OPPOSITE
The New York skyline forms a backdrop to this photograph of two Jewish emigrants to the USA, the 'land of hope'.

CHAPTER THIRTEEN

Heraldry and Family History

A basic knowledge of the principles of heraldry and of the somewhat archaic way in which arms are described is useful for those in search of their ancestry. In fact, much of heraldry can be described as pictorial genealogy, for its main purpose is to do with identification and inheritance. There is probably more nonsense and misunderstanding about heraldry than about any other aspect of genealogy and family history. Its value to the researcher is firstly to identify an individual or his immediate connections, and then to place him into the appropriate slot in a pedigree.

The origins of heraldry date from the eleventh century and arose from the need for personal identification on the battlefield and through the use of seals on legal documents. The emblems adopted for shield and seal were handed down from father to son over generations and thus became an integral part of each family's history. Shields are still used by companies and corporate bodies though almost never by individuals.

In order to introduce some order into the assumption, granting and registering of arms, colleges of heralds arose, who worked on behalf of the sovereign who was generally recognized as the fount of honour. The heralds were given power to settle disputes and to legalize grants of arms and to make new grants. Every coat of arms must first have been granted, or, if it had been assumed before the institution of the College of Arms, have been recognized by, or on behalf of the sovereign, and its transmission or destination (usually in the male line) follows that set out in the original patent or confirmation, just like most hereditary titles. In Scotland, only the eldest son inherits his father's arms, but all younger sons have the right to matriculate a differenced version of their paternal arms. Thus someone of the same surname as you has no more right to bear your family's arms than someone named Howard has the right to call himself Duke of Norfolk.

Most people think of heraldry as something exclusive to the nobility and

OPPOSITE

Drawing of a pursuivant by Sir Peter Lely.

1. Achievement of Drury in a decorated oval cartouche, showing sixteen quarterings.

2. Achievement of Wentworth with supporters, commemorating the issue of Sir Thomas Wentworth and Margaret, daughter of Sir Adrian Fortescue by Ann Stonor, one of the co-heirs of John Neville, Marquess of Montagu.

3. Achievement of Chetwode impaling Drury with two crests and showing twelve quarterings.

4. Achievement of Smith with quartering in decorated oval cartouche, which commemorates Frances Smith.

Lady Katherine Howard, the wife of the Duke of Norfolk, who died in 1452, is shown in this etching of her memorial in Stoke Church, Suffolk, surrounded by family coats of arms.

1

2

3

4

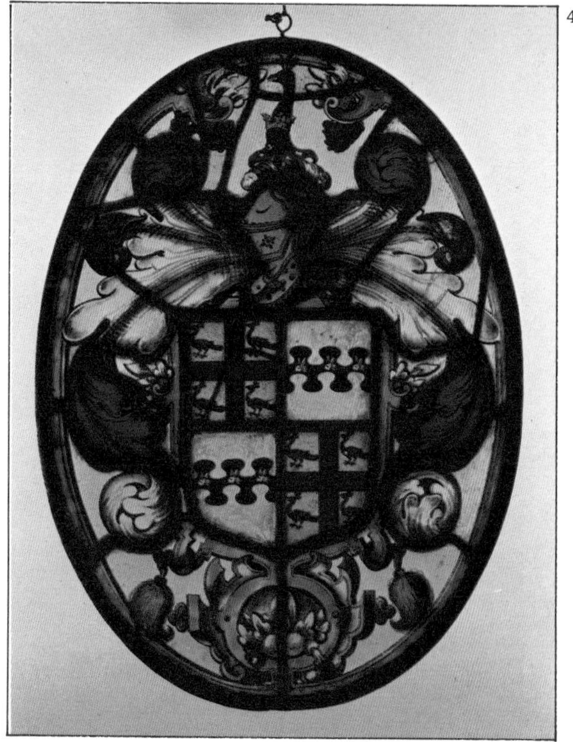

gentry. In practice, however, it is not like this at all. The junior branches of some noble houses have over the space of four or five generations fallen on hard times and sunk in the social scale. Many new families have risen from humble origins and applied for grants of arms in the recent past. Social mobility, therefore, ensures that heraldry is widely disseminated.

The two main categories of importance to genealogists are familial and individual heraldry. The former is practised throughout Europe, and we shall be saying a little about continental heraldry below. Familial heraldry pertains to a family rather than to an individual, whereby all male descendants of the original grantee bear the same family arms undifferenced, in much the same way as all the children of a Count of the Holy Roman Empire, for example, would be counts and countesses themselves. Such a system is only practical where there are a great many surnames, though it is a mistake to believe that there is a coat of arms for every surname.

The College of Arms in London is responsible for all aspects of English and Welsh heraldry and for much of Irish and Commonwealth heraldry too. Many Americans apply to the College for coats of arms or the right to bear the arms of families from whom they are descended. It is an independent and semi-private body of kings of arms, heralds and pursuivants responsible to the sovereign through the Earl Marshal.

Individual heraldry, as the name implies, means that an individual is granted a unique coat of arms which allude to factors such as his position in the family, ownership of fiefs, baronies or other titles, or as happens in Spain and Portugal, his four grandparental quarterings can be marshalled together. By its very nature, individual heraldry is therefore of much help to the genealogist.

In Scotland individual heraldry is seen at its best. The high proportion of its nobility to the total population, the clan system and the relatively small number of surnames, its feudal system of land tenure and the precision of the Scottish temperament, have encouraged people to know their relative position vis à vis their clan chiefs. These tendencies are vividly illustrated by the large attendances at International Gatherings of the Clans whenever they are held. Scottish heraldry takes a rather more liberal view regarding women, who are frequently recognized as Clan Chieftains and Lairds. This tends towards the assumption by male heirs of their mothers' surname and arms when familial succession has to pass through the female line.

Grants of titles of nobility on the Continent differ greatly from the system adopted in Britain. In France families able to trace their descent to 1400 or earlier were entitled to consider themselves the equal, or peers, of the King, and were known as feudal families. Quasi-feudal families were those able to prove an uninterrupted descent coupled with the possession of a fief from before 1560, and were called gentlemen of rank, birth or blood and could assume titles at will. In England the lowest rank of the peerage is the baron, in France the écuyer or esquire. The term 'Seigneur' is the equivalent of the English Lord of the Manor, and no matter whether you were a seigneur or a duc, you owed your nobility

The Grand Gathering of the Clans for the Braemar Games of 1851.

(noblesse) to the fact that you were an écuyer. Whether you called yourself Baron, Vicomte, Comte, Marquis or Duc depended upon the number of seigneuries you owned. Thus nobility and titles depended upon the size of your property, not, as in England, on a grant by the sovereign. It was the land or 'terre' which was deemed to be a Baronie, Comté or Marquisat, not the individual who possessed it. It did not follow that the son of a Marquis was a Comte or the son of a Comte a Vicomte as in England, where an individual or family rises through the ranks of the peerage so that a member of the family of A could be ennobled as Baron B, and later becomes Viscount C, Earl of D and Duke of E. In noble English families, subsidiary titles are used by courtesy only, e.g. the Duke of Grafton whose subsidiary titles, which may be borne by his eldest son and grandson until he inherits the dukedom, are Earl of Euston, Viscount Ipswich, and Baron Sudbury.

The use of heraldic arms in France has never been as strictly controlled as it has been in England and there is no French equivalent of the College of Arms. Arms, therefore, were not the privilege of noblemen. In 1696 Louis XIV instituted a General Armorial of France to register all coats of arms of gentlemen as well as

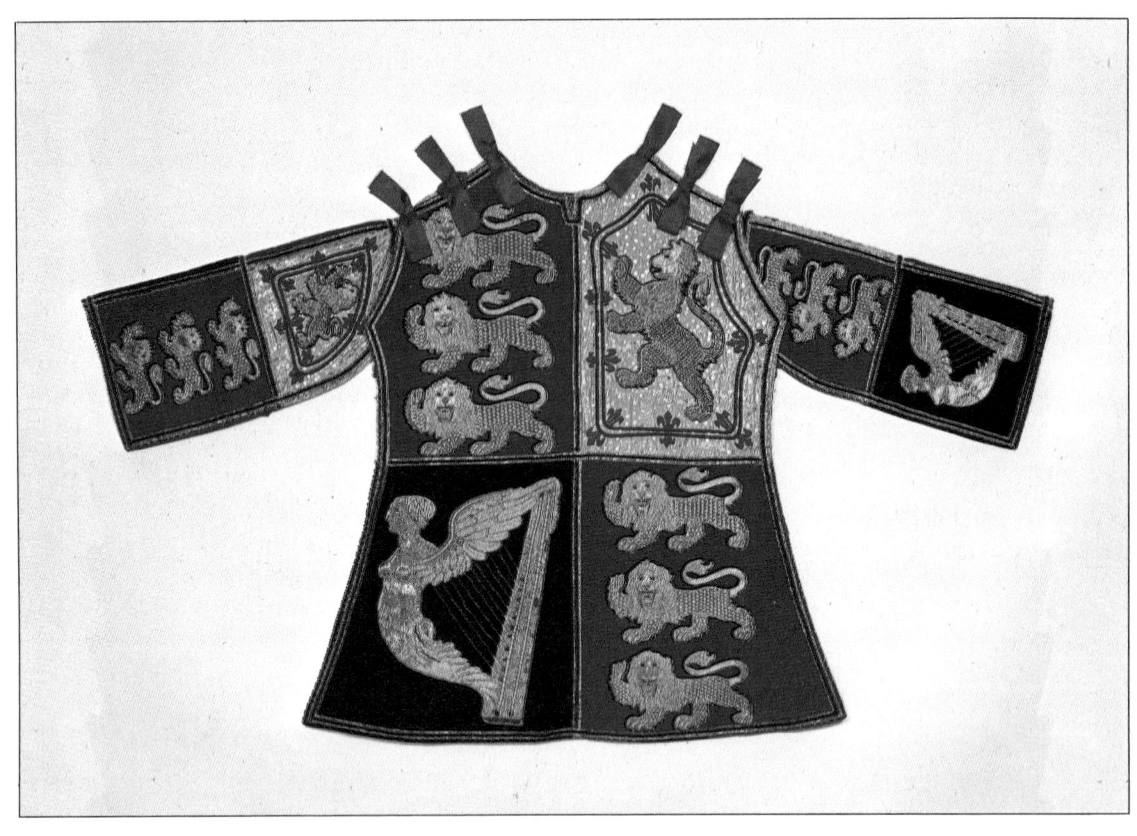

A Herald's tabard showing the arms of England, Scotland and Ireland. Tabards are still worn on State occasions by officers of the College of Arms, which is part of the Royal Household and not a department of state or public office.

Many of the 323 quarterings of this coat of arms are those of Welsh chieftains living in the ninth century or earlier. It encapsulates the family's history in visual form.

The Basic Geometry of Heraldry

Forms of shield

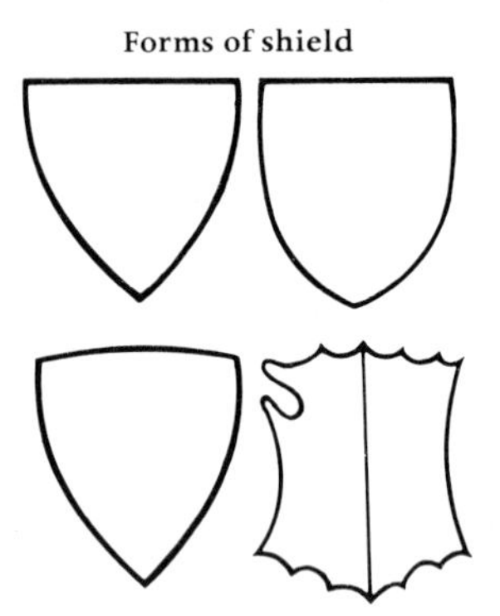

The parts and points of an heraldic shield

A *Chief*
B *Base*
C *Dexter Chief*
D *Sinister Chief*
E *Middle Chief*
F *Dexter Base*
G *Sinister Base*
H *Middle Base*
● *Honour Point*
■ *Fess Point*
▲ *Nombril (or Navel) Point*

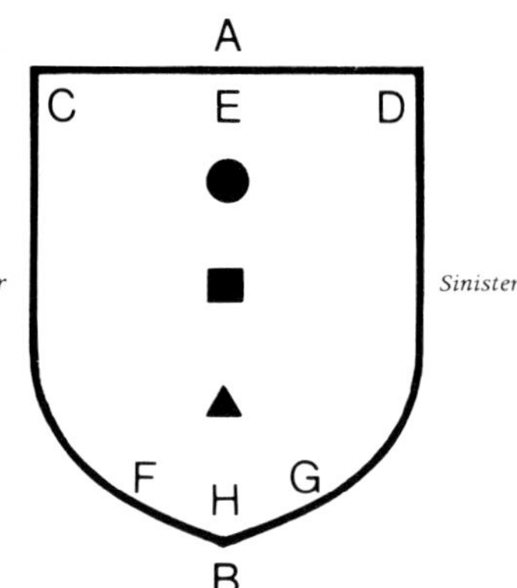

Tinctures (i.e. the colours, metals or furs used on an heraldic shield)

Azure (Blue)

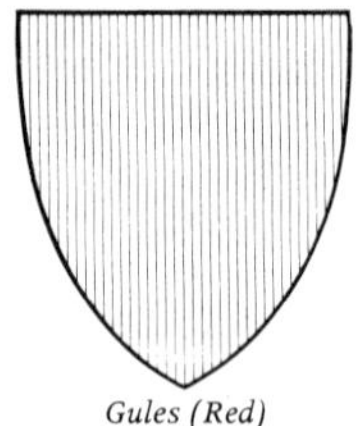
Gules (Red)

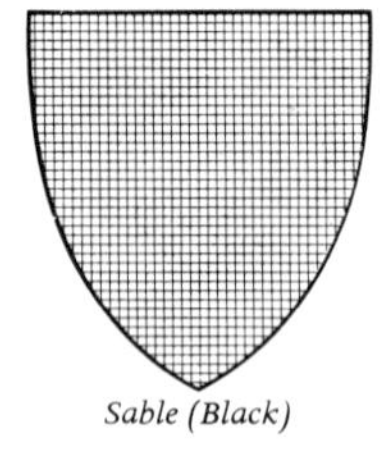
Sable (Black)

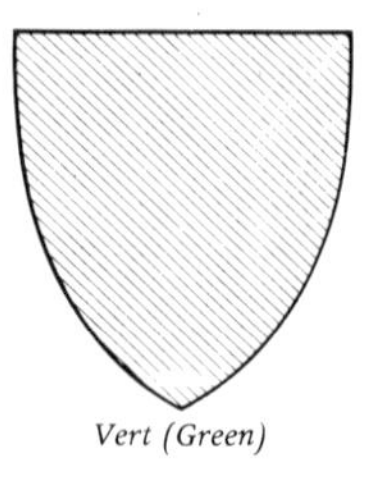
Vert (Green)

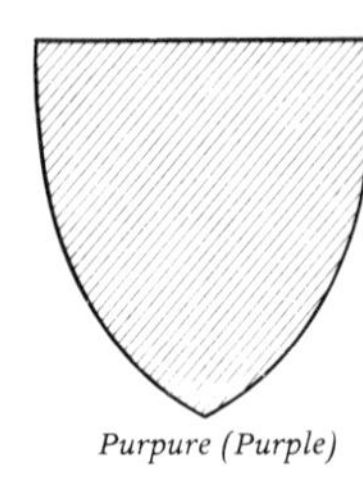
Purpure (Purple)

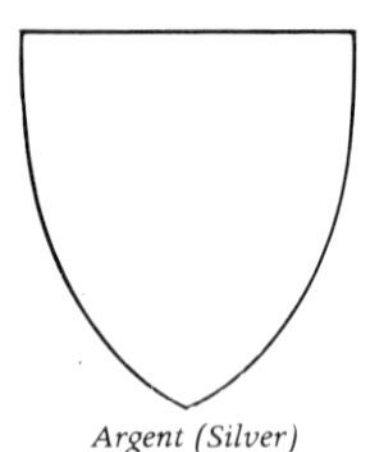
Argent (Silver)

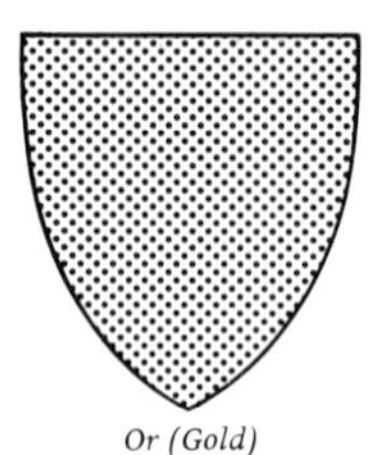
Or (Gold)

Ermine

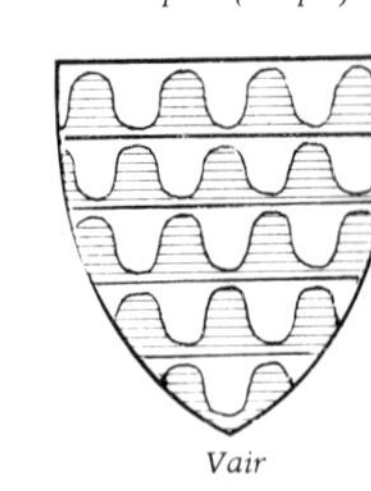
Vair

Forms of line used on an heraldic shield

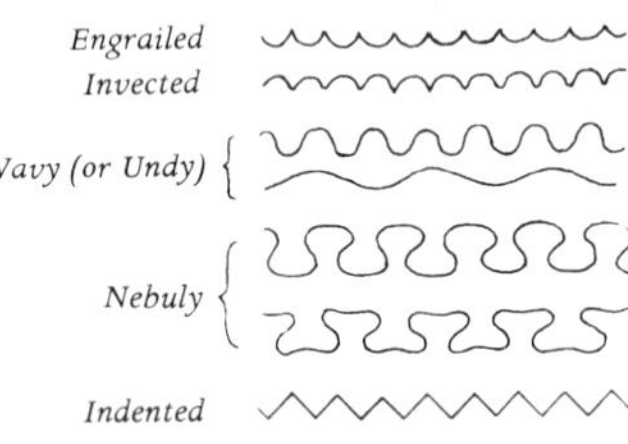

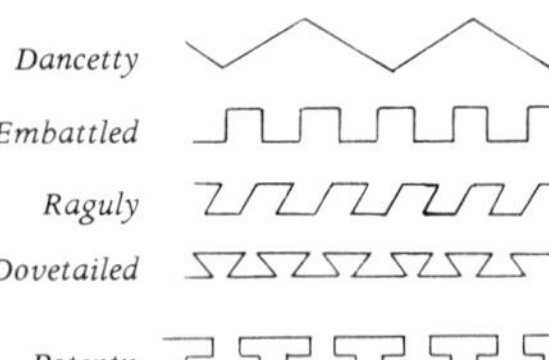

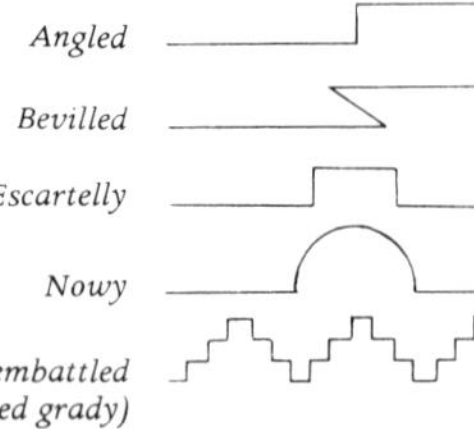

The shield can be divided in various ways:

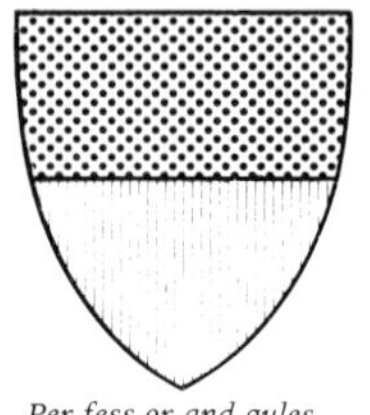
Per fess or and gules

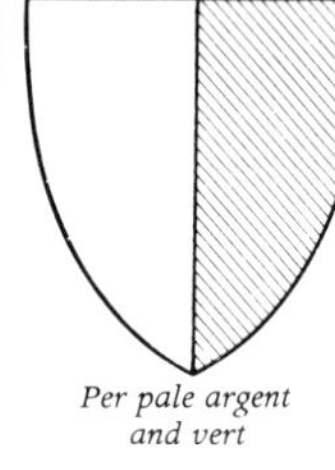
Per pale argent and vert

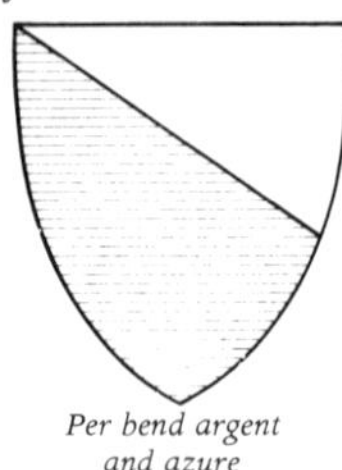
Per bend argent and azure

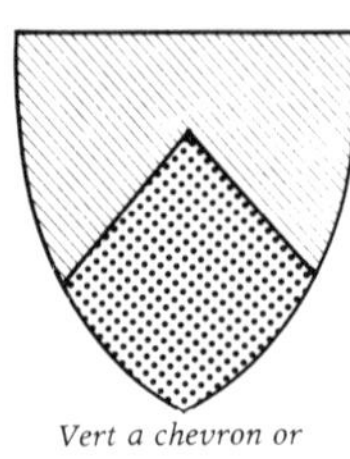
Vert a chevron or

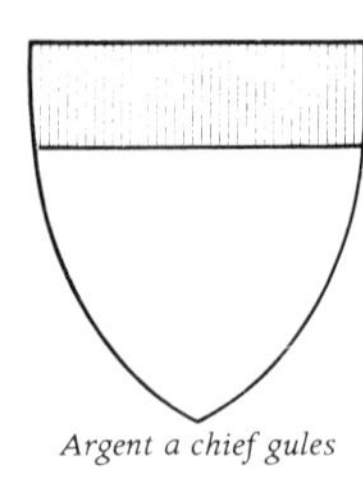
Argent a chief gules

Or a fess sable

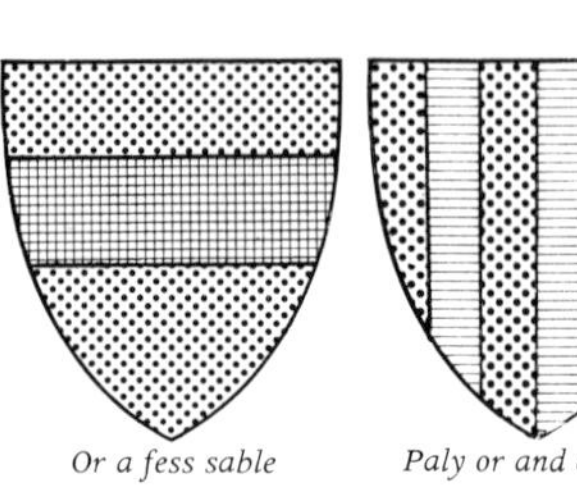
Paly or and azure

Other fields used include the following:

Per saltire

Bendy

Quarterly

Paly

Barry

Among more varied fields are the following:

Gyronny

Fusily

Chevronny

Checky

Lozengy

rdinaries can be 'cotised' or 'charged'.

Fess · Bend · Fess cotised · Bend cotised · Fess charged · Bend charged

Chevron · Saltire · Chevron cotised · Chevron charged · Saltire charged

ing which is displayed on a shield, e.g. beasts, flowers or inanimate objects is a 'charge'.

oss couped · Cross botonny · Cross flory · Cross patee (or formee) · Cross parted and fretty · Maltese Cross

le of heraldic lions

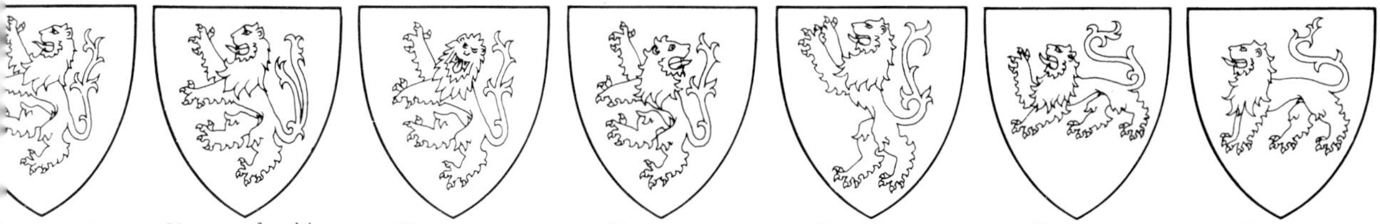

n rampant · Lion queue fourchée · Lion rampant guardant · Lion rampant reguardant · Lion salient · Lion passant · Lion statant

Some other heraldic beasts, birds and monsters

ion sejant · Lion couchant · Lion dormant · Horse rampant · Fleece · Pegasus rampant · Unicorn rampant

Other charges

s head caboshed

Dragon passant

Eagle displayed

Rose slipped and leaved

Trefoil slipped

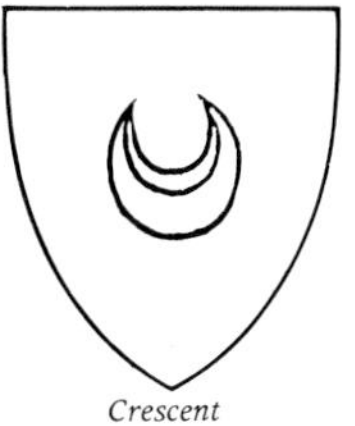
Crescent

Mullet or molet pierced (called a spur-rowel in Scotland)

' coronets

Duke

Marquess

Earl

Viscount

Baron

This wooden panel in the Royal Chapel, Granada depicts a Spanish herald from the last years of the reign of King Ferdinand I of Spain.

The royal coat of arms on Queen Victoria's Coronation Chair in the House of Lords.

SPE
RA TIDE,
SVSTINE.

those of ecclesiastics, burgesses and of those who enjoyed certain privileges and public rights.

In Austria and Germany since the sixteenth century the nobility has been divided into Fürsten (princes), Grafen (counts) and Freiherren (barons) which together comprise the landed class of the high nobility. The emperors tended to honour more and more families with hereditary titles to the extent that it is possible to talk of a kind of 'inflation' of titles. Much the same situation obtained in Italy, where the proliferation of small sovereign states within the Holy Roman Empire gave rise to a plethora of titled families. In Spain the titles of Vizconde, Conde, Marqués and Duque were first granted in the fourteenth century and made hereditary through primogeniture and by right of succession as in Britain. These titles, although personal, were founded either on domains that already had titles attached to them or on new lands granted by the sovereign. The right to bear arms was restricted in Navarre to the nobility. In 1595 Kings of Arms were introduced by Philip II with powers not unlike those enjoyed by their English and Scottish counterparts. The powers of this body were confirmed by law in 1951 so that arms may still be granted in Spain today much in the same way as they are in Britain.

OPPOSITE
Johann Francolin (1520–1586) was one of the first noblemen to become a herald of the Holy Roman Empire. His tabard bears the double-headed imperial eagle.

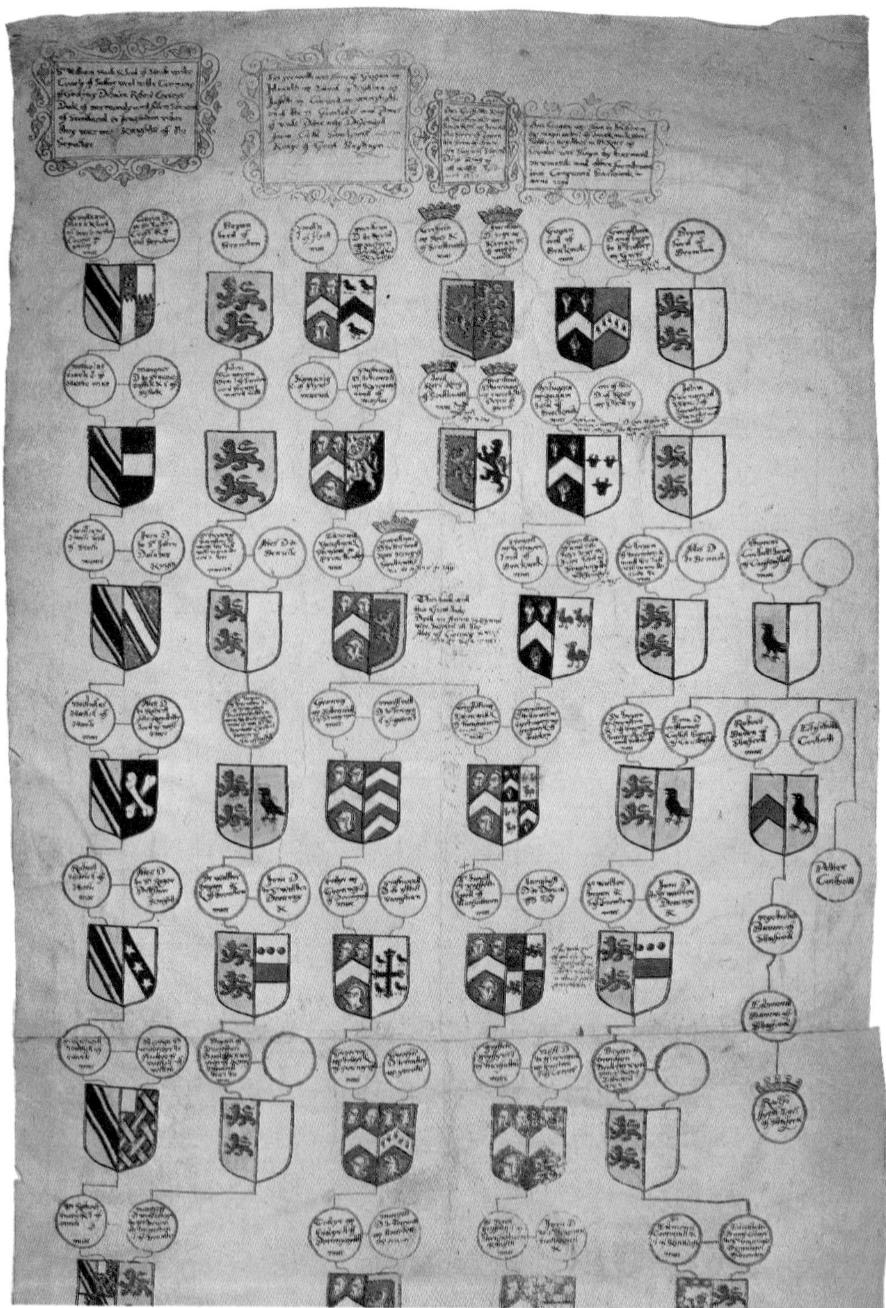

The pedigree roll of Anne Harle of Brompton, showing her descent from Edward Vaughan, Lord Steward of all Wales, by Thomas Jones, (1593).

CHAPTER FOURTEEN

Maps

Those who are fortunate enough to find that their ancestors lived in the same town or village for generations are comparatively few. In 1973, Dr Peter Spufford, in a paper given before the Society of Genealogists, quoted from Professor Chamber's findings from the Vale of Trent, that nearly half the people died in different parishes from those in which they were born, but that a very large proportion of them, including many who died in the same parish in which they were born, lived for many years in yet other parishes. He was referring to seventeenth and eighteenth century studies. Other demographers have shown that apart from the great flow of people to London, practically all movement was restricted to a very limited distance, less than twenty miles, and a great deal of it less than ten miles. Studies in France, Italy and Hungary amongst societies of very different structure, have shown similar movements of population from as early as the fifteenth century. Of course the Industrial Revolution increased migration of this kind, especially in England, where it began earlier and continued longer.

This movement, coupled with the loss of records or their inability to show where people came from, causes many family historians to give up their research. It is at this point that real detective work is needed, and every piece of evidence must be used. Among the most useful tools at this stage are maps.

The factors inducing people to move are many, so a detailed study of local history, especially with regard to the growth of industries and the increase in enclosures, coupled with the study of local maps is now vital. County archivists are usually equipped to help you find out the history of the neighbourhood in which you are interested.

The earliest maps are those printed in the fifteenth century, but not many of these survive. Christopher Saxton's are among the earliest, followed in the seventeenth century by John Speed's maps of England and Robert Morden's in the eighteenth.

Estate maps which date from about 1570 and continue to 1860 are very useful in showing the layout of towns and villages at any given time. A series of such

OPPOSITE
A seventeenth-century map of the English colonies in America showing the rivers along the banks of which the earliest settlements were located.

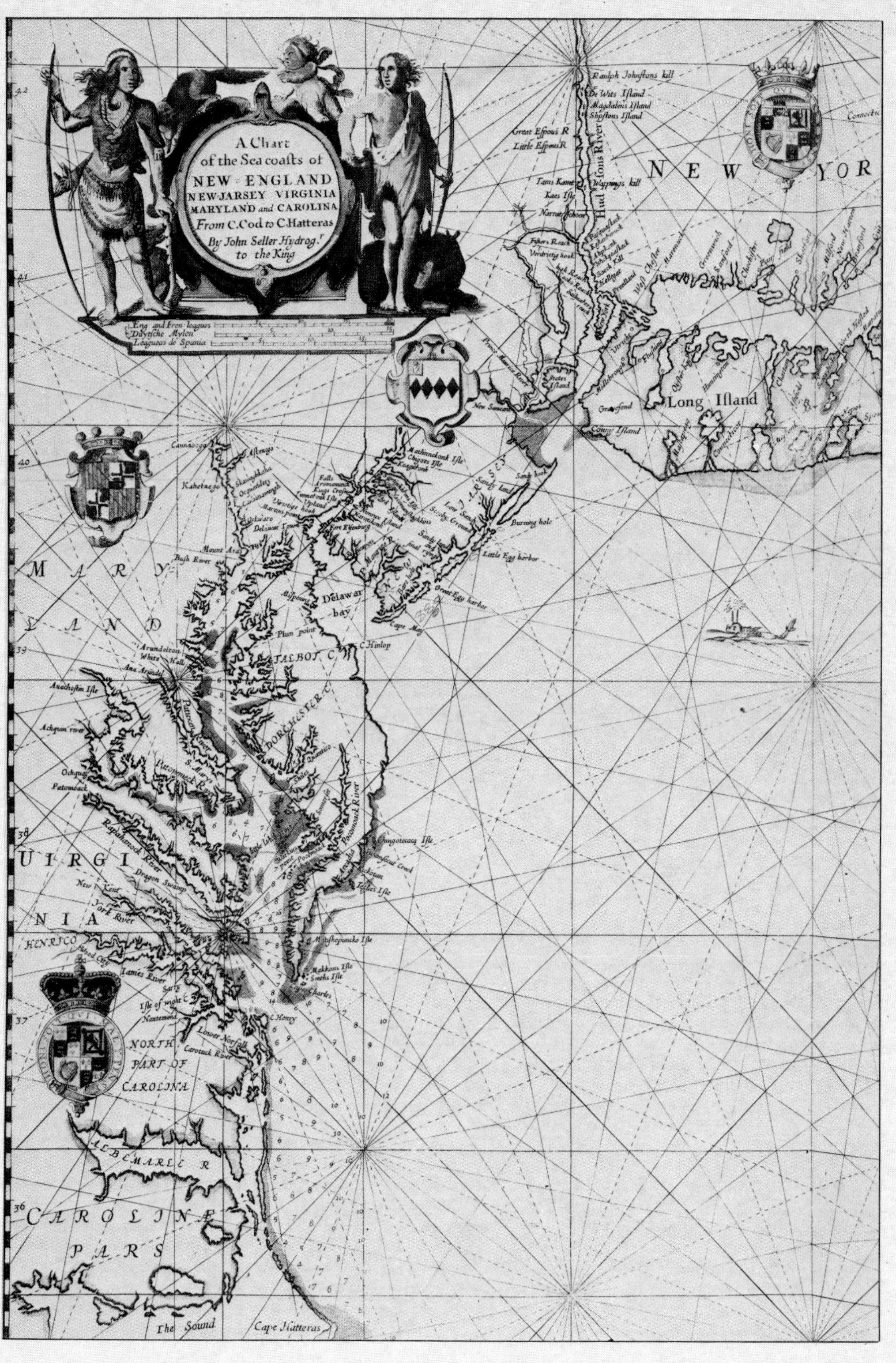

A Chart
of the Sea coasts of
NEW ENGLAND
NEW JARSEY VIRGINIA
MARYLAND and CAROLINA
From C. Cod to C. Hatteras
By John Seller Hydrog.r
to the King
Eng and Fren leagues
Duytsche Mylen
Leguoas de Spania
Raulph Johnstons kill
De Wits Island
Magdalens Island
Great Esopus R
Little Esopus R
Hudsons River
Wappings kill
NEW YOR
Long Island
Conny Island
Gravesend
Staten Island
New Sarum
Sandy hook
Burning hole
Little Egg harbor
Great Egg harbor
Delawar bay
Cape May
C Hinlop
MARY LAND
Bush River
Mount Aral
Fort Elsenburg
Delawar Towne
TALBOT C
DORCHESTER C
Arundelton
White Hall
Ana Arundel
Patomack
Patowmack River
Pocomock River
Chingoteague Isle
UIRGINIA
Rapahanock River
Dragon Swamp
York River
HENRICO
James River
Isle of wight C
Nantemond
C Henry
Lower Norfolk
Carotuck River
NORTH PART OF CAROLINA
ALBEMARLE R
CAROLINÆ PARS
The Sound
Cape Hatteras

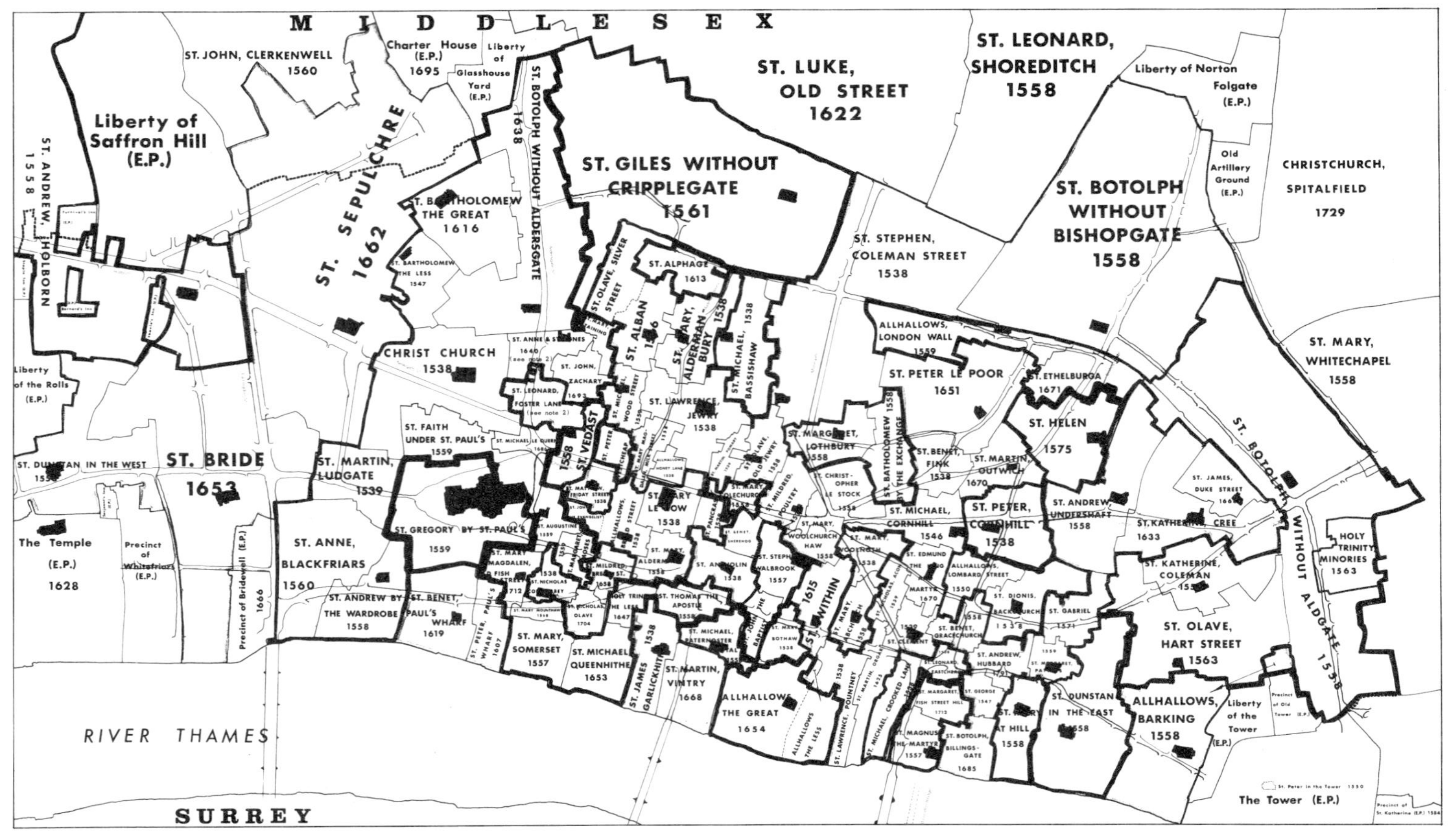

The county parish maps of London and Durham. These maps are taken from one of a series of maps of the Counties of England and Wales depicting parochial and probate jurisdiction boundaries with dates of registers, and appear by kind permission of the Trustees of the Institute of Heraldic and Genealogical Studies from whom copies may be obtained.

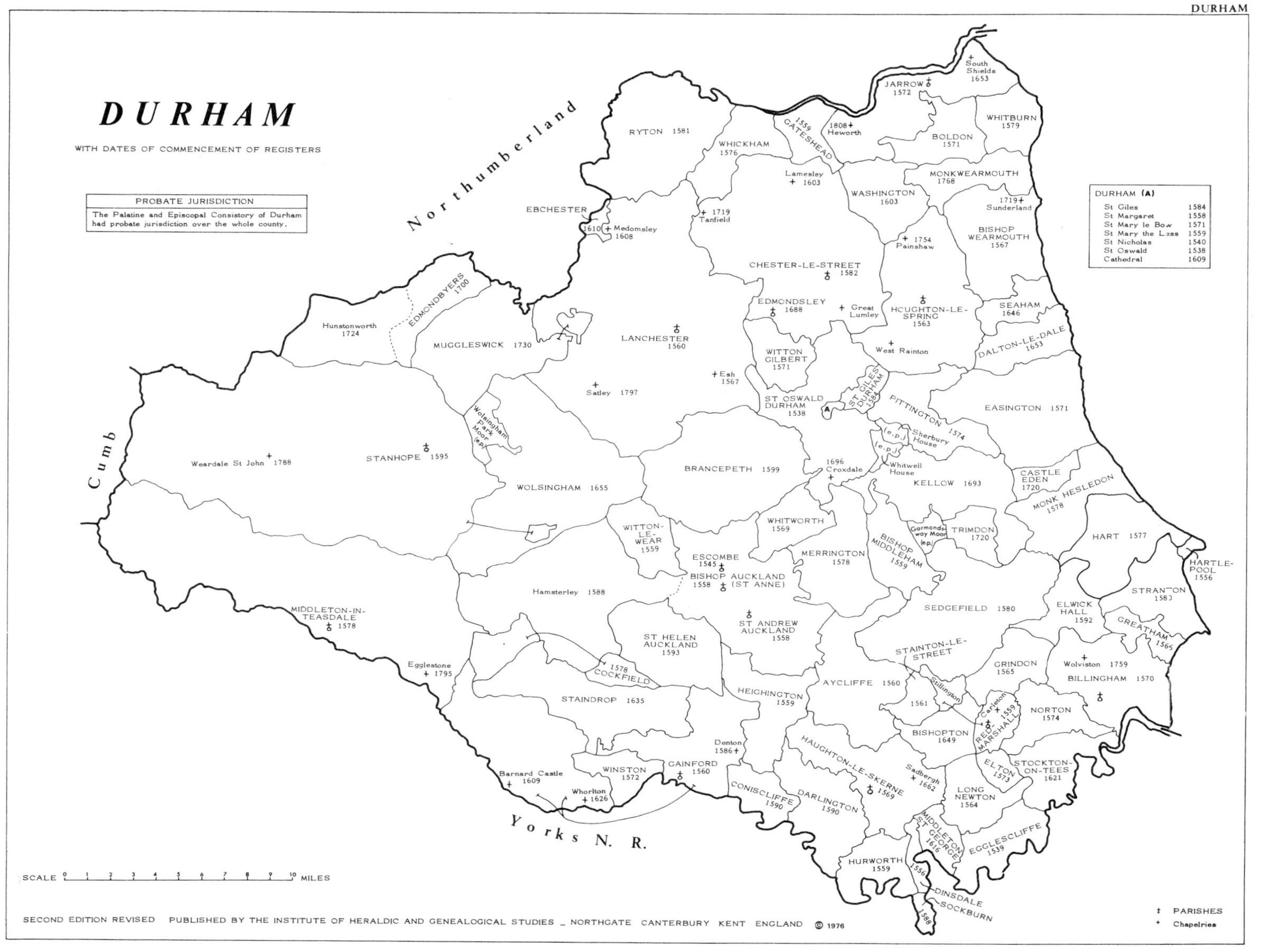
DURHAM
WITH DATES OF COMMENCEMENT OF REGISTERS
PROBATE JURISDICTION
The Palatine and Episcopal Consistory of Durham had probate jurisdiction over the whole county.
DURHAM (A)
St Giles 1584
St Margaret 1558
St Mary le Bow 1571
St Mary the Less 1559
St Nicholas 1540
St Oswald 1538
Cathedral 1609
PARISHES
Chapelries
HARTLE-POOL 1556
STRANTON 1583
GREATHAM 1565
HART 1577
BILLINGHAM 1570
Wolviston 1759
ELWICK HALL 1592
MONK HESLEDON 1578
CASTLE EDEN 1720
EASINGTON 1571
DALTON-LE-DALE 1653
SEAHAM 1646
BISHOP WEARMOUTH 1567
1719 Sunderland
MONKWEARMOUTH 1768
WHITBURN 1579
South Shields 1653
BOLDON 1571
JARROW 1572
1808 Heworth
WASHINGTON 1603
1754 Painshaw
HOUGHTON-LE-SPRING 1563
West Rainton
PITTINGTON 1574
Sherburn House
Whitwell House
KELLOW 1693
TRIMDON 1720
Garmondsway Moor
BISHOP MIDDLEHAM 1559
SEDGEFIELD 1580
GRINDON 1565
NORTON 1574
STOCKTON-ON-TEES 1621
ELTON 1573
Carlton
REDMARSHALL 1559
STAINTON-LE-STREET 1561
Stillington
BISHOPTON 1649
LONG NEWTON 1564
EGGLESCLIFFE 1539
MIDDLETON ST GEORGE 1616
DINSDALE 1556
SOCKBURN 1588
Sadbergh 1662
HAUGHTON-LE-SKERNE 1569
HURWORTH 1559
DARLINGTON 1590
AYCLIFFE 1560
HEIGHINGTON 1559
CONISCLIFFE 1590
Denton 1586
GAINFORD 1560
WINSTON 1572
Whorlton 1626
Barnard Castle 1609
STAINDROP 1635
COCKFIELD 1578
ST HELEN AUCKLAND 1593
ST ANDREW AUCKLAND 1558
ESCOMBE 1545
BISHOP AUCKLAND (ST ANNE) 1558
Hamsterley 1588
WITTON-LE-WEAR 1559
WHITWORTH 1569
MERRINGTON 1578
1696 Croxdale
BRANCEPETH 1599
ST OSWALD DURHAM 1538
WITTON GILBERT 1571
EDMONDSLEY 1688
Great Lumley
CHESTER-LE-STREET 1582
Lamesley 1603
1559 GATESHEAD
WHICKHAM 1576
1719 Tanfield
RYTON 1581
Esh 1567
LANCHESTER 1560
Medomsley 1608
1610 EBCHESTER
Satley 1797
WOLSINGHAM 1655
Wolsingham Park Moor (ep.)
MUGGLESWICK 1730
EDMONDBYERS 1700
Hunstonworth 1724
STANHOPE 1595
Weardale St John 1788
Egglestone 1795
MIDDLETON-IN-TEASDALE 1578
Northumberland
Cumb
Yorks N. R.
SCALE 0 1 2 3 4 5 6 7 8 9 10 MILES
SECOND EDITION REVISED PUBLISHED BY THE INSTITUTE OF HERALDIC AND GENEALOGICAL STUDIES _ NORTHGATE CANTERBURY KENT ENGLAND © 1976

The counties of England, Wales and Scotland before and after boundary reorganization.

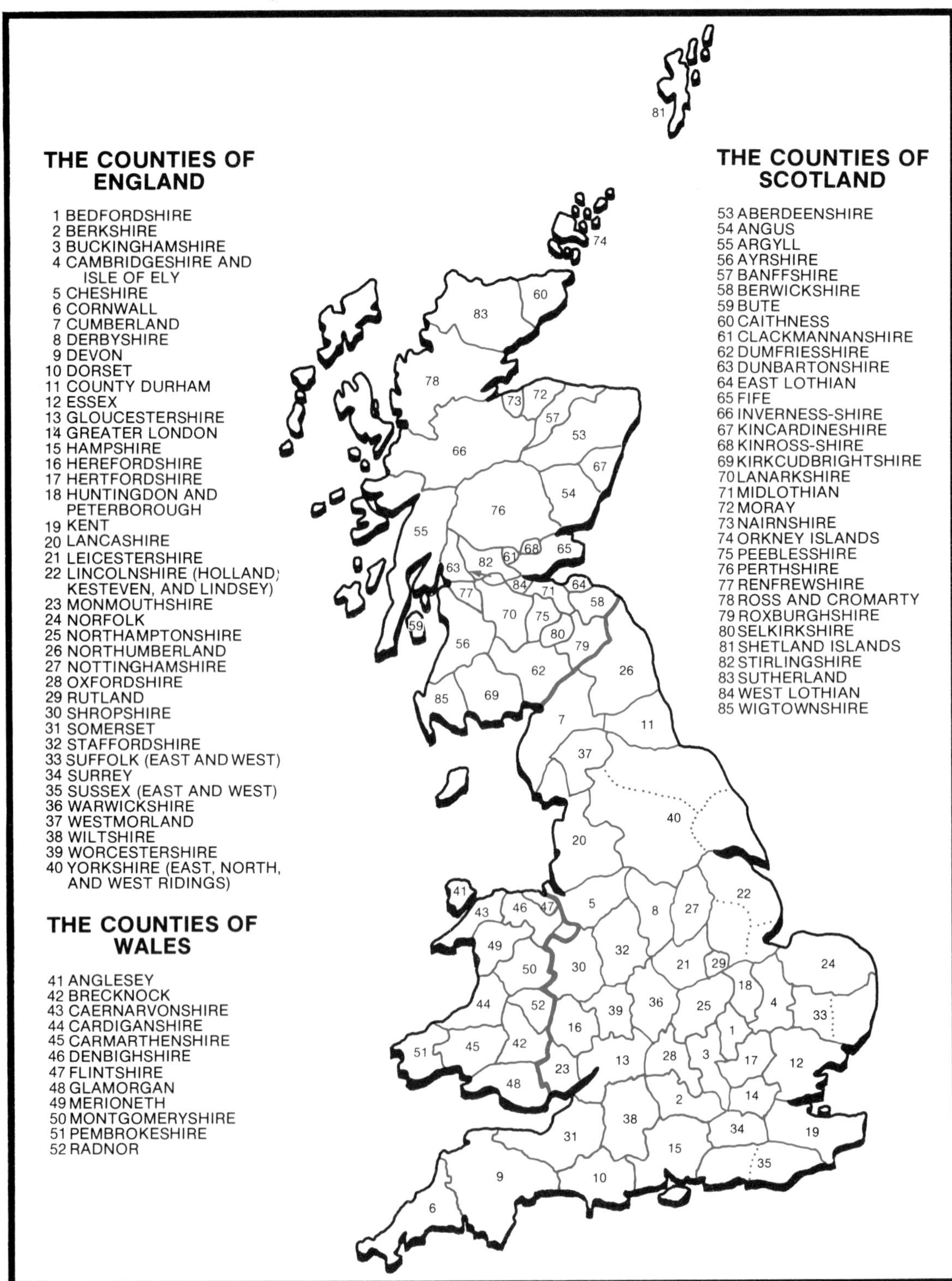

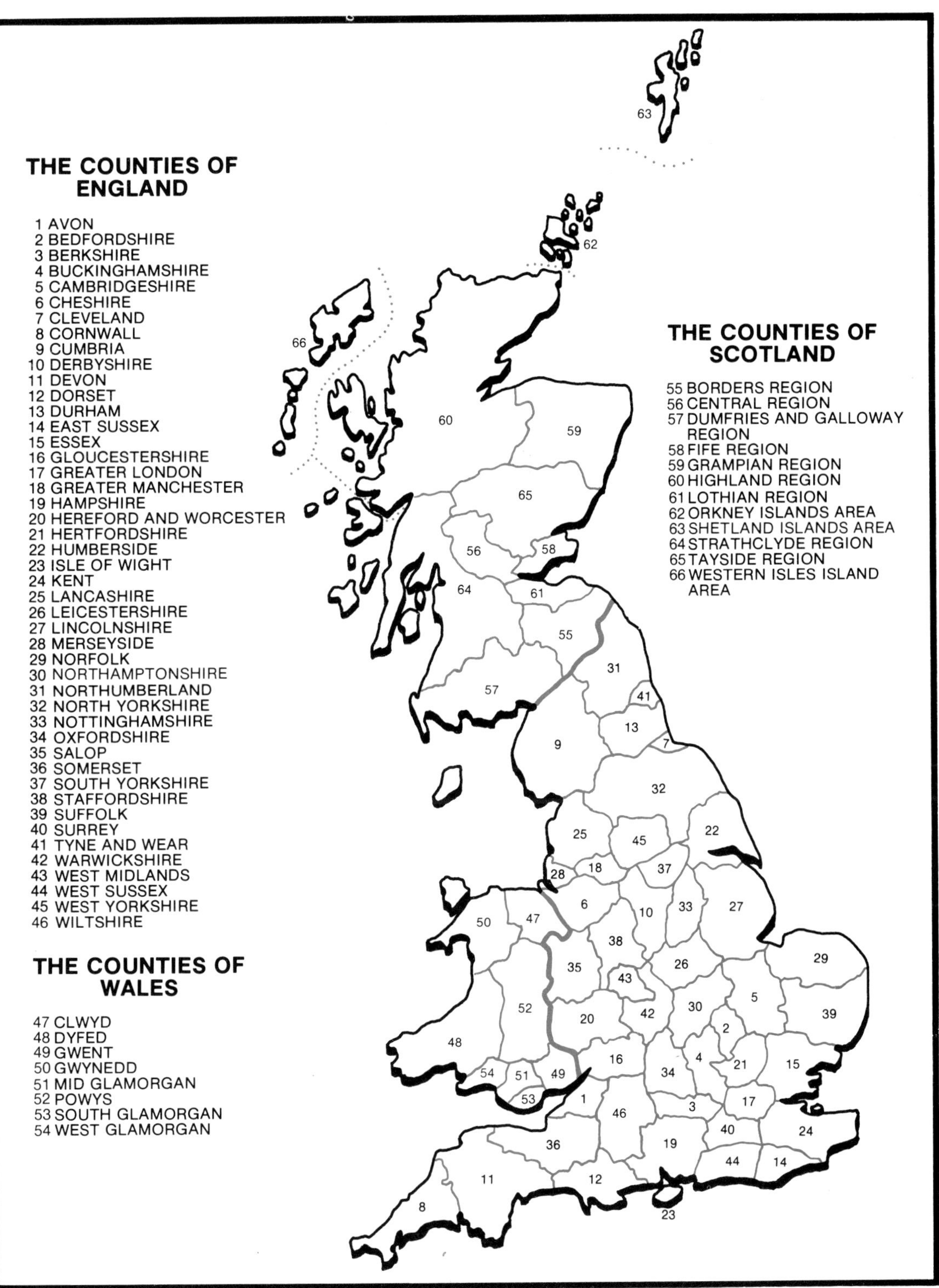
THE COUNTIES OF ENGLAND
1 AVON
2 BEDFORDSHIRE
3 BERKSHIRE
4 BUCKINGHAMSHIRE
5 CAMBRIDGESHIRE
6 CHESHIRE
7 CLEVELAND
8 CORNWALL
9 CUMBRIA
10 DERBYSHIRE
11 DEVON
12 DORSET
13 DURHAM
14 EAST SUSSEX
15 ESSEX
16 GLOUCESTERSHIRE
17 GREATER LONDON
18 GREATER MANCHESTER
19 HAMPSHIRE
20 HEREFORD AND WORCESTER
21 HERTFORDSHIRE
22 HUMBERSIDE
23 ISLE OF WIGHT
24 KENT
25 LANCASHIRE
26 LEICESTERSHIRE
27 LINCOLNSHIRE
28 MERSEYSIDE
29 NORFOLK
30 NORTHAMPTONSHIRE
31 NORTHUMBERLAND
32 NORTH YORKSHIRE
33 NOTTINGHAMSHIRE
34 OXFORDSHIRE
35 SALOP
36 SOMERSET
37 SOUTH YORKSHIRE
38 STAFFORDSHIRE
39 SUFFOLK
40 SURREY
41 TYNE AND WEAR
42 WARWICKSHIRE
43 WEST MIDLANDS
44 WEST SUSSEX
45 WEST YORKSHIRE
46 WILTSHIRE
THE COUNTIES OF WALES
47 CLWYD
48 DYFED
49 GWENT
50 GWYNEDD
51 MID GLAMORGAN
52 POWYS
53 SOUTH GLAMORGAN
54 WEST GLAMORGAN
THE COUNTIES OF SCOTLAND
55 BORDERS REGION
56 CENTRAL REGION
57 DUMFRIES AND GALLOWAY REGION
58 FIFE REGION
59 GRAMPIAN REGION
60 HIGHLAND REGION
61 LOTHIAN REGION
62 ORKNEY ISLANDS AREA
63 SHETLAND ISLANDS AREA
64 STRATHCLYDE REGION
65 TAYSIDE REGION
66 WESTERN ISLES ISLAND AREA

maps can show the progress of urban growth that accompanied the changes to many towns and villages during the Industrial Revolution.

The Enclosure Awards record the terms of enclosure and the disposition of all affected common land. An Award may be accompanied by a map which surveyors drew up to show how the common land was divided, and in some cases the whole village was shown in order to delineate the property in relation to the enclosure allotment that had been claimed. Medieval enclosures of open fields, moorland and meadow have often been agreed between the Lord of the Manor and other interested parties, but there were just as many enclosures made by stealth or even by brute force. In the sixteenth and early seventeenth centuries, the Courts of Exchequer and Chancery supervised enclosures, but after 1750 they were secured by Acts of Parliament. Since 1801 general Enclosure Acts have been made to facilitate enclosures.

The Anglo-Saxon tithes of one-tenth of the produce of land, stock or industry claimed by the church were a burden that led to disputes with farmers and landowners. The campaign to get them commuted into money payments finally resulted in the Tithe Commutation Act of 1836, and village meetings agreed on the value of tithes based on the average corn prices for the past seven years, and commissioners were appointed to award fair rents to be shared by all proprietors of land. Large-scale maps were drawn up by surveyors to show every parcel of land, path, garden, shed, outhouse, stream and factory, and apportionments set out in columns the names of owners and occupiers; description of each parcel of land; the state of cultivation and its acreage; and the tithe rent-charge. The Award, Map and Apportionment were fastened together and sealed. Three copies were produced, one for the Parish Chest, one for the Diocesan Registry, and one for the Land Registry. In 1936 rent charges were abolished, a stock fund was created to provide compensation, and all payments were planned to terminate in 1996.

Finally, there are the Ordnance Survey maps. These are probably the most frequently used by family historians. It is of course useful to have a copy of the current series for the area in which you are interested in order to locate places as they are today, but it is the first series of these maps that show what nineteenth-century Britain looked like. This edition is the one of greatest use in establishing the whereabouts of addresses obtained from census returns and civil registration certificates.

The Ordnance Survey, or Trigonometrical Survey as it was first named, was founded in 1791, its prime object being to produce a map of Great Britain to a scale of 1″ to the mile.

The first Ordnance Map, the 1″ to the mile map of Kent, was in fact privately published by William Faden, but the first official Old Series maps consisted of 110 sheets, mainly 36″ × 24″. This series was published between 1805 and 1873. These maps covered England and Wales, and, in terms of accuracy, are the least reliable. They should therefore be used critically. The New Series, or Second Edition, was started in 1840. There appears to have been a full-scale revision

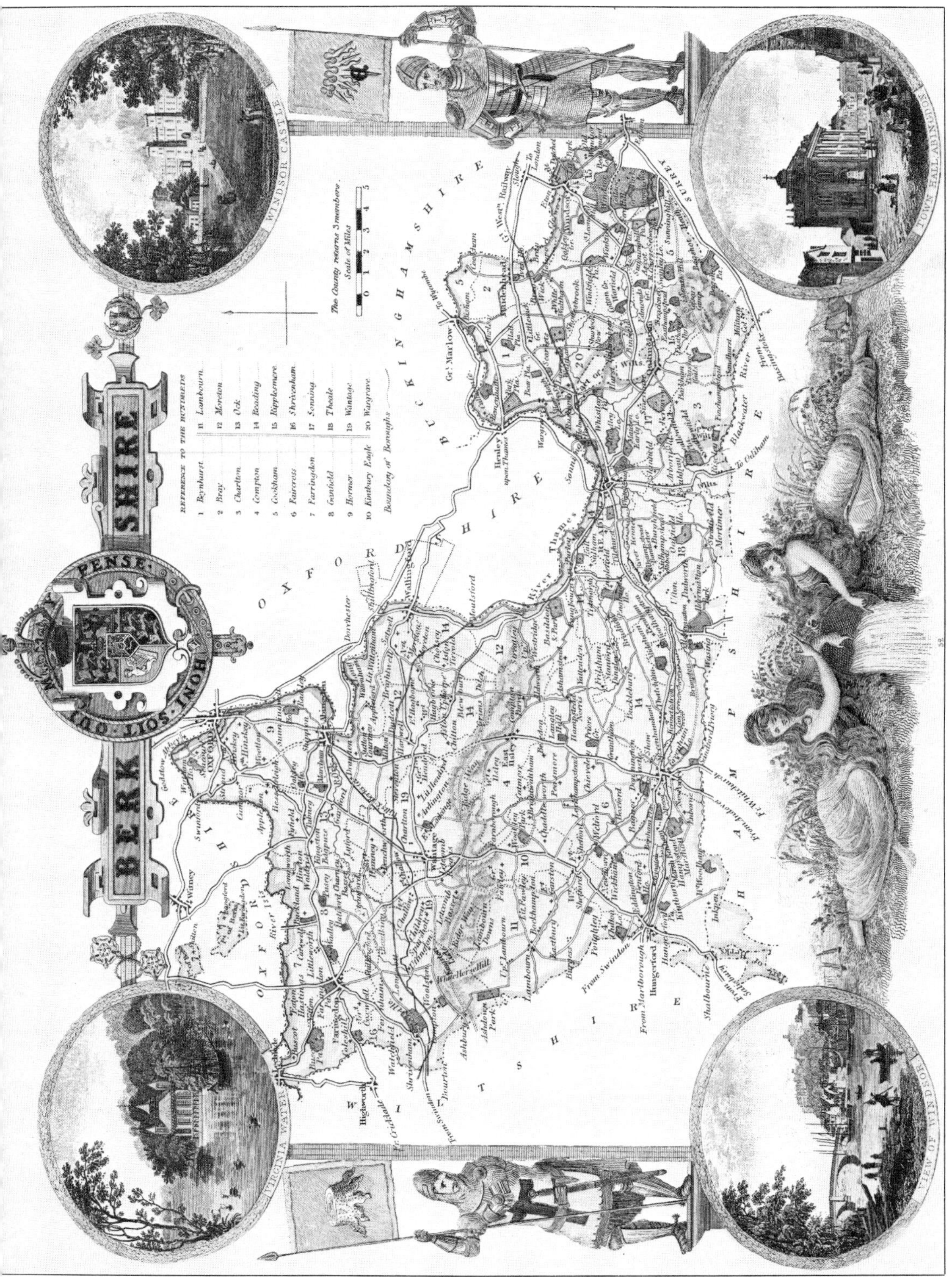

A map of the County of Berkshire (1837) by Thomas Moule.

between 1893 and 1898, but all 360 sheets (12″ × 18″) were published before 1899. The survey for the Third Edition began in 1901, with publication between 1903 and 1913, again comprising 360 sheets, 12″ × 18″. The survey for the Fourth Edition started in 1913 and was published between 1918 and 1926. This marked a departure from its predecessors as it consisted of 146 sheets, 18″ × 27″. Various revised Editions have been published since the Fourth Edition, but for the purposes of research it is only the latest series that have any obvious relevance.

Although the 1″ to the mile maps formed the original series, larger scale maps of 6″ and 25″ to the mile were introduced during the second half of the nineteenth century to cover the whole of Britain. The 6″ survey was started in 1840, and the 25″ in 1853. In spite of considerable controversy, both from vested interests, private surveyors and on the grounds of economy, it was decided to make the 25″ series for the whole country, except for the uncultivated districts which were to be surveyed on the 6″ scale. From the 25″ maps, 6″ maps were produced by reduction. The First Edition of this series was completed between 1888 and 1893, the 25″ maps being on sheets 38″ × 25⅓″. The 6″ maps published before 1881 were on sheets 36″ × 24″, but thereafter they appeared in quarter sheets 18″ × 12″. The first revision began in 1891 and was completed in 1914. The second revision survey began in 1904, but was drastically interrupted by the First World War. For this reason some areas were only partly revised, others not started, and the old system of revision was abandoned in 1922. Thereafter revision was confined to the 6″ sheets, and in 1928 this was replaced by continuous revision for areas of most rapid change. As with the 1″ series, these scales are available in the latest series.

It will be readily appreciated that the 1″ maps are most useful for research in a fairly large area, but once the exact place of interest has been located, it is essential to use the 6″ and 25″ maps for the very detailed information they can provide. The choice between the two larger scales will to a great extent depend on whether the area is urban or rural.

In addition to the main series of Ordnance Survey maps there are Town Plans found in a variety of scales and starting at different times; the first, for St Helens, was published in 1843. The usual and current sizes are those of 50″ to one mile, but all are worth examining for their superb workmanship and extensive detail. In some cases, even the number of seats within churches is shown.

There are of course other scales, in particular the 2½″ series, but for research purposes the above will invariably be sufficient.

Gazetteers are an essential accompaniment to maps. For the nineteenth century, the best is *Lewis's Topographical Dictionary*, which is divided into volumes covering England, Wales, Scotland and Ireland, each giving excellent details down to villages, hamlets and tythings. More recent publications are the Ordnance Survey and Bartholomew's Gazetteers which are adequate for use with current maps.

The British Library Map Library has one of the world's major historical collections of maps, charts, plans and topographical views, and also contains a comprehensive collection of modern maps of all countries. Similarly the copyright libraries—the National Library of Scotland, the National Library of Wales, the Bodleian Library at Oxford, Cambridge University Library and Trinity College Library, Dublin—hold extensive collections of maps, charts and plans. Indeed the best collection of Irish maps is at the library of Trinity College, Dublin. The Public Record Offices in London, Edinburgh, Belfast and Dublin, as well as the Royal Geographical Society, have their own unique and priceless collections.

County Record Offices have excellent collections for their own areas, including Ordnance Survey maps. In addition there are the county reference libraries, museums, and specialist societies. All these valuable and helpful sources can often be used in conjunction with other research, or specific lines of enquiry.

The Institute of Heraldic and Genealogical Studies, Canterbury, has published a very useful series of parish maps for each county of England and Wales. Each map shows the ancient parochial boundaries, the Probate Court jurisdiction affecting each area in colour, and the dates of commencement of the original registers of each parish to have survived. These maps can be obtained separately from the Institute, or bound in book form, from the publishers, Everton Publishers Incorporated, Logan, Utah, USA.

For those interested in colonial America, several seventeenth- and eighteenth-century maps are available, but if you wish to study or plot the boundaries of original holdings in, for example, Virginia, then the most useful are the 7·5 minute series (topographic), published by the US Department of the Interior Geological Survey. In British terms, the scale is slightly over $2\frac{1}{2}''$ to the mile.

If your line of research peters out in a particular place, and further documentary evidence is not available to indicate where you should search next, you will have to examine the records of neighbouring parishes in an ever-increasing circle for the next clue or link, to enable you to find the evidence you are seeking. As Gerald Hamilton-Edwards has pointed out: 'Villagers would often walk up the road in search of refreshment and change, and many a village lad met his future bride through first contacting her father or brother in the neighbouring "local".' With the higher classes this may well be the neighbouring county, but as these people are usually better documented, the problem does not so often arise until one gets back to the sixteenth century or earlier.

CHAPTER FIFTEEN

The Professional Approach

We at Debrett operate one of the world's larger professional ancestry-tracing services, and this gives us experience of family history research which the amateur researcher, working only on his or her own family, cannot normally expect to acquire. In addition a great many amateur researchers come to us with their problems after they have 'got stuck'. Indeed, we welcome such clients, as they have a good understanding of what we are doing. Our experience of where amateurs tend to run into problems points out, too, where emphasis is needed.

The first point where amateur researchers tend to err is in placing a too literal trust in documents and what they say. There is reluctance to accept variations in the spelling of a surname, forgetting that at a time when reading and writing were at best a rare effort for many people, and before modern documentation from driving licences to title deeds and cheque books, forced uniformity upon us, spelling simply did not matter, and even Shakespeare spelt his name in four different ways. Quite apart from errors and omissions by impersonal clerks and officials, people who were closely connected with the events could make errors. In one family Bible, great-grandmother began to record events following her marriage in 1871. She also copied entries from an older Bible recording the family from 1797; some of these dates did not agree with other records of the same events, and eventually it was discovered why, when the older Bible came to light. Great-grandma had simply made mistakes in copying out the entries.

Sometimes, too, records can be deliberately falsified. A common falsification was to exaggerate the age of a man enlisting in the army, who was really under the required minimum age, or of people marrying while minors without parental consent. Ages at death are often wrong simply because it is inevitably second-hand information, and indeed, no-one can personally remember when and where they were born, they simply repeat what they have been told. Feminine coyness about age is not new. For example one lady married three times; the first time she was aged eighteen and said she was twenty-one, the next time she married a man three years younger than herself and so reduced her own age by five years; at her third marriage to a yet younger man she reduced her age by another seven years. She lived with this until her death, when her gravestone recorded her age as being twelve years younger than the truth!

Method and the professional approach can best be described by recounting two case histories, those of former British Prime Minister Edward Heath and President Ronald Reagan of the United States.

Edward Heath's date and place of birth were known, in Kent. The records of the Registrar General took the descent back entirely conventionally to his grandfather born in 1860—the technique is that a birth certificate names the parents; the names of the parents lead to the marriage registration; this gives the ages of bride and groom and names their fathers which leads back again to the birth registration. The birth registration in 1860 gave us the address to locate the family in 1861, and the marriage certificate of George Weymouth Heath (Edward's great-grandfather) in 1857 combined to tell us that George had been born in a parish in Devonshire in 1830, and that he was son of Richard Heath, a Coastguard.

This opened the door to a wealth of government service records; the family career could be traced from Richard Heath's birth in Devon, through his interview and recruitment, to his posting to Kent in the Coastguard service. His pension records gave his address in retirement in Kent, and led to a census record, against which the Coastguard records could be double-checked.

This took the research to the parish of Cockington (near Torquay), where Richard proved to be one of the nine children born there to an earlier Richard Heath between 1789 and 1795. As the elder Richard had died in 1844 at the age of 81, he had been born around 1763, and parish poor relief records told much about the family in their poverty, down to the price of the children's shoes. But the problem was one of too many Richard Heaths born in south Devon to make identification easy. Indeed one pundit declared that the earlier ancestry could not be traced. However, given the facts of a coastal parish, and of poverty, research in 'Trinity House petitions' gave the answers. Trinity House is an organization which in addition to its well known care of lighthouses, also gave charitable relief to poor seamen. Richard Heath applied for this; to obtain it he had to set out in a petition his sea-going career in the Newfoundland fishery, with details of his birth, marriage, and children, supported by certificates from the respective parishes of register entries to corroborate it. This complete file of his family history led to Richard's baptism in 1763 in Paignton. He was one of the eight children of John Heath, a tailor who was described at his marriage as 'of Blackawton', a parish some fifteen miles away.

This reflects a point of some importance in researching the history of a poor family. The working of the English Poor Laws meant in essence that most paupers were supported by the parish where they were born, or where they were apprenticed; as individual parishes had to bear the cost of such relief, they took good care to record the place of origin of newcomers. Interestingly, not only did Paignton parish record John's origin in Blackawton, but Blackawton parish poor law records account for the family in Paignton, and in his old age John returned to Blackawton, where the Overseers of the Poor paid for his funeral and even for beer for the mourners.

John Heath was indeed baptised in Blackawton in 1734. Working back from this point in Blackawton parish registers, and those of the adjoining parishes, entirely straightforward research in registers, corroborated by several valuable records of householders such as the Hearth Tax of the 1660s and 1670s, and lists

The family tree of the Right Honourable Edward Heath, PC, MBE, MP.

RICHARD atte HETHE
of Aveton Giffard 1332

WILLIAM HEATH
of Cliston in
Blackawton Devon
there before 1524 d. 1

JOHN HEATH
of Cliston in
Blackawton d. 1569
= ALICE

AGNES TOLY
m. 1557
Blackawton
= RICHARD HEATH
of Cliston in Blackawton
b. *c* 1536 d. 1583

NICOLE
b. 1539 Blackawton
m. 1656 to
RICHARD SPARKE

ANDREW
b. 1544
Blackawton

ROBERT
b. 1546
d. infancy

WILLIAM
b. 1557
Blackawton

MARGERY
b. 1564 Blackawton
m. 1582 to
JOHN PHILLIPS

ALICE
b. 1567 Blackawton
m. 1595 to
RICHARD BURGESS

RICHARD HEATH
of Cliston in
Blackawton
= MARGARET GOO
m. 1594
Blackawton

MARGARET
- - - - -
d. 1672
Blackawton
= WILLIAM HEATH
of Cliston in
Blackawton
b. 1598 d. 1662

NICHOLAS
b. 1602
Blackawton

JOAN
b. 1606
Blackawton

HENRY
b. 1609
d. infancy

LUCY GILLERD
m. 1653 d. 1702
Blackawton
= RICHARD HEATH
of Cliston in
Blackawton
b. *c* 1626 d. 1699

WILMOT
b. 1630, d. 1689
Blackawton

MARGARET
b. 1635
Blackawton

AVIS
b. 1638
Blackawton

AGNES
b. 1641
Blackawton

WILLIAM
b. 1642
Blackawton

NICHOLAS
b. 1646
Blackawton

MA
b. 1
Black

JOHN
b. 1657
Slapton
d. 1668
Blackawton

MARY
NOSWORTHY
m. 1678
d. 1689
= RICHARD
HEATH jun
of Oldston
Blackawton
d. 1717
= MARY
JELLERD
m. 1692
d. 1693

MARY
b. 1668 Halwell
m. 1697 Blackawton
to WILLIAM
PERRING

JOHN HEATH
of Blackawton
b. 1671 d. 1709
= ALICE PARTRIDGE
m. 1693 Chivelstone
d. 1715 Blackawton

SARA
b. 16
Blackaw

RUTH
b. 1682
Blackawton

MARY
b. 1693
d. infancy

ROBERT
b. 1694
Chivelstone

ELIZABETH
FRANCIS
m. 1720
d. 1742
= JOHN HEATH
of Blackawton
husbandman
b. 1696 Chivelstone
d. 1773 Blackawton
= MARTHA
FORD
m. 1746

RICHARD
b. 1699
Blackawton

M
b.
Blac

RICHARD
b. 1722
Blackawton

ELIZABETH
b. 1727
Blackawton

ELIZABETH
HARRIS
m. 1759
Paignton
= JOHN HEATH
tailor
b. 1734 Blackawton
later of Paignton
d. 1810 Blackawton

SUSANNA
b. 1747

MATTHEW
HEATH
b. 1750 d. 1835
Blackawton
= MARY

JOHN
b. 1760
Paignton

THOMAS
b. 1761
Paignton

RICHARD HEATH
b. 1763 Paignton
later of
Cockington, mariner
d. there 1844
= SARAH BROWN
b. *c* 1764
m. 1785 East Ogwell
d. 1845

MARY
b. 1766
Paignton

NICHOLAS
b. 1769
Paignton

CHARLES
b. 1771
Paignton

WIL
b.
Paig

MARY
b. 1787
Cockington

JOHN
b. 1789
Cockington

NICHOLAS
b. 1791
Cockington

ELIZABETH
MORGAN
m. 1818
= WILLIAM
HEATH of
Cockington
labourer
b. 1793

SARAH
b. 1795
Cockington

RICHARD HEATH
b. 1797 Cockington
Coastguard, later of
Ramsgate, Kent; d. 1863
= SUSANNA WEYM
b. 1801 m. 18
St Marychur

SUSAN
b. 1823
Cockington

NICHOLAS
b. 1833
Cockington

GEORGE
b. 1836
Cockington

ELIZABETH
ARNOLD NEWING
m. 1860 St Mary
Sandwich, Kent
= GEORGE WEYMOUTH HEATH
b. 1830 St Marychurch
of Sandwich and Ramsgate
merchant seaman, later
pier man
= ELI
POT
m. 1
South

STEPHEN RICHARD HEATH
b. 1865 St Lawrence, Kent
later of Ramsgate, carrier
= JULIA LO
HOBDA
b. 186
m. 188
Ramsga

b—born/baptised
m—married
d—died/buried
numerous collateral lines
have been omitted

[MAR]GARET
[b.] 1547
[Blacka]wton

ALICE
b. 1550
Blackawton

WILLIAM HEATH = JOAN HARTE
of Blackawton
b. 1541 d. 1590

JOAN HARTE
m. 1564
d. 1618
Blackawton

ODO
b. 1552
d. 1558

NICHOLAS
b. 1556
Blackawton

RICHARD
b. 1565
d. infancy

JULIAN
b. 1569 Blackawton
m. 1595 to
THOMAS LUSCOMBE

WILLIAM
b. 1573
d. infancy

WILLIAM
b. 1574
Blackawton

TAMSEN
[Thomasine]
b. 1610
Blackawton

ROGER HEATH
of Woodleigh
b. 1613
Blackawton

RICHARD HEATH = MARIE COMBE
of Blackawton
b. 1600 later of
Cornworthy d. 1648

MARIE
COMBE
m. 1631
Blackawton

ROBERT HEATH = JOAN HURLE
of Blackawton
b. 1616

JOAN HURLE
m. 1640
Blackawton

[...]AN
[...] 1650
[...]wton

PASCHO HEATH = MARY
of Blackawton
b. 1628

MARY

MARGARET
b. 1632

MARY
b. 1635
d. infancy

RICHARD
b. 1636

NICHOLAS
b. 1638

REZA
b. 1641

RICHARD
b. 1645

JANE = ROGER HEATH
PRIM
m. 1680
Harberton

ROGER
HEATH
b. 1646

MARY
1654

HONOR
1661

[I]SAAC HEATH
of Blackawton
b. 1678
[M]ARGARET RIDER
[m.] 1706 Harberton

SARAH
b. 1674

ABRAHAM = MARY JEFFERY
HEATH
of Harberton
b. 1676
Blackawton

MARY
JEFFERY
m. 1697
Harberton

ELIZABETH b. 1677
d. infancy
MARTHA b. 1679
URANIA b. 1681
Blackawton

MARY
b. 1684
E. Allington

ROGER
b. 1686
Blackawton

JANE
b. 1689
Blackawton

NICHOLAS
b. 1691
Blackawton

[R]UTH
[b.] 1705
[Blac]kawton

SARAH
b. 1698
Harberton

ABRAHAM
b. 1699
Harberton

ISAAC
b. 1702
Harberton

JACOB
b. 1702
Harberton

MARY
b. 1704
Harberton

JOHN HEATH = MARY
of Cornworthy
b. 1706
Harberton

MARY

ELIZABETH
b. 1708
Harberton

MARY
b. 1754
Blackawton

JOHN HEATH
Sailmaker & Freeman
of Dartmouth
b. 1733 Cornworthy

WILLIAM
b. 1736
Cornworthy
d. 1820
Blackawton

ABRAHAM HEATH
Sailmaker & Freeman
of Dartmouth
b. 1739 Cornworthy

JACOB
b. 1739
Cornworthy

[B]ETTY
[b.] 1777
[...]ignton

JOHN HEATH
of Blackawton
Mason
b. 1785

MARY
b. 1788
Blackawton

SUSANNA
b. 1790
Blackawton

MATTHEW HEATH
of Blackawton
Mason
b. 1794 d. 1836

[TH]OMAS
[b.] 1801
[Coc]kington

JAMES HEATH = HANNAH HONEYWELL
of Torquay, painter
b. 1803 Cockington

HANNAH
HONEYWELL

CHARLES
b. 1804
Cockington

[other issue]

CHARLES HEATH
b. c Ramsgate

MARY JANE
[b.] 1860 Sandwich

[WIL]LIAM GEORGE HEATH = EDITH ANNIE PANTONY
b. 1888 Ramsgate
of Broadstairs, carpenter
and Master Builder

EDITH ANNIE PANTONY
b. 1888 St Peters, Kent
m. 1913 St Peters

EDWARD RICHARD GEORGE HEATH
b. 1916 Broadstairs

The Right Honourable Edward Heath PC, MBE, MP.

of inhabitants such as the Protestation Against Popery of 1642 (valuable records as they are a check-list of the family to corroborate conclusions drawn from parish registers) led us to a Richard Heath, baptised in Blackawton in 1571, the twelfth generation from the Prime Minister, and son of yet another Richard Heath and Agnes his wife who had married in 1557. What was interesting, and also gave support to the conclusions arrived at, was that in almost every generation a son was named Nicholas, a tradition which continued until 1791. (Perpetuation of rarer names in this way is valuable supporting evidence, as the traditional custom to do so was strong.)

The parish registers of Blackawton began in 1538, and so it was unlikely that one would find the baptism of Richard who had married in 1557. But there was a John Heath fathering children there recorded from the earliest page of the registers, and who named a son Nicholas, so it seemed probable that this was Richard's father.

At this point it was possible to turn to Manorial Court Rolls. These recorded John Heath in some detail (even to his being fined for insulting behaviour in the manor court) and yet earlier in 1524, his probable father William Heath. Interestingly John Heath is recorded in the parish registers as having been buried in 1569. Shortly afterwards, the court rolls record his death, and the admission to his copyhold lands of his son and heir Richard Heath—and so the fourteenth generation was established.

Research into the ancestry of President Reagan took an entirely different course, but the essential technique was the same, to progress backwards in time step by step, each step being soundly based and comprehensively researched, to give a firm foundation for the subsequent step.

American records in Illinois recorded his birth, and his parent's marriage. The death certificate of his father gave the birthplace of the deceased, and his parent's names. The indexed United States Census of 1900 listed the father John, born in July 1883 in Illinois, son of an English-born father, lodging with his aunt Margaret, recorded as born in England in April 1856. Further research in Illinois records and censuses, including death registrations, built up a picture of Michael Reagan, Catherine (née Mulcahy) his wife, both born in Ireland, and with three children born in England between 1852 and 1856, Thomas, Michael and Margaret; they had come to America in 1858, and had two more children born in Illinois.

The names of the children were important clues, as among the Scots and Irish there is a very strong tradition to name the eldest son and daughter of a marriage after the paternal grandfather and grandmother. Michael Reagan was farming his own freehold land, and employing (apparently) his two elder brothers.

English records of General Registration produced the marriage of Michael Reagan and Catherine Mulcahy in a Catholic Church; Michael signed his name, but interestingly his elder brother, a witness, was illiterate. This explains the younger brother in Illinois, a freeholder employing his elder brother as a labourer. Like many of the Irish in England, they failed to register the births of their children,

The family tree of Ronald Reagan, President of the United States of America.

THOMAS O'REGAN of Doolis in the parish of Ballyporeen, co. Tipperary, Ireland dead by 1852 = MARGARET MURPHY married in or before 1817

- NICHOLAS O'REGAN alias REGAN bapt. before 1817; later of Illinois, USA unmarried in 1860
- ELENA bapt. 5 July 1819 at Ballyporeen
- JOHN O'REGAN alias REGAN bapt. 24 June 1821 at Ballyporeen later of Illinois; unmarried in 1860
- MARGARET bapt. 29 Oct. 1823 at Ballyporeen
- ELIZABETH bapt. 13 Sept 1826 at Ballyporeen
- MICHAEL O'REGAN alias REAGAN of Peckham, London, Soapmaker; after of Fairhaven, Carroll co., Illinois, farmer. bapt. 3 Sept 1829 at Ballyporeen, d. after 1880 in Fairhaven = CATHERINE MULCAHY born *c* 1822/3 in co. Tipperary 31 Oct 1852 St George's Catholic Church, Southwark, England; d. after 1880 in Fairhaven, in Fairhaven, Illinois

Children of Michael O'Regan and Catherine Mulcahy:

- THOMAS REAGAN of Fairhaven, Ill., b. 15 May 1852 at Peckham. and bapt. 16 May 1852 at St George's, Southwark, England
- JOHN REAGAN of Fulton, Ill. grain elevator worker, b. 29 May 1854 at Peckham, and bapt. 4 June 1854 at St George's, Southwark; d. 1889 in Fulton = JENNIE dau. of PATRICK CUSICK of Fulton (b. *c* 1855/6 in Canada to father b. in Ireland) m. 1878
- MARGARET wife of ORSON G. BALDWIN of Bennett, Iowa, Dry Goods Merchant; b. April 1856 in England; brought up her nephew John Reagan
- WILLIAM REAGAN b. 1858/9 in Fairhaven, Ill. disabled
- MARY b. *c* 1864/5 in Fairhaven, Ill.

Children of John Reagan and Jennie Cusick:

- CATHERINE b. July 1879 in Fulton, Ill.
- WILLIAM REAGAN b. 1881 in Fulton
- JOHN EDWARD REAGAN of Tampico, Ill. salesman b. July 1883 in Fulton d. 1941 = NELLIE WILSON b. July 1883 in Illinois to a Scottish-born father and an English-born mother; m. 8 Nov 1904 at the Church of the Immaculate Conception, Fulton

Children of John Edward Reagan and Nellie Wilson:

- NEIL REAGAN b. *c* 1909
- RONALD REAGAN President of the United States of America b. 6 February 1911 at Tampico, Illinois

Ronald Reagan, the fortieth President of the United States of America.

but these were found recorded as baptisms in the registers of the Catholic church where they had married. The English Census also recorded Michael's age and county of birth, Tipperary in Ireland.

We were, therefore, able to turn to Irish records ready and prepared with a quantity of detail: we were looking for a Michael Reagan, born about 1829–30, son of Thomas and Margaret, with elder brothers John and probably Nicholas, all born in County Tipperary.

In Ireland there are two important lists of householders, the Tithe Applotment of about 1825–30, and Griffiths Valuation of about 1850. So our first step was to list all parishes in County Tipperary with Reagan (or, as usually spelt in Ireland, Regan, or O'Regan) families listed in the Tithe Applotment—of which the dates would fit the birth dates of Michael and his elder brothers.

From this nine Catholic parishes could be listed as 'possibles'. In only one of these was there a Michael recorded as born at about the correct date, baptised on 3 September 1829 and, very neatly, recorded as son of Thomas O'Regan and Margaret Murphy his wife. Michael's elder brother was John born in 1821, which tallied with American records, but it was not possible to confirm the eldest brother as the Catholic parish register did not begin until 1817.

However, the register recorded the townland, Doolis, in the Catholic parish of Ballyporeen (but in the Civil and Protestant parish of Templetenny—another trap for Irish research). A townland is a small area within a parish, in this case 229 acres, and the map showed twelve inhabited houses there in 1841 (when the O'Regans lived there). A visit to the place led to the discovery that, as so often is the case in rural Ireland, only three houses remained there, but old men remembered where the others were. Of those three houses, two had been long uninhabited and the third was now empty, and used as a hay store. Old men remembered the last of the O'Regans, and in the graveyard of the church built in 1824, where Michael had been baptised in 1829, a memorial reads 'Pray for the souls of the O'Regan family'.

Finally, to crown the research, a leading Gaelic scholar's work identifies the O'Regans of this district in Ireland as descendants of one Riagan, nephew of the great Irish king Brian Boru, who was killed in 1014.

The object lesson of this is the importance of sound and minutely detailed research in American and English records, so that one can move into Irish research knowing exactly what one is looking for, and not (as amateurs would attempt all too often) simply looking hopelessly for Michael Reagan born around 1829/30 'somewhere in Ireland', with nothing more known about him. This is the essence of the professional approach we use at Debrett, and this is what gets results.

OPPOSITE
The General Registry Office, St Catherine's House, Aldwych, London contains indexes of births, marriages and deaths from 1837 to the present day. Certificates can be obtained here for a fee, though searches through the indexes are free.

Appendix: Record Offices, Libraries and Societies

Before carrying out research, it is important to know where to find records, because these are not necessarily in the obvious place, the local county record office. The general principles about the whereabouts of archives need to be understood, in the first place. Church records in England and Wales are organized by dioceses which are not always the same as counties, although the majority of county record offices are in fact diocesan record offices as well. These are of primary importance since as well as parish registers and bishop's transcripts, wills were proved in church courts, and so are in diocesan archives. The records of the central government, including the armed forces, national courts, taxation, and the superior probate court, are in the Public Record Office, in London, while records of local administration like county quarter session courts are in county record offices. Many landowners are depositing their estate records in county record offices, but it is important to appreciate that some of these people owned property in several counties, and then generally their archives will be in the county where they lived, rather than the more obvious county where the land was. Another complication is the creation of new counties in 1974, which is confusing as earlier records tend to be kept according to the old counties. The maps on pages 180 and 181 show the old and new boundaries, and the list below is cross-referenced according to this.

In Scotland, the majority of archives of all types are collected centrally in Edinburgh, in two adjoining buildings, the Scottish Record Office and West Register House. In Ireland most records which have been brought into archive repositories

are in the various offices and libraries in Dublin and Belfast, and in both the Channel Islands and the Isle of Man, archives are generally centralized. It is important to remember that many church records are still held in the churches and chapels, in the custody of the respective clergymen, particularly in Ireland. Access to these records is not an automatic right for researchers, and their custodians have more important duties than accommodating family historians, who should remember the courtesies of both a prior appointment and a donation to church funds.

Anyone visiting a record office or library should acquaint themselves in the first place with whether the records in question are at that place, and also to confirm their availability. Opening hours may vary and in some places a prior appointment or reservation of a seat is necessary. The following is a list of useful guides to locating archives.

Record Repositories

Record Repositories in Great Britain (HM Stationery Office, London, 6th edition 1978) lists addresses, opening hours, and principal categories of archives held at each repository. It also lists any guides published to the individual record offices. In particular the *Guide to the Contents of the Public Record Office* (HM Stationery Office, London, 3 volumes 1963–1968) is important and can be found at most reference libraries.

Parish Registers

Original Parish Registers in Record Offices and Libraries (Local Population Studies, Matlock, 1974, with periodical supplements). This series of booklets lists original Church of England registers which have been deposited in record offices and libraries, only.

National Index of Parish Registers (Society of Genealogists, in progress, 12 volumes). When completed this will list details of all parish and other registers, and copies and indexes of them, in Great Britain, but much remains to be completed.

Guide to the Parish and Non-Parochial Registers of Devon and Cornwall 1538–1837 (Devon and Cornwall Record Society, 1979). A comprehensive guide with maps.

Parish Register Copies Part One—Society of Genealogists Collection and *Parish Register Copies Part Two—Other than the Society of Genealogists Collection* (Society of Genealogists, London) list copies of parish registers and their whereabouts.

In addition many county and other record offices publish lists of registers in their custody.

Wills

A. J. Camp's *Wills and their Whereabouts* (privately published, 1974) and J. S. W. Gibson's *Wills and Where to Find Them* (Chichester, 1974) are comprehensive guides but are both out of print. J. S. W. Gibson's *A Simplified Guide to Probate Jurisdictions* (Gulliver Press and the Federation of Family History Societies, 1980) is in print and is an adequate brief guide.

Manorial Records and other Landowners' Archives

There is no published guide but the Historical Manuscripts Commission maintains the Manorial Documents Register and the National Register of Archives, which list the whereabouts of such material where it is known. The indexes and catalogues may be consulted at Quality House, Quality Court, Chancery Lane, London WC2A 1HP.

Other Sources

Federation of Family History Societies Handbook lists addresses of all family history societies in the British Isles, and is obtainable from the Secretary, The Drovers, Cambridge, Gloucestershire. The Federation of Family History Societies and Gulliver Press publish jointly *Census Returns 1841, 1851, 1861, 1871 on Microfilm: a Directory to Local Holdings; Marriage Indexes: How to Find Them, How to Use Them, How to Compile One; Bishops' Transcripts and Marriage Licences: A Guide to their Location and Indexes*

The following list of record offices and libraries is not necessarily complete but includes those of most significance, in particular diocesan record offices and genealogical libraries. Cross references reflect county boundary changes in 1974, and the evolution of Greater London, but ignore other earlier changes of county boundaries.

The Round Room at the Public Record Office, Chancery Lane, London is one of the three search rooms that are open to the public. This branch of the Public Record Office houses pre-Victorian records. The indexes can be seen in the stacks which surround the central reading area. Admission is by reader's ticket, which is obtainable from the office.

England

Avon (see also Gloucestershire; Somerset)

Bath City Record Office, Guildhall, Bath BA1 5AW
Tel (0225) 28411 Ext 201

Bath Reference Library, 18 Queen Square,
Bath BA1 2HP
Tel (0225) 28144

Bristol Record Office, Council House,
College Green, Bristol BS1 5TR
Tel (0272) 26031 Ext 441/2

Bedfordshire

Bedfordshire Record Office, County Hall,
Bedford MK42 9AP
Tel (0234) 63222 Ext 277

Berkshire (see also Buckinghamshire; Oxfordshire)

Berkshire Record Office, Shire Hall,
Shinfield Park, Reading RG2 9XD
Tel (0734) 85444

Windsor Muniment Room, Guildhall, High Street,
Windsor SL4 1LR
Tel (075 35) 66167

Buckinghamshire (see also Berkshire)

Buckinghamshire Record Office, County Hall,
Aylesbury HP20 1UA
Tel (0296) 5000 Ext 588

Buckinghamshire Archaeological Society,
The Museum, Church Street, Aylesbury

Cambridgeshire (includes former county of Huntingdonshire; see also Northamptonshire)

Cambridge County Record Office, Shire Hall,
Castle Hill, Cambridge CB3 0AP
Tel (0223) 58811 Ext 281

Cambridge County Record Office, Grammar
School Walk, Huntingdon PE18 6LF
Tel (0480) 52181

Cambridge University Archives,
University Library, West Road,
Cambridge CB3 9DR
Tel (0223) 61441

Cheshire (see also Derbyshire; Greater Manchester)

Cheshire Record Office, The Castle,
Chester CH1 2DN
Tel (0244) 602574

Chester Archaeological Society, Chester Public Library, St John Street, Chester
Tel (0244) 21938

Chester City Record Office, Town Hall, Chester CH1 2HJ
Tel (0244) 40144 Ext 2108

Cleveland (see Durham; Yorkshire)

Cornwall

Cornwall County Record Office, County Hall, Truro TR1 3AY
Tel (0872) 3098

Royal Institution of Cornwall, County Museum, River Street, Truro TR1 2SJ
Tel (0872) 2205

Cumberland (see Cumbria)

Cumbria (includes Cumberland, Westmorland, parts of Lancashire and Yorkshire)

Cumbria County Record Office, The Castle, Carlisle CA3 8UR
Tel (0228) 23456

Cumbria County Record Office, County Offices, Kendal LA9 4RQ
Tel (0539) 21000

Cumbria County Record Office, Duke Street, Barrow in Furness LA14 1XW
Tel (0229) 31269

Derbyshire (see also Cheshire)

Derbyshire Record Office, County Offices, Matlock DE4 3AG
Tel (0629) 3411 Ext 7347

Devon

Devon Record Office, Castle Street, Exeter EX4 3PQ
Tel (0392) 79146

Devon and Cornwall Record Society, c/o Westcountry Studies Library, Castle Street, Exeter EX4 3PQ
Tel (0392) 53422

Exeter Cathedral Library, Bishop's Palace, Exeter EX1 1HX
Tel (0392) 72894

West Devon Record Office, 14 Tavistock Place, Plymouth PL4 8AN
Tel (0752) 28293

Dorset (see also Hampshire)

Dorset Record Office, County Hall, Dorchester DT1 1XJ
Tel (0305) 3131 Ext 4411

Durham (see also Cleveland; Tyne and Wear; Yorkshire)

Durham County Record Office, County Hall, Durham DH1 5UL
Tel (0385) 64411

Dean and Chapter Library and the Prior's Kitchen, The College, Durham DH1 3EH
Tel (0385) 62489/64561

Durham University Library, Palace Green, Durham DH1 3RN
Tel (0385) 61262

Essex (see also Greater London)

Essex Record Office, County Hall, Chelmsford CM1 1LX
Tel (0245) 67222 Ext 2104

Gloucestershire (see also Avon)

Gloucestershire Record Office, Worcester Street, Gloucester GL1 3DW
Tel (0452) 21444 Ext 277/8

Hampshire (see also Dorset; Isle of Wight)

Hampshire Record Office, 20 Southgate Street, Winchester SO23 9EF
Tel (0962) 63153

Portsmouth City Records Office, 3 Museum Road, Portsmouth PO1 2LE
Tel (0705) 29765

Southampton City Record Office, Civic Centre, Southampton SO9 4XL
Tel (0703) 23855 Ext 251

Hereford and Worcester (see also West Midlands)

Hereford and Worcester Record Office, Shirehall, Worcester WR1 1TR
Tel (0905) 23400 Ext 521

Hereford Record Office, The Old Barracks, Harold Street, Hereford HR1 2QX
Tel (0432) 65441

St Helen's Record Office, Fish Street, Worcester WR1 21IN
Tel (0905) 23400 Ext 440/443

Hertfordshire (see also Greater London)

The exterior and Search Room of the Public Record Office at Kew. This ultra-modern building houses post-Victorian public records and is designed to give a fast efficient service to readers.

Hertfordshire Record Office, County Hall, Hertford SG13 8DE
Tel (0992) 54242

Humberside (see also Lincolnshire; Yorkshire)

Humberside County Record Office, County Hall, Beverley HU17 9BA
Tel (0482) 887131 Ext 393/4

Huntingdonshire (see Cambridgeshire)

Kent (see also Greater London)

Kent County Archives Office, County Hall, Maidstone ME14 1XH
Tel (0622) 671411

Canterbury Cathedral Archives and Library and City Record Office, The Precincts, Canterbury CT1 2EG
Tel (0227) 63510

Lancashire (see also Cumbria; Greater Manchester; Merseyside)

Lancashire Record Office, Bow Lane, Preston PR1 8ND
(Tel 0772) 58347

Leicestershire (includes Rutland)

Leicestershire Record Office, 57 New Walk, Leicester LE1 7JB
Tel (0533) 539111

Lincolnshire (see also Humberside)

Lincolnshire Archives Office, The Castle, Lincoln LN1 3AB
Tel (0522) 25158

Greater London

Record Offices and libraries in Greater London are a complex subject and, being the capital, it is not always possible to draw a clear distinction between local and national archives. The following list is not necessarily complete and deliberately omits repositories of minor importance. There are many specialist societies and libraries, and local reference libraries, not in this list but which may be of value for individual and specialist needs.

NATIONAL AND GENERAL ARCHIVES AND LIBRARIES

Army Records Centre, Bourne Avenue, Hayes, Middlesex.
Tel 01-573 3831 Ext 116

British Library Department of Manuscripts, Great Russell Street, London WC1B 3DG
Tel 01-636 1544

College of Arms, Queen Victoria Street, London EC4V 4BT
Tel 01-248 2762

General Register Office, St Catherine's House, Kingsway, London WC2B 6JP
Tel 01-242 0262

House of Lords Record Office, House of Lords, London SW1A 0PW
Tel 01-219 3073

India Office Library and Records, Foreign and Commonwealth Office, 197 Blackfriars Road, London SE1 8NG
Tel 01-928 9531

Lambeth Palace Library, London SE1 7JU
Tel 01-928 6222

Principal Registry of the Family Division (*Probate and Divorce*), Somerset House, Strand, London WC2R 1LP
Tel 01-405 7641

Public Record Office, Chancery Lane, London WC2A 1LR (*Medieval, Legal, Probate and Nonconformist records*)
Tel 01-405 0741

Public Record Office, Portugal Street, London WC2A 3PH (*Census Records*)
Tel 01-405 3488 Ext 335

Public Record Office, Ruskin Avenue, Kew, Richmond, Surrey TW9 4DU (*Departmental Records*)
Tel 01-876 3444

Royal Commission on Historical Manuscripts, Quality House, Quality Court, London WC2A 1HP
Tel 01-242 1198

Society of Genealogists, 37 Harrington Gardens, London SW7 4JX
Tel 01-373 7054

LOCAL LONDON ARCHIVES

Greater London Record Office, County Hall, London SE1 7PB
Tel 01-633 6851

Corporation of London Records Office, Guildhall, London EC2P 2EJ
Tel 01-606 3030 Ext 2251

Duke Humphrey's Library at the Bodleian Library, Oxford houses records of the diocese of Oxford, including wills, as well as many manuscript collections of a more general nature. Admission is by reader's ticket only.

Guildhall Library, Aldermanbury,
London EC2P 2EJ
Tel 01-606 3030

Lambeth Archives Department, Minet Library,
52 Knatchbull Road, London SE5 9QY
Tel 01-733 3279

Lewisham Archives and Local History Department,
The Manor House, Old Road, Lee,
London SE13 5SY
Tel 01-852 5050

Westminster City Libraries Archives Department,
Victoria Library, Buckingham Palace Road,
London SW1W 9UD
Tel 01-730 0446 Ext 23

Westminster Abbey Muniment Room and Library,
London SW1P 3PA
Tel 01-222 4233

RELIGIOUS DENOMINATIONAL ARCHIVES

Baptist Union Library, 4 Southampton Row,
London WC1
Tel 01-405 2045

Society of Friends Library, Friends House,
Euston Road, London NW1 2BJ
Tel 01-387 3601

United Reformed Church History Society,
86 Tavistock Place, London WC1H 9RT
Tel 01-427 8644

Unitarian Church Headquarters, Essex Hall,
Essex Street, London WC2
Tel 01-240 2384

Westminster Archiepiscopal Archives (*Roman Catholic*), Archbishop's House,
Ambrosden Avenue, London SW1P 1QJ
Tel 01-834 1964

Dr Williams's Library, 14 Gordon Square,
London WC1H 0AG
Tel 01-387 3727

(*Methodist Archives are now at the John Rylands Library, Manchester*)

Greater Manchester (see also Cheshire; Lancashire; Yorkshire)

John Rylands Library, University of Manchester,
Oxford Road, Manchester M13 9PP
Tel 061-834 5343

Manchester Central Library, Archives Department,
St Peter's Square, Manchester M2 5PD
Tel 061-236 9422 Ext 269

Wigan Record Office, Town Hall,
Leigh WN7 2DY
Tel (0942) 672421 Ext 65/6

Merseyside (see also Cheshire; Lancashire)

Liverpool Record Office, City Libraries,
William Brown Street, Liverpool L3 8EW
Tel 051-207 2147 Ext 34

West Midlands (see also Staffordshire; Warwickshire; Worcestershire)

Birmingham Reference Library, Central Libraries,
Birmingham B3 3HQ
Tel 021-235 4219

Dudley Archives and Local History Department,
Central Library, St James's Road, Dudley DY1 1HR
Tel (0384) 56321

Middlesex (see Greater London)

Norfolk

Norfolk Record Office, Central Library,
Norwich NR2 1NJ
Tel (0603) 22233

Northamptonshire (see also Cambridgeshire)

Northamptonshire Record Office, Delapré Abbey,
Northampton NN4 9AW
Tel (0604) 62129

Northumberland (see also Tyne and Wear)

Northumberland Record Office, Melton Park,
North Gosforth, Newcastle upon Tyne NE3 5QX
Tel (0894) 262680

Nottinghamshire (see also Yorkshire)

Nottinghamshire Record Office, County House,
High Pavement, Nottingham NG1 1HR
Tel (0602) 54524

Nottingham University Manuscripts Department,
University Library, University Park,
Nottingham NG7 2RD
Tel (0602) 56101 Ext 3437

Oxfordshire (see also Berkshire)

Oxfordshire County Record Office, County Hall,
New Road, Oxford OX1 1ND
Tel (0865) 815203

Bodleian Library, Oxford OX1 3BG
Tel (0865) 44675

Rutland (see Leicestershire; Northamptonshire)

Salop (see Shropshire)

Shropshire

Shropshire Record Office, Shirehall,
Abbey Forgate, Shrewsbury SY2 6ND
Tel (0743) 222406

Somerset (see also Avon)

Somerset Record Office, Obridge Road,
Taunton TA2 7PU
Tel (0823) 87600

Staffordshire (see also West Midlands)

Staffordshire Record Office, Eastgate Street,
Stafford ST16 2LZ
Tel (0785) 3121 Ext 7910

Lichfield Joint Record Office, Public Library,
Bird Street, Lichfield WS13 6PN
Tel (054 32) 56787

William Salt Library, Eastgate Street,
Stafford ST16 2LZ
Tel (0785) 52276

Suffolk (see also Norfolk)

Suffolk Record Office, Ipswich Branch,
County Hall, Ipswich IP4 2JS
Tel (0473) 55801

Suffolk Record Office, Bury St Edmunds Branch,
School Hall Street, Bury St Edmunds IP33 1RX
Tel (0284) 63143

Surrey (see also Greater London)

Surrey Record Office, County Hall, Penrhyn Road,
Kingston upon Thames KT1 2DN
Tel 01-546 1050 Ext 3561

Surrey Record Office, Guildford Muniment Room,
Castle Arch, Guildford GU1 3SX
Tel (0483) 73942

East Sussex (see also West Sussex)

East Sussex Record Office, Pelham House,
St Andrew's Lane, Lewes BN7 1UN
Tel (079 16) 5400

West Sussex (see also East Sussex)

West Sussex Record Office, West Street,
Chichester PO19 1RN
Tel (0243) 85100

Tyne and Wear (see also Durham; Northumberland)

Tyne and Wear Archives Department,
Blandford House, West Blandford Street,
Newcastle upon Tyne NE1 4JA
Tel (0632) 26789

Warwickshire (see also West Midlands)

Warwick County Record Office, Priory Park,
Cape Road, Warwick CV34 4JS
Tel (0926) 43431 Ext 2508

Shakespeare Birthplace Trust Records Office,
Henley Street, Stratford-upon-Avon CV37 6QW
Tel (0789) 4016

Westmorland (see Cumbria)

Isle of Wight (see also Hampshire)

Isle of Wight County Record Office, 26 Hillside,
Newport PO30 2EB
Tel (098 381) 4031 Ext 19

Wiltshire

Wiltshire County Record Office, County Hall,
Trowbridge BA14 8JG
Tel (022 14) 3641 Ext 3500

Salisbury District Council Muniment Room,
Council House, Bourne Hill, Salisbury
Tel (0722) 6272

Worcestershire (see Hereford and Worcester; West Midlands)

YORKSHIRE

Prior to 1974, this county was divided into three Ridings, North, East, and West. By the changes made in 1974, the county of Humberside takes in most of the former East Riding, together with part of Lincolnshire; the county of Cleveland takes in part of the former North Riding, together with part of county Durham; the county of North Yorkshire includes the remainder of the former North Riding, apart from a small area transferred to Cumbria, together with the northern part of the former West Riding, and the remainder of the former East Riding; the remainder of the former West Riding now forms the two counties of South Yorkshire and West Yorkshire (the former taking in also a small part of former Nottinghamshire), apart from small areas transferred to Lancashire and Greater Manchester.

North Yorkshire

North Yorkshire County Record Office,
County Hall, Northallerton DL7 8SG
Tel (0609) 3123

York University, Borthwick Institute of Historical
Research, St Anthony's Hall, Peasholme Green,
York YO1 2PW
Tel (0904) 59861 Ext 274

The West Suffolk Record Office in Bury St Edmunds is typical of amny local record offices. It houses collections of parish registers and wills dating back to the sixteenth century as well as many local parish histories compiled by amateur and professional writers.

York Minster Library, Dean's Yard,
York YO1 2JD
Tel (0904) 25308

South Yorkshire

South Yorkshire County Record Office,
Cultural Activities Centre, Ellin Street,
Sheffield S1 4PL
Tel (0742) 29191

Sheffield City Libraries, Archives Division,
Central Library, Surrey Street, Sheffield S1 1XZ
Tel (0742) 734711

West Yorkshire

West Yorkshire Record Office, Registry of Deeds,
Newstead Road, Wakefield WF1 2DE
Tel (0924) 67111 Ext 2352

Calderdale Metropolitan Borough Archives
Department, Central Library, Lister Lane,
Halifax HX1 5LA
Tel (0422) 65105/60425

Leeds Archives Department, Chapeltown Road,
Sheepscar, Leeds LS7 3AP
Tel (0532) 628339

Yorkshire Archaeological Society, Claremont,
Clarendon Road, Leeds LS2 9NZ
Tel (0532) 456362

Wales

Wales now includes the former county of Monmouthshire, which was formerly part of England. Until recent years the National Library of Wales, Aberystwyth, was the principal repository, and the only one authorized for church records. Although local record offices have now been established, the National Library remains predominant, and *inter alia* holds all probate records and bishops' transcripts. Welsh counties have also been reorganized; the former counties of Cardigan, Carmarthen and Pembroke now form the single county of Dyfed; the former county of Glamorgan, together with small parts of Brecon and Monmouth, forms the three new counties of West, Mid and South Glamorgan which are served by a single record office; the remainder of Monmouthshire is now called Gwent; the remainder of Breconshire, with Radnorshire and Montgomeryshire, forms the new county of Powys; Flintshire, most of Denbighshire, and a small part of Merioneth form the new county of Clwyd; and finally Anglesey, Caernarvonshire, the remainder of Merioneth and a small part of Denbighshire form the new county of Gwynedd.

Clywd

Clywd Record Office, The Old Rectory, Hawarden, Deeside CH5 3NR
Tel (0244) 532364

Clywd Record Office, 46 Clywd Street, Ruthin LL15 1HP
Tel (082 42) 3077

Dyfed

National Library of Wales, Department of Manuscripts and Records, Aberystwyth SY23 3BU
Tel (0970) 3816

Dyfed Archives, Carmarthenshire Record Office, County Hall, Carmarthen SA31 1JP
Tel (0267) 31867

Dyfed Archives, Ceredigion Record Office, Swyddfa'r Sir, Marine Parade, Aberystwyth
Tel (0970) 617581

Dyfed Archives, Pembrokeshire Record Office, The Castle, Haverfordwest
Tel (0437) 3707

Glamorgan, Mid, South, and West

Glamorgan Archive Service (for Mid, South and West Glamorgan), County Hall, Cathays Park, Cardiff CF1 3NE
Tel (0222) 28033 Ext 282

Gwent

Gwent County Record Office, County Hall, Cwmbran NP4 2XH
Tel (06333) 67711

Gwynedd

Gwynedd Archives Service, Caernarfon Area Record Office, County Offices, Shirehall Street, Caernarfon LL55 1SH
Tel (0286) 4121

Gwynedd Archives Service, Dolgellau Area Record Office, Cae Penarlag, Dolgellau
Tel (0341) 422341 Ext 261

Gwynedd Archives Service, Llangefni Area Record Office, Shire Hall, Llangefni, Gwynedd LL77 2TW
Tel (0248) 723262

Scotland

Although regional and other archives have been formed recently outside Edinburgh, in general these hold specialized material which will be needed only when that in Edinburgh has been exhausted. For most practical needs of the amateur family historian the following two addresses are sufficient: lists of other repositories will be found in *Record Repositories in Great Britain*, mentioned above.

Scottish Record Office, HM General Register House, Edinburgh EH1 3YY
Tel 031-556 6585

The General Register Office for Scotland, West Register House, Edinburgh EH1 3YT
Tel 031 556-6585

The Isle of Man

General Registry, Finch Road, Douglas
Tel (0624) 3358

Manx Museum Library, Kingswood Grove, Douglas
Tel (0624) 5522

The Channel Islands

Alderney

Clerk to the State, Court House, Alderney
Tel (048 182) 2816

Guernsey

Greffe, Royal Court House, St Peter Port, Guernsey
Tel (0481) 25277

La Société Guernesiaise, Guilles-Allès Library, St Peter Port, Guernsey
Tel (0481) 20556

Jersey

Judicial Greffe, States Building, Royal Square, St Helier, Jersey
Tel (0534) 33201 Ext 214

La Société Jersiaise, Museum and Library, 9 Pier Road, St Helier, Jersey
Tel (0534) 22133

Sark

The Greffier, Sark
Tel Sark 12

Ireland
(including Northern Ireland and the Republic of Ireland)

Although Northern Ireland (part of the United Kingdom) and the Republic of Ireland (Eire) have been politically separate from 1922, their former union means that their archives are not separate. In particular many archives relating to Northern Ireland are in the Republic, and the reverse applies to a lesser extent.

Northern Ireland

Public Record Office of Northern Ireland, 66 Balmoral Avenue, Belfast BT9 6NY
Tel (0232) 661621/663286

General Register Office (for Northern Ireland), 49–55 Chichester Street, Belfast BT1 4HL
Tel (0232) 35211

New Library, Trinity College, Dublin. Students of Irish genealogy will find much of value here. Trinity College largely escaped the great damage done to Irish records during the 'Troubles'.

Presbyterian Historical Society, Assembly House, Fisherwick Place, Belfast
Tel (0232) 23936

Friends Meeting House, Lisburn, Co Antrim

Republic of Ireland

Public Record Office, Four Courts, Dublin 7
Tel (01) 72-52-75

National Library of Ireland, Kildare Street, Dublin 2
Tel (01) 76-55-21

Registry of Deeds, King's Inn, Henrietta Street, Dublin 1
Tel (01) 74-89-11

Office of the Registrar General, Custom House, Dublin 1
Tel (01) 74-29-61

Genealogical Office, Dublin Castle, Dublin 2
Tel (01) 75-12-84

State Paper Office, Dublin Castle, Dublin 2
Tel (01) 71-17-77

Royal Irish Academy, 19 Dawson Street, Dublin 2
Tel (01) 76-25-70

Trinity College Library, Trinity College, College Green, Dublin 2
Tel (01) 71-36-49

Library of the Church Representative Body, Braemor Park, Dublin 14
Tel (01) 97-99-79

Friends Meeting House, 6 Eustace Street, Dublin 2
Tel (01) 77-80-88

Irish Manuscripts Commission, 73 Merrion Square, Dublin 2
Tel (01) 76-16-10

Cork Archives Council, The Courthouse, Cork
Tel (021) 50-90-12

Acknowledgements

It is impossible for a single author to do justice to a subject as complex as genealogy. We have, therefore, been fortunate in being able to assemble contributions from many specialists, but I must especially thank my colleague, Royston Gambier for his invaluable help in the compilation of this book. His experience both as a practising genealogist and as a teacher, as well as a former chairman and co-founder of the Federation of Family History Societies is of a very special character. Without his assistance and critical attention to detail it would not have been possible to produce this book in the time at our disposal. I am likewise indebted to Hugh Peskett and Charles Teviot for their valuable contributions on Celtic ancestry and on the records of the services and professions as well as to Sir Iain Moncreiffe for his thought-provoking Introduction. I must also acknowledge my special gratitude to Peter de V. B. Dewar FSA (Scot) for his valuable assistance in preparing the chapter on heraldry and to Jane Paterson for her contribution on handwriting.

Among the many whom I consulted by letter and through their published works I must thank in particular Margaret Audin, Count Camajani, Professor Hans Eysenck, Sebastian de Ferranti, Francis Leeson, Isobel Mordy, Hugh Montgomery-Massingberd and Edgar Samuel.

I am especially grateful to Susan Quince for typing the manuscript under exceptionally difficult conditions, and to Anne-Marie Ehrlich for her indefatigable help with the illustrations.

PUBLISHER'S NOTE

PICTURE CREDITS

The author and publishers would like to thank the following for supplying illustrations:

Colour

The Bodleian Library 46 (above & below), 47; The College of Arms 166, 167; Jerome Dessain 39 (above); E. T. Archive 162, 171; Foto Mas, Barcelona 170; Michael Holford Library (British Museum) 42, (Victoria & Albert Museum) 43; Kunsthistorisches Museum, Vienna (Meyer KG) 35 (above right); London Editions 163; Museo del Prado, Madrid 34 (above); The National Library of Wales 174, 175; Spectrum Colour Library 39 (below).

Black & White

Amsterdams Historisch Museum 93; E. T. Archive Ltd 40, 60, 61, 62, 64, 131, 134, 148, 150, 153, (Jewish Museum, London) 92; Bavarian State Library, Munich 172; The British Library 68–69; The British Museum 15, 29, 41; The British Tourist Authority 10; Camera Press Ltd 189, 191; David Campbell 94, 95; Church of Jesus Christ of Latterday Saints 98–99, 100; City of Aberdeen, Department of Information and Tourism 30; Department of the Environment 138, 193, 197; Bord Failte Photo 140, 204; Foto Mas, Barcelona 25; John Freeman & Co. 143; Guildhall Library, London (Godfrey New Photographics Ltd) 90; Michael Holford Library (British Museum) 53; Library of Religious Society of Friends 88; Mansell Collection frontispiece, 27, 109, 129, 165; Museo del Prado, Madrid 34 (below), 35 (above left); Museum of the City of New York (E. T. Archive Ltd) 154, 155; The National Library of Ireland 139; The National Maritime Museum 137, 177; The National Monuments Record 96, 199; The National Portrait Gallery (Smithsonian Institution, Washington DC) 24; The New York Public Library 151; Osterreichische Nationalbibliothek, Vienna 35 (below left); Harry T. Peters Collection, Museum of the city of New York (E. T. Archive Ltd) 156; John Piercy Ltd 152; Private collection 126; Provost of Southwark 84, 85; The Public Records Office 80, 81, 107, 110, 113, 117, 118, 119, 121, 122, 132, 133, 146, 195; Maurice Quick 17, 35 (below right); The Royal Commission on Historical Monuments (England) 71; Ronald Sheridan 11; Lady Soames (Her Majesty's Stationery Office) 73; The Society of Genealogists 37, 65, 86, 115; Brian Steven (Monmouth Historic Prints) 183; Suffolk Record Office 202; Monique Tremeau 79; The Trustees of the Institute of Heraldic and Genealogical Studies 178, 179; Victoria & Albert Museum, London 66, 67, 161; John Watt (The Black Watch Regimental Archives) 124; Josiah Wedgwood & Sons 36; The Wiener Library Photo Archive 158; The Yivo Institute for Jewish Research 28.